The *Abbé Breuil*

PREHISTORIAN

Breuil at Lascaux, 1940

ALAN HOUGHTON BRODRICK

THE ABBÉ BREUIL
PREHISTORIAN
A Biography

HUTCHINSON OF LONDON

Auckland Bombay Toronto
Johannesburg New York

★

First published 1963

*This book has been set in Garamond type face. It has
been printed in Great Britain by The Anchor Press
Ltd., in Tiptree, Essex, on Antique Wove paper.*

Contents

Illustrations

Except where mention is made of another
origin the photographs have all been kindly
furnished by the Musée de l'Homme, Paris.

Foreword

In this book I have made use, first of all, of my own recollections, but I also owe much to information received from those who knew Breuil better than I did. I must express my gratitude to Professor Millot, Director of the Museum of Man, for permission to quote from documents preserved in the *Fonds Breuil* and the property of his museum. Among the material which I have utilized from this source are the text of the speech the Abbé delivered at his old school in 1953; a description of the Somme and one of the La Magdaleine grotto (from *Quaternaria*, 1954 and 1955); considerable portions of Chapter 6 (as well as isolated passages elsewhere) come from the pamphlet *Science and Religion— are they Incompatible?* published (n.d.) by Breuil at Maseru in Basutoland. Some of the description of Lascaux in Chapter 12 (as well as a quotation in Chapter 7) has been taken from an article by the Abbé in the *Bulletin de la Société préhistorique française* (June–August 1950). In Chapter 13 I have drawn on Breuil's article 'Les Roches peintes de l'Afrique australe' (in *L'Anthropologie*, Vol. 53, 1949) as well as on his presidential address to the South African Archaeological Society.

In Chapter 13 I also have embodied some material relating to African prehistoric art which Breuil wrote in 1949 when reviewing my book *Prehistoric Painting*. The article appeared in the British review *The Month* and my thanks go to Father Caraman, s.j., for permission to quote from it.

The quotations in Chapter 3 relating to Breuil's painting come from an unpublished autobiographical account entitled *Comment j'ai appris à dessiner* in the possession of Dr. Léon Pales, who has kindly allowed me to make use of it. The valuable descriptions of Breuil's African explorations (notably Chapter 13) come, as I state in the text, from some of the Abbé's letters to me.

This book could not have been written without the aid and assistance of a number of friends both of his and of mine. First of all I must express my grateful thanks to the Abbé's sister, Mme de Mallevouë, who not only communicated many interesting details about her brother's early years but also gave me the impressive photograph taken at Burg Wartenstein in 1960. I was much indebted to my old friend the late Harper Kelley, the Abbé's close associate for more than thirty years. I have also received invaluable assistance from a number of others who knew Breuil well, notably from Dr. Léon Pales and M. Pierre Champion, Assistant Director of the Museum of Man, who from his childhood was well acquainted with the Abbé.

I should like also to express my gratitude to the staff of the photographic archives of the Museum of Man and also to Mlles de Barante and Debroise of the Centre de Documentation et de Recherches Préhistoriques in Paris.

A.H.B.

Paris

I

The Fires of Choukoutien

O<small>N A</small> winter's day in 1930 Breuil was sitting smoking in
his office when the door opened and a tall man with a
clerical collar stepped in and placed a small object on
the desk.

'What do you make of that?'

It was a piece of bone. The Abbé examined it and said: 'It is a
portion of a stag's antler. It was, when still fresh, exposed to fire
and it was worked with a crude stone implement, probably not
of flint, some sort of primitive chopping-tool.'

'But that's impossible. It comes from Choukoutien.'

'I don't care where it comes from, it was fashioned by a man,
and by a man who knew the use of fire.'

A chance meeting, then, between two priests in Paris led to
one of them changing radically our ideas about Man's past. This
identification of the Choukoutien implement as having been fired
was but one of the many discoveries we owe to a man who during
his long lifetime was to revolutionize prehistory and so our views
of Man's past. But his life was not that of an aloof, cloistered man
of science. He was a great traveller, an explorer, one who
delighted in mingling with his fellow-men of all sorts and kinds;
in fact, a remarkable human being. I have tried to show the Abbé
Henri Prosper Edouard Breuil not only as someone who had to
tell things which concern and interest us all, but at the same time
as a personality. . . .

The bit of horn came, in fact, from a site in the Western Hills, some thirty-five miles south-west of Peking, where had been found, during the preceding three years, portions of the skulls and other bones of a sort of man who had not been quite satisfactorily classified but who obviously lived a very long time ago. It was, in fact, some 400,000 years ago. And no one in 1930 suspected that this Peking Man had used fire. Man's mastery of fire was thought to have been achieved much later on in our history. Indeed, until comparatively recent years some held that fire did not enter into men's lives—at least as a servant—until the time of pots and pans, earthenware; that is to say, in New Stone Age or neolithic cultures, which even in the Near East did not begin until some 8,000 or 10,000 years ago at the most, and not until very much later (about 2500 B.C.) in Britain.

But although in 1930 it was known that the Neanderthaloids used fire, maybe a hundred centuries ago, no one had supposed that the much more primitive Peking Man had been a fire-maker, and as learning to control fire was the first great step towards Man's mastery of his surroundings—for such control enabled him to see in the darkness and to penetrate into new areas—obviously men, a very long time ago, were much more advanced in coming to terms with their environment than had been thought probable.

But, despite Breuil's reputation as the greatest living authority on early Man's implements—and, indeed, on prehistory in general; that is to say, mankind's history before the invention of writing—the visitor was unconvinced. His name was Teilhard de Chardin, who, as Breuil wrote, was 'very limited in his knowledge of early Man's implements'. And Breuil was to be proved absolutely right. His deduction of a great fact from a tiny bit of bone was indeed one of his more spectacular achievements. For the proof he gave that hominids (a less question-begging term than men) hundreds of thousands of years ago used fire revolutionized some of our ideas about our remote ancestors and threw light on one of the most puzzling problems in our whole history.

The great apes and ourselves are the only mammals to snore in the sense of keeping up a buzz-saw noise while they sleep. As a look-out man is no good in the dark, and while moonlight, when there is any, plays strange tricks with our eyes, it is fairly clear that Man did not occupy caves until he knew the use of fire and could light a blaze to keep off prowling beasts attracted by those rattling grunts which are just another proof of our cousinage with gorillas, chimpanzees and orang-outangs.

Yet men seem to have occupied caves from very early on in their career; in some parts of the world at least, though there is little evidence that our ancestors in Europe used caves as homes before about 150,000 years ago, maybe less; anyway, during that last Interglacial or warm period between two Ice Ages. But then until the last Ice Age (or 'Würm'), beginning some 70,000 years ago, men did not, it would seem, live much in Europe during the great cold. We are tropical animals, although we have learned during the ages to manufacture, by various devices, artificial climates, letting us survive and even prosper where our remote ancestors did not venture.

However, sparks from flint-chipping, lightning and volcanic eruptions all offered Man flames very early on in his story. Maybe men played about with fire before they learned to use it.

'There are indications that fire not only appeals to Man's cortical or rational mind but that it has a deep, subconscious or sensual appeal. The fact that the Philippine tarsier' (a primitive sort of animal probably representing a stage of evolution leading to apes and men) 'has been named *Tarsius carbonarius* on account of its propensity for picking up hot embers from camp-fires suggests to me that Man's ancestors . . . may have been attracted to natural fires and toyed with burning matter just as rooks and some other birds exhibiting the so-called "anting behaviour" seek fires and smoke' (Dr. K. Oakley).

The gorgeous dancing tongues, orange, red, golden and implacable, have always fascinated mankind and maybe there are pyromaniacal tendencies deep down in our subconsciousness.

Breuil not only recognized the Choukoutien implement as having been fired, but, later on in China, he was to prove his diagnosis by tracing out for himself at the site the *cendres rubanées*, the striped ashes, coloured green, blue, pink, yellow and sometimes brown, which weave their way right through the layers of fillings which piled up in those ancient Chinese caves.

No hearths have, with certainty, been identified earlier in date than those of Choukoutien, but old charcoal soon weathers in the open air and so is rare. However, Fontéchevade Man (see p. 169) is about the most ancient European we know of who used fire. In fact, his remains were discovered among kitchen refuse, and he was very probably eaten, perhaps even roasted. But Fontéchevade Man lived much later than the Peking Man of Choukoutien, the latter dating back to about 400,000 and the former to around 100,000 years ago. These datings are approximate only, since the radio-carbon dating method (most useful for charcoal) can be applied only to remains less than 70,000 years old.

It is one of the prime puzzles of our history that Man—well described as a 'foetalized ape'—managed to survive at all. A long, helpless infancy, feeble physical means of defence, outrun and out-distanced by most of the animals on which he fed—a two-day-old vicuña can run faster than a man—still our ancestors did manage to survive, although we must imagine them until comparatively recent times as rather rare animals.

No doubt Man's prolonged childhood, which exposed him to so many dangers, had, on the other hand, immense spiritual advantages, since it is during infancy that the mother-child relationship is formed. Mere physical care of an infant is not enough to secure its development as an individual. Constant affection and what we may call psychical care are imperative, since it is doubtful whether when we are very young we possess much instinct at all in the sense of innate ability to adapt ourselves to environment. We have to be taught everything. And it is by that teaching we develop the complicated emotional reactions lying at the base of social life.

Maybe the key to the puzzle of Man's survival is fire.

For Breuil held that Man used fire very early on indeed, in fact that our forbears possessed fire from the time they began to chip stones over a million years ago. Sparks flew off from flint-working then as now. Breuil also thought that fire was kept alive (for the remaking of it must have been an arduous task) rather in dry grasses, where it would smoulder for hours, than among wood.

In any case, since the men of Choukoutien knew how to light a blaze it is a fair guess that others of their kind in Africa and in Europe, getting on for half a million years ago, also knew how to keep the wolf from the door.

And if fire-taming was, so to speak, a by-product of stone-instrument making, we may ask, 'What led Man to make implements?'

Maybe 'meat-eating' is the answer to that one.

Apes and monkeys are vegetarians (except in rare circumstances), but all men are meat-eaters—when they can get the meat. The evidence points to the earliest hominids as having lived in dry, open country, certainly not in forests (though the myth of our tree-climbing forefathers dies hard), and to survive in such conditions men had to become, at least partially, meat-eaters. It is likely that the lowly Australopithecines (see p. 211) who flourished in various parts of Africa from maybe as long ago as 2,000,000 years, were scavengers before they became hunters. Wooden bludgeons, bits of rock and daggers of broken bone, plus a good deal of hullabaloo, thumping, banging and shouting, would sometimes have sufficed to drive off animals from a kill and to secure half-mangled carcasses.

But between using tools and making tools there is a great difference. The fashioning of a tool implies a good deal of conceptual thought, and is, in fact, an intellectual training. Flesh-eating creatures with small teeth and weak jaws need some sort of sharp tool for cutting through skin and muscle when it is no longer a question of dealing with half-devoured corpses but with an intact, large animal.

Meat-eating, then, led to knife-making and to all the other manufactures of mankind—from the pebble-tools of the Australopithecines to electronic computers and nuclear fission.

2

Breuil's Beginnings

'WHY', runs a saying of rather bitter Hebrew wisdom, 'do we so often like our grandchildren better than our own children?' Answer: 'Because our grandchildren have the same enemies as ourselves.'

Those who are lucky enough when young often to be with affectionate, understanding and intelligent grandparents generally realize poignantly enough how much they owe to people who no longer cherish absurd ambitions or demand impossible achievement. Then, grandparents often fade away before we are soured, hardened, engrossed or become sceptical, before life has made us less kind and less responsive to kindness in others.

Henri Breuil was among those who owed a good deal to a grandparent: to a grandmother who had a country estate in the Aisne department, a region of undulating plains, woods and rich pastures where ways of life had not changed much for generations. She was interested in botany, she painted flowers in her spare time, lived on good terms with her neighbours and seems to have been gently strong-willed. She and her grandson were alike physically and maybe also in character; anyway, she certainly had some influence on young Henri, though even when a youth he showed an independence of mind that was to mark all his life. She does not seem wholly to have approved of Henri's decision to become a priest and it was in deference to her wishes that he never wore the *soutane* or cassock until he entered the seminary of Saint-Sulpice in Paris and was being prepared for ordination.

The boy's first formulated ambition was to become a physician, but his indifferent health ruled out such a career. Even in youth Breuil was slightly round-shouldered, and this condition, no doubt congenital, was, by one of those usual family fables, attributed to a fall downstairs when he was very young.

It was to his poor health that he owed a marvellous sabbatical year during which he was left alone to find himself; a year which had, most certainly, a determining influence upon his whole life.

'When, in 1894, I left Saint-Vincent . . . my health was so bad that the doctors insisted I take a whole year's rest—much to my delight, I may add. A whole year during which I was not to open a textbook or make any notes, but a whole year for fishing, botanizing, hunting butterflies and beetles to my heart's content . . . what a piece of luck! I enjoyed every minute of the time I spent exploring the countryside, making my way into most hidden places, into thickets and woods and among marshes. I would crouch motionless, watching and listening to animals and birds which had no suspicion I was anywhere near. Quite alone I plunged into wild nature where were no human beings at all. I harkened to the birds' song, to the bees buzzing in the thyme, to the throbbing life of beasts and plants. Although, of course, I had no idea of what I was doing I was really learning to let myself think and throughout my life I have never ceased to do that . . . in the hundreds of murky caverns I have explored, in the wildest parts of Spain or when making my way along never-ending tracks through Africa when I crossed the paths Livingstone had cut through the bush . . . indeed before I was ten years old I had devoured the account of his exciting explorations as contained in a book called *Le Tour du Monde* at the home of my young friend, Jacques Ansart.'

This sabbatical year, then, was a period of discovery of self, of imaginings, of spiritual and physical freedom, of delight in the sights and sounds of the countryside—and no doubt of planning for the future. The sort of break that is often of incalculable benefit to those fortunate enough to enjoy it during their most impressionable years.

When we look back most of us realize that some apparently trivial incident, some object, some chance conversation, triggered off a chain of thought urging us towards a path we were to tread. *Le Tour de Monde*, with its highly imaginative and romantic woodcuts, had fascinated young Henri Breuil. Maybe one day he would explore Africa. Well, he did do just that, though his adventures had not much in common with those of Dr. Livingstone.

Henri Prosper Edouard Breuil was born on 28th February 1877 at Mortain in Normandy, though he was no Norman. His father, Albert Breuil, was a lawyer then practising in that town, but in 1878 he was appointed *procureur de la République*; that is, public prosecutor, at Clermont de l'Oise, a town some forty miles north of Paris. It was at Clermont that Henri Breuil spent his childhood and had his earliest schooling.

Although it seems there was a tradition in the Breuil family that they came originally from Spain, the name is essentially French[1] and the earliest known ancestor was Breuil's great-grandfather, who was a native of Palaiseau some twelve miles south of Paris, a town full of Jansenist memories, surrounded by market gardens and famed as the setting for Coigniez's *La Pie Voleuse* and Rossini's opera *La Gazza Ladra*, founded on the tale. Palaiseau is in the most French part of France, in the Île de France itself, the region round Paris, and the little town is the

---

[1] 'Breuil' is a common place-name all over France, but especially in the north. The word (in a score of different spellings: Breuille, Bruille, Brule, Bruoll, Broil, Broeil, Broel, Broal, Breuil, Brual, Bréal, Breil, Bril, Brul, Bruil, etc.) means a wood, a coppice or a thicket. *Breuil*, in the modern French jargon of forestry, signifies 'a wood enclosed with fences serving as a game-preserve'.

gateway to the delightful country known as the Vallée de Chevreuse, dotted with country houses ranging from the splendours of the Duc de Luynes' Dampierre to the rustic delights of the Moulin de la Tuilerie, belonging to the Duke of Windsor, at Gif.

As far back as we can go, then, Breuil's father's family was not only northern French but almost Parisian. The ancestral Breuil from Palaiseau bought himself a notary's practice at Amiens and thus started the family connection with Picardy. He had three sons, one of whom was in the consular service; another, Auguste, sometime president of the Picardy Antiquarian Society, a friend of Boucher de Perthes (see p. 30) and a playwright in his spare time; the third son, Edouard, a lawyer, was the father of Albert Breuil who married Lucie Morio de l'Isle of a Bonapartist family. Her father was until the fall of the Second Empire sub-prefect at Compiègne (where the Emperor and Empress often resided) and he himself was the son of a general officer under the great Napoleon. There was not, then, either on Henri Breuil's father's or mother's side, any ecclesiastical tradition.

Albert Breuil retired from the public service in the 'eighties but continued to live at Clermont until his death between the two world wars. Besides Henri there were two other children: a son who followed the family tradition and became a lawyer—he died childless—and a daughter still living, Mme de Mallevouë, who also has no children.

Albert Breuil was rather a severe parent. He looks stern enough in his portraits: strong features in a square face barred by an imposing cavalry moustache and showing little or no resemblance to his famous son. The Abbé would say he owed his punctuality in general and his fussiness about punctual meals to his father's training. He would also hint that Albert Breuil retired 'too soon'; maybe this was a delicate way of implying that he was rather tiresome about the house, as are many men who retire early. Still, although there does not seem to have been much sympathy between father and son, there was no tension in the family, and Breuil was much attached to his mother, to whom he wrote regularly every week of his life from wherever he happened to be until her death in 1928.

Henri Breuil was a reserved and contemplative child. One of his masters at Clermont described him as sitting about musing 'like a little old man'. This teacher, by the way—who set the lad aged ten as the subject of an essay the 'Neolithic burial in the Aurignac Cave'—was still living when Breuil was elected professor at the Collège de France in 1929.

In 1887 Henri was sent to the Collège Saint-Vincent at Senlis, a town some distance south of Clermont and about thirty-five miles north-east of Paris. Senlis is in the heart of the historic Valois country that gave its name to the race of French kings which ruled from 1328 to 1589. It is a delightful, old-world town with a fine Gothic cathedral and is, even today, fairly quiet and provincial.

The school was, and is, housed in the buildings of an abbey, some parts of which date back to the eleventh century when it was founded by Queen Anne, the Russian wife of Henri I of France. The college was run by members of the Marist Order. It is still thought, in some French circles, and not without justification, that in the church schools the teaching is as thorough as in the state-supported ones, while the moral and social training is a good deal better. There is, of course, in neither set of schools any corporal punishment (this may surprise the British, if not Americans), and in both pupils are addressed as 'Monsieur So-and-so' (this may surprise both Americans and British). Masters are 'Monsieur' alone, which means 'Sir', whereas 'Monsieur So-and-so' is just 'Mr. X'.

The atmosphere of at least one of these *écoles libres* (i.e. 'free schools' but 'free' only in the sense of not being state-controlled) is well reproduced in Michel de Saint-Pierre's *Les nouveaux Aristocrates* ('The New Aristocrats'), but there is a difference between the conventions of today and those of nearly eighty years ago when Breuil went to Senlis.

There is also in the preference for an *école libre* a certain amount of class-feeling involved. At some of the Jesuit colleges, and at a school, such as, for instance, that of the Oratorians at Juilly (where Jerome, Napoleon's youngest brother, was educated), the boys are more or less hand-picked.

Young Breuil was put in the *sixième*; that is, the lowest class; and he was, as he himself said, 'feeble in health and with a detestable memory'. He meant, I think, by 'detestable' that his verbal memory was bad; he had difficulty in learning by rote (pedagogues have a tendency to like fools with good memories) —his memory for facts, for events, could hardly have become so remarkable afterwards had it been so 'detestable' at the age of ten. He seems to have been bullied a good deal; naturally enough since he was small and weak—until the other boys learned to leave him alone, for he was full of courage.

When men become famous and re-visit, in mature age, their old schools it is conventional for them to praise their schooldays as the 'happiest time' in their lives. Breuil was not one to stoop to such soothing lies. On St. Vincent's Day 1953, when he was seventy-six years old, he was the guest of honour at the prize-giving. His start-off was rather odd, for he remarked he felt like visiting a 'family vault'; then, after a passing reference to the 'elegant tower, the noble cloisters and the flowery gardens' near which he spent 'seven years of my youth', he went on to reminisce about his old masters:

'Father Perrault who made me realize how important it is to articulate clearly when speaking in public and how great is the difference between a lecture droned out and one delivered in a natural tone of voice . . . Father Hinault who endeavoured, all too early, to awaken in me some taste for literature . . . Father Bresson who managed to cram into my childish head the principles of French composition informed with logic, order and clarity . . . Father Falquet who did arouse in me something of the philosophic spirit . . .'

We may note how much of all this is concerned with speaking, writing, composition; in fact with the problems and difficulties of communication. In this connection there is a passage in a letter from Carl J. Burkhardt, the Swiss writer, to Hugo von Hofmannsthal:

'Everyone here' (that is Paris) 'is intelligent, even the fools, so we have a situation quite different from that in our countries' (i.e. Switzerland and Austria). 'Everyone possesses a very definite fund of prefabricated, already prepared formulae which serve to prevent much useless reflection. Everyone is caught up in the works of a thinking-machine that is infallible, of unimaginable subtlety, informed with good taste and prudent limitations. This thinking-machine is the language whose influence none can escape. Words impose their limits, words in all their perfection.'

Maybe this is worth bearing in mind when we are considering the career of an eminent Frenchman and his impact on his fellows.

After these few words about his old teachers Breuil got more candid: 'I was a weakly lad, unable to make a sustained effort. I was dreamy and more interested in nature and in wild life than in all the scholastic fustian . . . the adventurous life of a missionary attracted me. I also dreamed of being a scientist. . . .'

In fact, as he went on to state very plainly, what he liked by far the best during his schooldays was getting away from school.

'On holidays I went to Clermont de l'Oise. An omnibus took us to Creil, where we caught a train before day-break. It brought us back at night amid a dreadful clanging and jangling of windows as it pitched and tossed through the dark forest, often in freezing cold weather. . . . Clermont station was at the foot of the hill and my father's house was right on the top of it. The long Station Road running between interminable high walls and feebly lit by a few miserable street-lamps echoed to my footsteps in a most

alarming way. I was afraid; and I was ashamed of being afraid.
So, to overcome my fears, I made it a habit to take a quite dark
and very lonely short cut which led up the Chatelier, a wooded
walk, planted with great elms whose tall branches stood out
against the sparkling night sky. In this way I taught myself to
master my terrors and prepared myself for other and much
greater solitudes which I was, later on, to endure for long periods
at a time in Spain and in Africa.'

Senlis is surrounded by delightful woods and forests, such as
that of Halatte, where in the springtime the trees rise from an
unending carpet of daffodils, jonquils and narcissi that is unique,
I think, in France. When Mme de Sévigné picnicked there with
Louis XIV and the court *tout estoit parfumé de jonquilles*—'everything was perfumed with the scent of jonquils'. Into these forests
Henri Breuil would flee when he could.

'My walks out from Senlis were an escape into Nature. Sometimes
I would follow a hunt and glimpse a stag. At other times in the
Ermenonville woods we would chase squirrels from pine-tree to
pine-tree. Once I grabbed in its hiding-place among the heather—
and then as soon let free again—the only red-leg partridge I
ever saw north of Paris. . . . Near Le Tomberet I discovered a
pool with the round-leaved pyrola of which I have seen only
two specimens since. Near the Butte d'Aumont in a plantation
of leafless oaks I lighted one day upon a swarm of *Bombyx tau*.
The males, like russet leaves borne upon the wind, were flopping
about looking for females . . . and that reminds me of what
happened to my friend Eugène Parmentier—who was killed
during the 1914–18 war—a female *Vanessa io* [great peacock
moth] had come out of her chrysalis inside a cage of cocoons
hanging in his garage. Attracted by the effluvium of the captive
hundreds of males rushed in and frightened a footman out of his
wits since he took them for bats. . . . At Senlis some were huge,
you could see them at Fair times flying at the tops of the tall

trees in the esplanade. In all my long life I have never again seen a *Bombyx tau* nor another rare and superb Bombycide, the "Dead Poplar Leaf", that I discovered, just emerged from its chrysalis, on the coping of a wall near the Roman arena . . . in some years when a late date for the *bachot* examination kept us at school after prize-giving we could witness the mass-murder of the drones by the bees that lodged in the wall around the Seniors' Yard (the *cour des grands*).'

All his life Breuil remained a keen entomologist and one large filing-case (in the library of the Scientific Research Centre) is filled with his published notes and articles on butterflies, moths and beetles.

The examination for the *baccalauréat* (the *bachot*; that is, the matriculation for entrance to the university, though stiffer than equivalent tests in Britain or the U.S.A.) is taken in two successive parts and, nowadays, usually when a boy or girl is seventeen and eighteen. Seventy years ago the *bachot*—which it is said now creates 'an atmosphere of demented tension'—was tackled in more leisurely fashion. There were, of course, not nearly so many candidates, for with changing social conditions it has become the ambition of many more French families, especially in the towns, to get one, at least, of their children through the *bachot*, which is, indeed, an absolutely essential diploma for all who want a university education, its equivalent, or any sort of job with a future to it, except maybe in business. And even when the *bachelier* gets into a university he must, after one year, take the dreaded *propédeutique* examination. Those who fail in this are dropped.

Young Henri passed his examination for *bachelier de rhétorique* easily enough, at least as far as the natural sciences were concerned. He did not do so well in Latin verse, in German or in literature. His was, in fact, rather an 'unliterary' nature. He wrote readily enough, he was often lively, his style generally straightforward, his vocabulary rich and apposite, but he did not always take the trouble to arrange his material so as best to be understood by the ordinary reader—but then he wrote mostly for specialists. His more popular works are well arranged and clear, and he avoided the facile generalizations and peremptory judgements so common in French writing; in fact, he would sometimes shake the 'thinking-machine' and make it work a little differently. He liked to let facts speak for themselves, but in what may be called his non-scientific writings (many of which were either not published or were published and are now impossible to find) he would at times wax rather lyrical.

In his last year at Senlis he passed the second part of his *bachot* —the 'philosophy'. The main subject was aesthetics. Either he had not attended or not attended to the lessons in this recondite matter. So, as he said, he 'made it all up'. Maybe he thought aesthetics so much 'scholastic fustian'. He passed, though the shrewd Marists knew well enough he was bluffing, but he bluffed so well they just had to let him through.

Then came the sabbatical year from July 1894 to the end of September 1895. Except for some lessons in water-colour painting (that came in useful later on) and in piano-playing (he disliked music and could hardly tell one note from another) he was free to do what he wished: collect flowers and plants, hunt, fish, shoot, chase butterflies and burrow for beetles—and dream of what he would be in life.

However, before the sabbatical year the young man's range of interests had broadened out to beyond bugs and moths. Sometimes during vacations he would be invited to stay at a country house in the Somme department and right up in the region where the science of prehistory was born. At this château de Bouillancourt-en-Séry lived an aunt married to a cousin of Geoffroy d'Ault du Mesnil, an excellent geologist and archaeologist, though remembered now mostly as the man who aroused Henri Breuil's interest in the problems of prehistory, and of Man's origins and of the tale earth can be made to tell. In a turret-room of the château was a small collection of fossils gathered together no one could remember by whom. It was in handling and examining these specimens that d'Ault gave Breuil some idea of the puzzling problems you can dig out of the soil.

Geoffroy d'Ault du Mesnil, by the way, had a curious background. His father was a country gentleman of means who began his career as a violent conservative and colonialist. He served in Algeria and had a radical prescription for curing that country's ills: 'The conquest of Algeria will never be complete until the Moslems are all either killed off or converted to Catholicism.' His advice was not taken; as recent events have shown, the conquest never was 'complete'. Later, however, the elder d'Ault changed his opinion, became a close friend of Lamennais and held with him that 'Catholicism is a dead or dying form of the elemental religion'.

It may have been during his sabbatical year that Henri Breuil made up his mind that if he could not be a doctor or a missionary he would be a priest and a scientist. In any case he seems to have taken the decision himself. His family appears to have thought his health so indifferent that he would not make old bones in any case, so that it was best to let him have his own way. In October 1895 he entered the seminary at Issy-les-Moulineaux, then a dependency of that of Saint-Sulpice in Paris. Not all those admitted to Issy necessarily became priests; some of the seminarists would decide—or have decided for them—that they had no 'vocation'. Still, Issy was the step to Saint-Sulpice itself, where were admitted only those who were recognized as having 'vocations' or at least as being determined to be ordained.

Issy is today a dingy and rather depressing industrialized Parisian suburb whose main street (now called the rue Ernest-Renan) is dominated by an immense stone pile, half palace, half prison in appearance, which is built upon the site of a castle where ended her days the Reine Margot, Henri IV's first wife, famed for her beauty, her learning, her literary talent and her extremely loose conduct.

The chapel of the seminary is copied from that of Versailles, while near to it is a small chamber in rusticated style where in 1695 Fénelon, the high-bred churchman of Quietist leanings, met and discussed theological matters with his senior, the bourgeois genius Bossuet, who but two years afterwards was to become Fénelon's most dangerous opponent and the man who procured the disgrace of his enemy.

In the crypt of the chapel is preserved the wall against which in 1871 the Communards shot the hostages in Paris—including Mgr. Darboy, the liberal-minded Archbishop of Paris, who voted against the proposition of Papal Infallibility at the Vatican Council.

Seen from the back the seminary (which is now the Catholic Theological Institute) is not quite so grimly imposing. The ground rises, and over a narrow road is a large, leafy and flowery garden, maybe that of the Superior. All here is quiet and provincial even today. It is a little oasis. Here and there a cassocked figure on a bicycle. Renan was a poor scholar at Issy, and in later life, estranged from the Church as he was, he praised the excellent education he got there. So also Breuil: 'I owed my real educational training as well as the development of my literary and artistic tastes to my time at Issy . . . my masters, but more, perhaps my fellow-students, helped in the formation of my thought, my inclinations, my character.'

Issy was to be Breuil's home for the next two years; however: 'Life in the seminary cut me off from general society with which even later on, owing to my explorations and my scientific work, I was not much brought in contact.' Yet, as a matter of fact, Breuil, in his middle and later years anyway, seemed to be at his ease in any company, though he never did trouble to assume the special professional suavity so many ecclesiastics display.

At Issy the master who had the greatest influence on him, the man who must, with d'Ault du Mesnil, count as young Breuil's guide to his career, was the Abbé Guibert, who encouraged a bent towards natural history and expounded the theory of evolution. When we hear it stated, as something remarkable, that Teilhard de Chardin was a 'priestly evolutionist' we may remember that Guibert was just that before Teilhard was born. It was Guibert who agreed young Henri could, as a priest, follow his scientific bent. Guibert's words were, 'There's a lot to be done in prehistory—you ought to tackle it.' He lent Breuil Mortillet's works and afterwards made him a present of the complete set of twenty-two volumes of Mortillet's anthropological review.[1]

At Issy also Breuil was to make a friend for life in Jean Bouyssonie, who came from Brive in the Corrèze department (not far from Lascaux and the other prehistoric sites of the Vézère Valley). Canon Bouyssonie was an exact contemporary of Breuil's and is still living as I write this; his name is linked with one of the most important of anthropological discoveries (see p. 70) and of him Breuil wrote: 'He is the only man who sometimes equalled me in the reproducing of palaeolithic engravings. In the drawing of artefacts he surpassed me.' High praise from the Abbé, who had, quite justifiably, a very definite opinion of his own ability as a draughtsman.

During his vacations from Issy, Breuil again met d'Ault du Mesnil, who in 1896 had recovered from the Somme gravel-pits fossil bones of hippopotamus, rhinoceros and an ancient type of horse—indicating a mild climate. The deposit in which these were found dates back, in fact, to the warm Interglacial between the first (Günz) and the second (Mindel) Ice Ages, and thus to over 400,000 years ago. In those days, however, prehistoric chronology could not be said to exist, though d'Ault and his friend d'Acy had in 1895 declared that 'Chellean' implements

---

[1] This was afterwards bought by Cartailhac and merged into the still flourishing *L'Anthropologie*, the most authoritative and reliable of European anthropological reviews. It was Mortillet who adopted the terms still used for the various culture-phases of our history, e.g. 'Chellean', 'Solutrean' or 'Magdalenian', instead of Lartet's old, rather vague, designations of 'Hippopotamus', 'Great Bear' or 'Reindeer' Age.

came before 'Acheulian' and these latter were more ancient than 'Mousterian'—and this was a sound piece of observation.

Breuil often said that 'It was d'Ault who initiated me into the mysteries of the Somme gravel-pits', and it was the evidence from those pits which formed the starting-point of much of the Abbé's work on the time-table of the Pleistocene period.

It was, indeed, lucky for young Breuil that each year he and his family moved to Amiens (there to stay with grandfather Breuil), since the capital of Picardy was the place where first was recognized the evidence proving the great antiquity of Man. There were plenty of people who thought the world had been 'created in 4004 B.C.' or some other date even later—when civilizations were flourishing in the Near East. Even the day of the month was stated: somewhere in September or October.

Boucher de Crèvecœur de Perthes not only bore a strange and rather improbable name but his life was a curious one. The family of Boucher de Crèvecœur was supposed to go back to the fifteenth century, while his mother claimed descent from one of Joan of Arc's brothers. Jacques Boucher was a tall, good-looking man, very careful of his appearance and not, it is said, 'showing that coldness and reserve which might have been expected from his noble origins'. He was 'benevolent, always polite and on occasion affable'. When he was no more than seventeen years of age he met, at Genoa, Pauline, the highly temperamental sister of Napoleon, and years later, in 1852, Boucher published love-letters said to have been exchanged during this romantic interlude.

Boucher de Perthes was even more of a jack-of-all-trades than most of the early archaeologists: he was government employee (he succeeded his father as head of the Abbeville customs house), man-about-town, novelist, poet, playwright (none of his plays ever got acted), 'metaphysician', pamphleteer, social reformer, philanthropist, candidate for parliament, although he was never elected. His political profession of faith was a prose-poem. Boucher wooed the electors with promises of 'universal peace, liberty of conscience, less taxation, lowered cost of living, encouragement for agriculture, abolition of the death penalty, old-age pensions, etc.'.

At Abbeville, described in the first half of the nineteenth century as being a town of 'narrow, filthy streets with some quaint specimens of domestic architecture', Boucher (who was for years president of the local Société d'Emulation, a scientific and literary club) had friends, some of whom were interested in the 'natural sciences'. His own researches into what we should now call 'prehistory' began in 1837. Queen Victoria had just ascended the throne of Great Britain and Van Buren was President of the United States in a time of financial crisis.

Boucher had observed that man-made objects were being thrown up by a dredger along the Somme Canal and that one of these polished axes was hafted in stag-horn. Meanwhile a friend of his called his attention to 'Celtic remains' (anything pre-Roman was dubbed 'Celtic', whatever it might be) discovered in the local gravels.

During the sixteenth, seventeenth and eighteenth centuries some people seem to have realized that the so-called 'thunder stones' —that is, prehistoric chipped-stone implements—resembled the artefacts made by American Indians; while in the early nineteenth century men in Belgium, France and England thought they had found man-made implements in association with the fossil bones of animals long extinct in, or long migrated from, Europe. But all the popular prejudice of those days was against the possibility of Man having existed in very remote epochs. In France the eminent naturalist Cuvier was firm in his protests that there 'was not, and could not be, any such thing as fossil Man'.

Anyway, Boucher began a collection of chipped-flint tools unearthed by workmen in the Moulin-Quignon, Menchecourt and L'Hôpital gravel-pits just outside Abbeville. These pits were in the 'high terrace' of the Somme River and the most striking pieces found were large, flattish stones, in outline somewhat like a pear and chipped to an edge on both faces (hence the name they bear of 'bifaces'), usually known in English by the misleading name of 'hand-axes', for anyone who employed them with his bare hand would damage it a good deal. The 'hand-axes' found in the Somme deposits were, as a matter of fact, of two main classes, though this was not realized until afterwards. There was a coarser, more 'primitive'-looking, sort of biface and there were better-worked and more-finished implements.

The Somme Valley is a region of white chalk (containing natural flints) and its average width between Amiens and Abbeville is about one mile. The geological formation of this area is indeed very similar to that of south-eastern England; moreover, until about 10,000 or 8,000 years ago the two regions of France and England were joined together. Still, the ice-front did not reach France during the glaciations, whereas, at times, the sheet did touch the Thames, and to such an extent that the river's course was, at certain ages, deflected.

In 1847 Boucher published a book entitled *Celtic and Diluvian Antiquities* in which he gave an account of and a commentary on his discoveries, but the volume met with little approval. Some scientists were put off by Boucher's preoccupation with the biblical Flood, while fundamentalists, of course, would not entertain his theories at all. There was current at the time an idea (also held by Cuvier) that the earth had been subjected to a series of 'cataclysms', after each of which there was a new crop of 'creations'. The theory lingered on, in some quarters, for a good many years.

Few people declared outright that Boucher was a liar and a forger, but it was suggested he had been fooled by workmen in the pits and that he had allowed his enthusiasm to get the better of his judgement. As a matter of fact, the rewards he offered did encourage some of the more resourceful pit-men to do a little chipping on their own account.

In 1854, however, Boucher made a convert of note. A Dr. Rigollot of Amiens, a shrewd and keen amateur archaeologist, went to confound Boucher at the Saint-Acheul and Saint-Roch gravel-pits just outside Amiens—and there himself unearthed hand-axes from the ground. Little by little, some of the more open-minded French scientists came round to Boucher's views: namely, that Man had existed in ages so remote that all ideas about human history must be revised.

And if we are inclined to wonder why there was so much scepticism regarding the evidence of the terraces, maybe the words Breuil wrote as recently as 1948 are worth pondering: 'The very great antiquity of Man and the less great (but still immense, speaking from the stand-point of history) antiquity of the art of the caverns and the painted rocks are still unrealized except by a few among the learned.'

The hand-axes found in such great quantities near Abbeville and Amiens lay in the 'high terrace' of the river and therefore must be very ancient. And this is the reason: rivers, as they make their way across flood-plains, lay down gravels, sands and loamy clays. When the streams scooped out deeper valleys (the volume of water varied, of course, with the climate) patches of such deposits would be left alongside the rivers' courses as 'terraces', which from the geological formation, the fossil bones and man-made implements they contain tell of past climates and their succession—in fact we are provided with a sort of time-table, admittedly one often puzzling to read, but still a time-table.

Obviously, therefore, the oldest terrace will be the top one, and in any given terrace the oldest remains (fossils and implements) will be at the bottom and the more recent at the top of that terrace.

Here are Breuil's own words on the Somme at work:

'As each glacial period brought about a considerable lowering of the sea level, the river also deepened its bed . . . at the same time, especially during the wet phase at the beginning of a

C

glaciation, solifluxion[1] swept along . . . the material dragged from the river's banks . . . during the succeeding Interglacial the rise in sea level put an end to this process.'

However, although the credit for recognizing man-made implements as very ancient goes to Boucher de Perthes, the fact is—and this Breuil was always ready to recognize—the undoubted authenticity of Boucher's discoveries was established by British men of science: Falconer a palaeontologist, Prestwich a geologist, Evans a paper-manufacturer (the father of the Evans who revealed ancient Crete) and active archaeologist, and Lyell the author of the *Antiquity of Man* (1863). They visited Saint-Acheul, unearthed man-made implements for themselves and when they returned to England found similar artefacts in the Thames Valley gravels.

So now came the question: What sort of men made these hand-axes? Why, of course, men just like ourselves. Practically no one in the 'fifties of the last century imagined there could ever have been on this earth any kind of man but *Homo sapiens*; in fact *Homo sapiens* was Man created (more or less) in God's image, and Man was *Homo sapiens*. The few odd bits and pieces of strange-seeming types (what we now call neanderthaloid) were just pathological or maybe monkeys. . . .

And how long ago had the makers of the hand-axes lived? There was the wildest disparity between the various guesses at the length of time which had elapsed since the creatures (that is, animals) whose fossil bones had been discovered near the hand-axes had been alive.

The duration of the Pleistocene[2] might have been anything

---

[1] Breuil attached great importance to the phenomenon of 'solifluxion' and demonstrated how worked flints, crushed and carried to the foot of slopes or rolled in rivers, may be found in deposits side by side with more recent types of implements (intact). Hence the rule 'a specimen showing signs of solifluxion is always older than the deposit in which it is found'.

[2] The Pleistocene (now enlarged to take in the Villafranchian, the period during which, as far as we can see, the whole story of Man was played out until the fringe of historic times) lasted over 2,000,000 years.

from 10,000 to 1,650,000 years. The 'Ice Age'[1] came to an end 4,000 years ago—or maybe it was 100,000 years. . . .

What sort of man made the ancient implements in the Somme Valley? Boucher could not say, nor could he meet the challenge of those who declared that if the worked flints he produced were really man-made why were there no human fossils found with the implements? So Boucher offered 200 francs ($40 or £8 gold) to any of the workmen who should find human bones embedded in the pleistocene formations. On 28th March 1863 Boucher was shown a human lower jaw stuck in the gravel about fifteen feet from the surface of the ground and thirty metres (98 feet) above the level of the Somme River. Boucher himself dug out the specimen. Obviously the mandible was contemporary with the hand-axes of the Somme's high terrace. The find was one of importance, of such importance that an international committee, or rather a Franco-British committee, met in Paris to decide whether the Moulin-Quignon jaw was or was not authentic; that is to say, of remote antiquity, for, strangely enough, the mandible was quite indistinguishable from that of a modern Frenchman, but, then, why not? A man was a *Homo sapiens*, any other sort of creature was not a man at all. The British members of the committee, however, were sceptical and concluded that the jaw was not a fossil of great age. The French members, on the other hand, accepted the specimen as very ancient, since the president of the committee was a Frenchman and had the casting vote, Moulin-Quignon was, for a time, accepted. One French anthropologist, Pruner Bey (who left some racy descriptions of sexual habits among various peoples of the world), indeed opined that the 'Moulin-Quignon race' was still represented by

[1] The 'Ice Age' was thought of as one (more or less long) period of glaciation. It was not until well into this century that a succession of Ice Ages during the Pleistocene was recognized.

such 'primitive peoples as the Lapps and Basques' (!) of a type once wide-spread 'all around the shores of western Europe'. In vain was it pointed out that in 1346 there had been at Moulin-Quignon a mass-burial of plague-victims.

But the Moulin-Quignon jaw was a hoax and has been conclusively proved (by fluorine tests) to be quite modern.

What sort of man, then, did make Acheulian hand-axes several hundred thousand years ago by the banks of Somme and Thames?

It took a long time to find an answer.

Boucher de Perthes turned his *vaste hôtel*—'huge mansion'—into a museum—it was entirely destroyed during the 1939–45 war—where in addition to his prehistoric implements (most of which were moved in 1862 to the château of Saint-Germain-en-Laye, near Paris, where they form the nucleus of the prehistoric collection) he had a large number, 'over 1,600', paintings of 'the Flemish, Dutch and French schools—mostly fakes', so he never did get quite clear of forgeries.

His work did, however, receive some recognition during his lifetime. Napoleon III made him an *officier* of the Legion of Honour (see p. 50) as a reward for presenting his collection to the State—and Boucher de Perthes was even decorated with the cross of Commander of the Order of Civil Merit of Mecklenburg-Schwerin.

At the time of his death in 1865 the storms of controversy had by no means died down, and although his local municipal council had given his name to a street, the stuffy, provincial society of Abbeville looked on him as a dangerous radical who had advocated state-supported welfare schemes, care for the working classes and democratic control. Then, again, he never married. He left most of his fortune to be distributed among deserving poor working women in twenty French towns.

After his death his family (in disgust, maybe, at being cut out

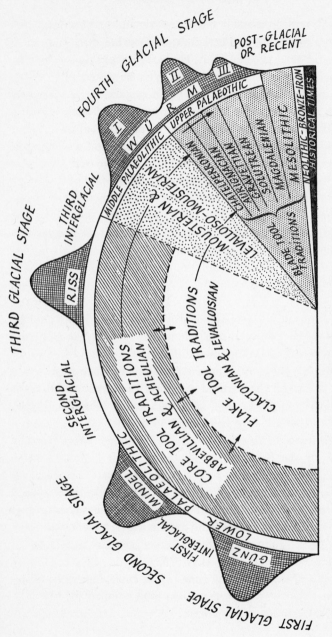

PREHISTORIC AGES. AN ATTEMPTED CHRONOLOGY AND CORRELATION OF GLACIAL STAGES AND INDUSTRIES.

(MUSÉE DE L'HOMME, PARIS)

of his will) withdrew his books from sale and had them, as well as his papers, pulped. Furthermore, Boucher had one most peculiar and even sinister habit. He bathed every day of his life, even when away from home. At Abbeville he would swim in the Somme and have the ice broken when necessary. In fact, this odd addiction nearly cost him his life. A man out wild-duck shooting took Boucher's head for a bird and fired pot-shots at it.

Obviously Boucher was an unreliable man and a dangerous innovator, but when Breuil presided at Abbeville over the meeting held to celebrate the centenary of the confirmation of Boucher's discoveries, and paid a handsome tribute to the memory of Prestwich, Lyell, Falconer and Evans, the people of Abbeville knew well enough that Jacques Boucher de Crèvecœur de Perthes was by far their most illustrious citizen.

After Amiens and Abbeville, d'Ault du Mesnil took young Breuil off to the Campigny site, where they met Capitan (see page 55) and where Breuil dug for the first time, distinguishing himself, moreover, by identifying the skeletons of three marmots, a feat that attracted the amused attention of Albert Gaudry, an eminent palaeontologist, and of a man called Marcellin Boule, with whom Breuil was to have much to do later on.

Though it was d'Ault du Mesnil who 'initiated' Breuil into the mysteries of the 'Quaternary alluviums' it was Capitan who introduced the young man to the study, the analytical study, of man-made implements, an art in which Breuil was to become a past-master. And it was Capitan who said that the men who had chipped the Chellean coarse hand-axes in the Somme Valley were perhaps of the same type as the makers of similar implements in other lands even as far away as Africa.

But it was also a very long time before even a guess could be made as to what was the sort of men who chipped the Chellean (Abbevillian) hand-axes anywhere.

As we have seen already, the hand-axes from the Somme terraces were of two sorts: 'Chellean' (Abbevillian)[1] and 'Acheulian'—named from the Saint-Acheul gravel-pits outside Amiens. Both types of implement lasted for long ages and display a number of variations in form. The 'Abbevillian' in north Europe dates back to the Interglacial between the First (Günz) and the Second (Mindel) Ice Ages; that is to say, a dating in the general order of 500,000 years; while the 'Acheulian' flourished all through the Mindel-Riss Interglacial and to as late as midway through the Riss-Würm Interglacial; say, from 400,000 to 100,000 years ago. Hand-axe users seem to have disappeared from parts, maybe from all, of western Europe during the Mindel glaciation, but they continued in Africa. In the Mindel-Riss Interglacial hand-axes were back in Europe, but as almond-shaped or pointed 'Acheulian' artefacts.

In October 1897 Breuil moved to the Saint-Sulpice seminary. Now, for the first time, he had to wear the *soutane*. In the Issy class-photographs his is the only figure in 'civilian dress'.

The seminary of the Company of Saint-Sulpice no longer exists, though its building (since 1906 a branch of the Ministry of Finance) still occupies all the south side of the old-world

[1] The 'Chellean', so called from Chelles to the east of Paris, was renamed, by the Abbé Breuil, 'Abbevillian', since he maintained that the artefacts at Chelles were not in their proper place but were 'derived', i.e. had been brought down by natural agencies from some other site. It says much for Breuil's authority that he was able to effect this change in nomenclature, since it is a fixed rule that once named by the finder an object must remain saddled with the appellation. Typical Abbevillian artefacts made from flint nodules are found in the Somme forty-metre terrace, generally regarded as of Günz-Mindel dating. Comparable implements in Morocco are found in the raised beaches ninety metres above sea level and are probably just pre-Günz. It may well be that Abbevillian (pre-Chellean and early Chellean) implements may have developed in central Africa, but they spread out over that continent and into western Europe.

Saint-Sulpice square, in the centre of which rises the imposing Fountain of the Four Bishops where Bossuet and Fénelon sit in marble, enemies and fellow-prelates. But Fénelon was no match in intrigue, argument or orthodoxy for the genius of Bossuet:

> *'Défenseur et captif altier du rite ancien,*
> *Prophète du passé, tes lèvres sans souillure*
> *Du charbon d'Isaïe ont gardé la brûlure.'*[1]

The square and its surrounding streets still seem a little provincial (they form an oasis between the conservative 'noble faubourg' Saint-Germain to the west and the Quartier Latin to the east), but perhaps it is rather something of the Sulpician spirit—compounded of sound learning, modesty, good manners and self-confidence—that hovers in the air. You need but a little imagination to see a stooping, effacive figure gliding along into the huge Italianate church—Renan in his early days. Saint-Sulpice church is cold and gritty and overwhelming; its saving grace is Delacroix's masterpiece 'Jacob wrestling with the Angel' in the first chapel to the right.

Breuil gazed on this picture a hundred times and maybe glanced at it on the fateful day when he was ordained—the Abbé was always fascinated by the technique of drawing and painting. All his life he kept on sketching and always had paper and pencil in his pockets. From his Saint-Sulpice days dates the amusing portrait of one of his Sulpician masters, a portly ecclesiastic called Monsieur Roby.[2]

---

[1]'Defender and proud captive of the ancient rite,
Prophet of the past, thine unsoiled lips
Still burning from Isaiah's flaming coal.'

[2] Sulpicians are exceptional in that although priests they are addressed simply as 'Monsieur'. The late Cardinal Verdier, Archbishop of Paris, jumped from plain 'Monsieur' to 'Eminence' when he was selected by the Pope from the Company of Saint-Sulpice.

Breuil also registered as a student at the Faculty of Science of the University of Paris.

In the summer of 1897 Bouyssonie invited Breuil to Brive, a town which now advertises itself as the 'Blossoming Gateway of the South', spelt out in flowers at the railway station. On 1st July came for him the revelation of Les Eyzies, the 'Capital of Pre-history', in the broad Vézère Valley and surrounded by stratified cliffs topped with greenery, with concave rock-faces elephant grey, overhanging ledges, the smoothed surface of stone, and caves, caves, caves all around. At the Auberge de la Gare Breuil met a young schoolmaster, one Denis Peyrony, who was to play a capital part in archaeological discovery of the Dordogne department.

Then Breuil took a quick look at Pair-non-Pair and on 17th July joined Piette at Brassempouy (in the Landes) where was found the beautiful ivory Venus (see p. 93). Piette invited young Henri to stay at Rumigny (in the Ardennes of north-eastern France), Piette's home from 1890 until his death in 1916. Before going north, however, Breuil visited the Mas d'Azil down in the Pyrenean foothills. The Mas d'Azil is a huge natural tunnel some 200 feet high and about 500 yards long, through which run both a river and a highway. The site where Piette found his famed 'Azilian' objects (including the painted pebbles) is a little farther along the river-banks. After the Mas d'Azil Henri saw the prehistoric cavern of Gargas, filled with dozens of mysterious imprints of hands (see p. 229).

By September Breuil was at Rumigny and 'thunder-struck' by Piette's marvellous assemblage of Magdalenian art-objects, ivories, sculptures, bas-reliefs, engravings on reindeer-horn and stone, statuettes and implements.[1] Henri, there and then, decided

[1] Most of Piette's collection was bequeathed to the Saint-Germain museum, but what remained at Rumigny was dispersed during the 1940 invasions.

to devote himself to the study of the 'Reindeer Age', when the peoples of Europe were still living in a hunting and food-gathering economy and Man was rather a rare animal.

In 1898 Breuil did another 'Tour of France' when he dug both at Cro-Magnon and at La Madeleine. The Cro-Magnon rock-shelter, where were recovered the first skeletons of the 'Cro-Magnon' type of man (such as were found at the Baoussé Roussé[1]), is now masked by the Cro-Magnon Hôtel at Les Eyzies, but the rock-face of the shelter has been left to form the back wall of the building, and it is strange to walk along the first-floor passage past the beautifully smooth pale grey limestone that was part of our ancestors' lodging 15,000 years ago and more.

The next year Breuil was in England and looked over the British Museum collection of French Magdalenian objects. He also stayed with John Evans at Nash Mills in Hertfordshire. Some of us who met Sir John in his old age did not realize we were being introduced to one who had known Boucher de Perthes.

Two books he acquired in England helped to fix Breuil's attention on the mysteries of art-evolution, the spread of art-traditions and the development of art-styles. I do not know whether on this occasion he met their authors, probably not, though he got to know them well later. They were Henry Balfour, an Oxford man, distinguished and affable despite arthritis that so crippled his hands they resembled gnarled and knotted tree-roots; and A. C. Haddon, an outstanding ethnologist whose shock of thick white hair in advanced age was so surprising that he would lead off by saying 'No, it's *not* a wig' and take a hearty tug at his forelock.

Breuil was ordained sub-deacon on 9th June 1900 and priest in the church of Saint-Sulpice on 21st December of the same year, thus ten days before the dawn of the new century.

[1] See page 91.

What was the Abbé Henri Breuil to do?

His thoughts were running on Magdalenian art and not on running a parish. The Abbé Bielle, who had been his director of conscience at Saint-Sulpice, offered to get him a job in Paris, but before anything could be done Bielle died very suddenly and Breuil had no one in whom he cared much to confide, since Bouyssonie was doing his military service in the Army. Normally the young priest would have been sent as curate to some church or other, but this was just what he did not want at any cost. So he applied to Mgr. Douais, the Bishop of Beauvais, for permission to be attached to his diocese, but with leave of absence to allow of Breuil continuing his studies in prehistory—after all, Douais was himself an historian and had occupied a chair at Toulouse University, surely he would understand. But historians often fight shy of prehistory, which does not lend itself so easily to doctrines about the 'logic of history', the overall 'pattern' or 'design' in the human story and so forth. History starts with the Romans, or the Greeks, or the Egyptians or the Sumerians— rarely with palaeolithic Man. Anyway, the Bishop refused the young Abbé's request. Curiously enough, it was one of Douais's successors who conferred upon Breuil the only ecclesiastical promotion he ever received. In 1947 the Abbé was appointed honorary canon of Beauvais Cathedral, but he never used the title.

He found a more sympathetic listener in Mgr. Deramecourt, the Bishop of Soissons, in whose diocese the young man had a number of relations. Mgr. Deramecourt fell in with Breuil's wishes and excused him from all parochial work for four years. The dispensation was to last a lifetime. Breuil never held any ecclesiastical post, nor did he receive a regular stipend from the Church, unless one can count his salary for the few years he was a professor at the Catholic University of Fribourg (Switzerland). However, despite the Abbé's being formally attached, with leave of absence, to the diocese of Soissons, he, like all other Catholic priests, was subject to the general authority of the ordinary (that is, the bishop) of any diocese in which he happened to be at any given time.

Meanwhile Breuil went on reading for his degree and in October 1903 was received *licencié ès sciences naturelles* at the University of Paris. The subjects were geology, geography, physics, botany and physiology. Note the absence of anthropology or prehistory—these were not, in those days, considered usually as 'natural sciences'.

The *licence* is a degree above *bachelier* and below *docteur*. The *licence ès sciences* may be compared with the B.Sc. degree in America or Britain. Breuil never did trouble to contest a thesis for a doctorate (though some of his books would have sufficed) but he was an honorary doctor of Oxford, Cambridge, Edinburgh, Lisbon and Cape Town universities—though of no French one. The Abbé, who at times was rather inclined to complain that his work was more highly appreciated abroad than at home, would no doubt have valued an honorary doctorate from his own university of Paris, but the French universities (and this is especially true of the Sorbonne) do not distribute as many 'caps' as do the British and American, while most of the French honorary doctorates seem to go rather to foreigners than to French citizens.

Here, then, we have Henri Breuil on the threshold of his career. What did he look like? What sort of a man was he? Well, he was short, not more than about five feet five inches. A good height for longevity. All centenarians are small. Few or no men of six feet or more, it seems, ever lived to be over ninety, much less a hundred; there must be some compensation for lack of inches. He was slight, rather round-shouldered, with small expressive hands, flashing brown eyes, broad forehead, rather wide and not very long face, dark hair (most of which he lost fairly early on in life). His profile, as so often with highly intelligent men and women, was somewhat wedge-shaped, that is to say his pointed and inquiring nose stood out between a sloping forehead and a lower jaw with rounded chin. His long, rather sinuous mouth smiled readily even when the eyes remained critical, probing, penetrating. However, quite the most exceptional of his physical features was an extraordinarily long head—that in later years resembled somewhat a great Spanish water-melon—which can be noted in a photograph taken of him at Issy, though his lank hair somewhat masks the sharp curve inwards from the back of the head to the neck.

Breuil's general appearance was Mediterranean both in the strictly anthropological sense and in the ordinary use of the word. Mediterranean also was his lively and at times turbulent temperament. All this is the more strange when we remember he was of northern stock, but he took after his mother's side of the family and I have been told (though I have no documentary evidence for it) that the Morio de l'Isles were of Corsican origin, certainly they were Bonapartists, and Breuil would not have looked out of place in the *maquis*. I never heard the Abbé mention any southern origins, though he was communicative about his family. However, there is in France what may be called a 'Corsican complex'. It is one of the better-kept French secrets. Napoleon was a Corsican, but his fellow-islanders in more recent times are generally considered a pretty poor lot, providing an excessively large proportion of France's toughs and crooks and tending to embrace one or other of the closely allied professions of politician, policeman or pimp. Unless a man is what might be called a 'professional' Corsican, he generally does not advertise any remote connections he may have with the 'Isle of Beauty'.

Although the Abbé had plenty of what we like to think of as northern stability and perseverance, and even secretiveness at times, his demeanour was that of a southerner; his geniality, his vindictiveness, his vivacity, his rapidity of thought, his adaptability, his ease in social approach and his affectionate nature which he learned, as do all wise men, to keep well under control. These qualities were not such as to make it easy for him to get along with some of the more fussy, pretentious and narrow-minded of his fellow-countrymen. I have heard men complain the Abbé was 'difficult' and lacked 'ecclesiastical unction'. Indeed he did. But although he was an unusual sort of priest, outspoken (on most subjects), rabelaisian at times and with an almost medieval mingling of sacred and profane, he was also acutely conscious of belonging to a special caste. As though, perhaps, to offset his own exceptional career, he was ever indulgent to men of his cloth and would back them up even in cases where some of them were maybe not very worthy. I do not mean unworthy from the moral or even the theological standpoint, but from the scientific or intellectual—people with whom he probably would never have bothered his head at all had they been laymen. No doubt this attitude was a calculated one, for Breuil was shrewd enough. He meant never to lose the tacit approval of the Church or to man-œuvre himself into the entanglements that plagued Teilhard's later years.

Although he himself would hardly have claimed he felt a call to 'the cure of souls', or indeed much priestly vocation at all, his ecclesiastical character was part and parcel of his being, and to understand his career and some of his reactions we should consider the state of the French Church at the time of his ordina-tion—and later.

Before 1789 the French Church had been the richest, the most powerful and maybe the most imposing in Christendom, though there were many cracks in the edifice. At the Revolution the Church's property was confiscated, and France, in a measure, de-Catholicized. Though re-established by Napoleon (who held that religion kept people in order, prevented the poor from murdering the rich and generally made for good government), the Church never regained anything like its former position, though it slowly staggered back and, from fear of revolution, attracted at times active governmental support as well as a measure of adhesion by the propertied classes, great and small. To a degree, however, religion in France became politics and has so since remained.

The attitude of the Church towards the Third Republic was

imprudent at first, and this attitude had disastrous consequences, despite the later papal commands to accept the Republic. However, it must be admitted that the successive governments of the Third Republic (1870–1940) were more or less anti-clerical, and no politician of pre-1914 days could hope to go far if he were known to be a practising Catholic (it did not matter if he belonged to the small but powerful Jewish or Protestant minorities), while freemasons, who were influential in the old Socialist-Radical party that dominated the political scene, were by profession anti-clerical if not agnostic or atheistic. However, the Concordat (the agreement with the Vatican whereby the Church had been re-established) was not ended until 1905. The men, then, who trained and ordained Breuil were the members of an Established Church, but they were also men brought up in a defensive atmosphere. After all, three Archbishops of Paris had met violent deaths within the space of twenty-three years from 1848 to 1871.

Nevertheless, during the late nineteenth and early twentieth centuries the Church closed its ranks and gathered in strength. It survived the defection of Lamennais and it retained Lacordaire and Montalambert. It weathered the storms raised by Renan's and Loisy's probes into Christian origins. After the First World War the banished religious Orders returned to France. The intellectual standing of some of the French clergy is high, while some members of the Orders, especially the Dominican and Jesuit, are men of remarkable achievement. The Church indeed is a good deal more healthy now than it was in 1905 and it could not have regained so much of the lost ground had its ministers not enjoyed a measure of intellectual prestige. In France nothing can take the place of intelligence.

Diplomatic relations were re-established with the Vatican, while the menace of Communism has led many to rally round the Church as a bulwark against social, political and economic extremists. An appreciable amount of the Church's income is today contributed by Big Business, whose magnates no doubt share Napoleon's judgement. Expressions of violent anti-clericalism have died down—you might search a long time today in the book-boxes along the Seine before you come across a copy of *La Bible Comique*. And to take what may seem to be a trivial example: some 'advanced' municipalities used to consider that a suitable place for a public urinal was against the walls of a church.

Some Paris churches, and Saint-Roch among them, are filled at the hour of High Mass, and not solely with older people and women; but, then, there are, for the numbers of the population, comparatively few churches in Paris; one need not suppose that all of those who go to church are necessarily very pious. Maybe a proportion of them fits into the *pratiquant non croyant*, 'practising, not believing', class. On the other hand, whole regions of rural France are as good as lost to the Church, while the urban industrial workers are to a man—and a woman—indifferent in religious matters. A sort of 'Gallup poll' taken in 1960 revealed that not one out of a hundred believed in God, an after life or the existence of human souls. There are some 8,000,000 urban workpeople out of a total population of about 46,000,000.

This, then, is the situation that matured and took shape during Breuil's lifetime. When he was ordained it was into an Established Church. The secular clergy were paid by the State, as were the bishops—important official personages. And Breuil lived through a period of active anti-clericalism to see the attacks die down and to be succeeded by indifference. But he also lived to see the Church regain lost prestige and occupy a position of greater respect than it had enjoyed maybe since 1789, and he was able to see also the Head of the State a practising Catholic.

Breuil did not, I think, pay very much attention to these matters, but he could not be unaware that ecclesiastics are often regarded as social and political reactionaries or that among most scientists a religious profession is thought of as something distinctly odd.

Just before the outbreak of war in 1939 the late André Sieg-fried, a distinguished economist, professor at the Collège de

About 1898 at Saint-Sulpice

Drawings made in class, 1897–8, from memory

France and member of the French Academy, and I were discussing the relative merits of Guignebert and Goguel, then the outstanding authorities on and critics of the history of Christian origins. 'Of the two,' said Siegfried, 'Goguel is the more intelligent, but he thinks Jesus was something more than a man, whereas Guignebert is like you and me, he holds that Jesus was only a man.' And Siegfried knew nothing at all about my religious opinions.

However, despite what their personal prejudices may be, most Frenchmen still retain, if only embedded in the language they use, some expression of deference for the pomp and circumstance, the historic significance, of the Church. Not only would it be grossly impolite, but also bad French, to address a priest other than as *Monsieur l'Abbé*, unless it were *Mon Père* or *Monsieur le Curé*.[1] I once saw Breuil, though slightly wincing, bear without comment the onslaughts of an English-speaking foreigner (he was our host, so the Abbé was disarmed), who, having read, maybe, that in some circumstances, and in the eighteenth century, some people addressed young, unattached priests as *L'Abbé* (without any *Monsieur*), persisted in so speaking to Breuil, a man of late middle age and world-wide fame.

Even in encounters less than amiable the formulae of politeness will be employed. In his later years the Abbé once took part in the inauguration of an exhibition which was to be opened by a member of the Cabinet. The politician was late. One of the French habits some foreigners often find trying is that adopted by persons in positions of some influence; it is the habit of being late for appointments and of keeping visitors kicking their heels. The conviction of these status-seekers is that if they keep you waiting long enough not only will you be duly impressed by their importance but you will probably become angry, nervous or

[1] The title *Abbé* is not the equivalent of 'Abbot'—the French words for this are *Père Abbé*. *Abbé* during the seventeenth and eighteenth centuries came to designate an unattached priest, one who is neither vicar nor rector (*curé*) nor curate (*vicaire*), nor a member of a monastic or other religious Order who is addressed as *Mon Père* and called *Le Père X*.

D

dispirited; in any case easier to bluff, rebuff and dress down. The French as a rule (if they think it expedient or profitable) are singularly patient in the face of such behaviour. But Breuil was not at all patient, and without waiting for the politician he began an explanation of the exhibits. When the great man did turn up he was rather peeved, and, after introductions, remarked, 'Do you know, *Monsieur l'Abbé*, you've just shaken hands with a freemason?'

Breuil countered, 'Well, *Monsieur le Ministre*, I have during my long life met all sorts of people, of all colours, races and faiths, or lack of them—one freemason more or less doesn't make much difference to me.' The words evidently went home, for the politician held up for a number of years the Abbé's nomination as a Commander of the Legion of Honour. This *cravate*—since the decoration is worn hanging from a ribbon round the neck— is the insignia of the Order's lowest rank which really counts as a distinction—though in France *cravates* are not less common than plain knighthoods in Britain. There are countless members of the Legion of Honour's lower ranks—*chevalier* (this humble bit of red ribbon 'just means', as a disgruntled friend of mine said with only slight exaggeration, 'that you've not been in jail during the past five years') and *officier*. So numerous indeed are the holders of these decorations that Bismarck's contemptuous remark 'You can't get common civility in France unless you have a bit of ribbon in your buttonhole' no longer has any point.[1]

As it was, Breuil did not get his rank of *commandeur* until within three years of his death, whereas plenty of less eminent scientists, not to mention journalists, political professors, business men, political jobbers, actors and indifferent writers, get their *cravates* in middle life.

---

[1] The Legion of Honour has been so debased by indiscriminate bestowal that in 1962 General de Gaulle created a new Order, the *Mérite de France*, and it is said no civilian will be considered for nomination even as *chevalier de la Légion d'Honneur* until he has held for a number of years the rank of *officier* in the *Mérite de France*—but such rules and regulations tend to have a short life.

3

Into the Field

'. . . à travers des forêts de symboles
Qui l'observent avec des regards familiers . . .'
('. . . through forests of symbols
Which watch him with familiar looks . . .')

THERE are French beaches on which you may gather
pebbles marked with natural striations making designs
resembling the letters of our alphabet. These objects
date, of course, from times long before any man-like creature
walked this earth. Still, some people have suggested that the
unknown (probably Phoenician) inventors of our A B C may
have discovered their signs and symbols ready-made for them on
the sea-shore—all nonsense, of course. I showed some of these
'alphabetic' pebbles to Breuil and we amused ourselves by com-
posing short words. One I made was a rather impolite one of
five letters which I suggested was fair comment on Piette's
theory that his Azilian stones were 'alphabetic'. If one has plenty
of goodwill one can find a sort of M, a T, a U, a V, and a Greek
theta and other 'letters' on the painted pebbles. But Breuil,
quite early on in his career, questioned a number of Piette's
conclusions, much to the older man's disgust, for like all of us
he was inclined to think that the good luck or good management
which leads a man to find something, also necessarily ensures that
his interpretation of what he has found shall be 100 per cent
valid.

As a matter of fact, the red-ochre-painted symbols on these Azilian pebbles are derived from stylized figures (many representing the male and female genitalia). At the end of the Ice Age the climate changed, the storm-tracks shifted, thick forests covered most of Europe, while the sea level rose; rose indeed by about three feet a century between 12,000 and 4000 B.C., or a total of some 240 feet. The change, then, was slow. About 6000 B.C. the so-called 'Boreal Phase' gave way before a warmer 'Atlantic' one (which maybe favoured the growth of wild cereals)—this was the time when the last land-bridge was severed between France and England, but here again the seepage of the sea was slow and gradual, each winter bringing more marsh and less solid earth. Between about 5000 and 3000 B.C., indeed, the sea level was higher than it is now, for this was the epoch of 'optimum climate' when it had not been so warm in Europe since the Riss-Würm Interglacial maybe 100,000 years before.

During the Mesolithic, the time of the 'Azlilian' pebbles, men were more or less confined to sea-shores and river-banks—there were no tools suitable for tree-felling on any large scale. They became fish-eaters (it would be interesting to know whether the switch-over to sea-food tended to lengthen men's lives, but we have not enough comparative material to judge) and they created no pictorial art. As Breuil said:

'The same or similar peoples to those who produced the splendid art of the European Late Old Stone Age, lived, during mesolithic times, on sea-shores and fed on fish and crustaceans and produced no art at all comparable with that of the big-game hunters, and left behind them only diagrammatic figures which increased in number and variety among peoples who derived much of their subsistence from the practice of *incipient* agriculture. These men prepared, all unconsciously, the advent of writing.'

Food conditions all our activities and here is a thought from a present-day scientist:

'It is the salt contents and the calcium contents of the food and water of a locality which largely influence the development and appearance of individuals who live in that locality. . . .'

Although the young Abbé did not take Piette's 'alphabetical' stones seriously, and although he would not accept Piette's extravagant idea that the horse was 'semi-domesticated' in Late Old Stone Age times, the older man bore no grudge and, moreover, paid Breuil for making drawings of objects in the collection. These were largely examples of chattel-art (*art mobilier*); that is to say, small engravings, carvings, decorated implements of everyday use—nearly all Magdalenian and dating, therefore, from the latest phase of western European Old Stone Age cultures (say 15,000 to 8000 B.C.).

Long before prehistoric painted caverns had been dreamt of Magdalenian chattel-art objects had been found and, of course, pronounced 'Celtic'. By the 'sixties of the last century the numbers of such things had increased considerably. Among them were bits of mammoth-tusk engraved with figures of mammoths, so obviously not only had there been hairy elephants wandering about France a long time ago but there had been men to sketch them.

Breuil did not turn at once to Reindeer Age objects; as soon as he had got his dispensation from Mgr. Deramecourt and had four years' respite before him, he was puzzled where to begin. D'Ault du Mesnil said, 'Start at the end'; that is, study the Bronze Age (in France from before 1500 to about 500 B.C.); so the Abbé set to work on such things, drawing them, cataloguing them, arranging them. He found this dull, for he could not get the memory of Piette's treasures out of his mind and quite soon he switched over to the Late Old Stone Age.

The Abbé had an inquiring mind and he could not handle evidence without attempting to interpret it. Moreover, even when he was quite young he was not over-impressed by what others said, thought or taught. Indeed, the more Breuil looked at the facts, the more he became convinced that the different prehistoric 'industries' (that is, types of stone implements) were arranged in an unsatisfactory way and, furthermore, that the various guesses made at dating the Old Stone Age were irreconcilable.

As the Abbé Guibert had said, 'There's something to be done in prehistory'. Breuil was getting down to tackling it.

First of all he spotted a major error in the then accepted sequence of industries. The mistake had been made by Gabriel de Mortillet, who regarded the 'Aurignacian' (named for that grotto in the Pyrenees which was the subject of Breuil's first 'scientific paper'—at the age of ten) as a minor and initial phase of the Magdalenian, whereas the Aurignacian was a long-lasting epoch separated from the Magdalenian (in France) by the Solutrean and the Perigordian (Gravettian) culture-phases. In fact the sequence then 'classical' was wildly inaccurate.

Breuil's first spectacular success in the prehistoric field was the winning of the 'Battle of the Aurignacian', though it raged fiercely for years. Breuil succeeded in placing the Aurignacian culture-phase in its right place and in stressing its importance.[1]

However, the Abbé's attention was soon to be attracted to quite another line of country—one that he was to make his own and in which he was to become the greatest authority: the world

---

[1] Here are a few facts and figures useful for an understanding of some aspects of Breuil's work. We are dealing here only with the Late Old Stone Age, the time when, as far as we know, the only sort of man in Europe was *Homo sapiens*:

Magdalenian (localized in France)	15,000 to 8000 B.C.
Solutrean	18,000 to 15,000 B.C.
Gravettian (Upper Perigordian)	22,000 to 18,000 B.C.
Aurignacian	28,000 to 22,000 B.C.
Chatelperronian (Lower Perigordian)	32,000 to 28,000 B.C.

The stone implements of these Late Old Stone Age cultures are all 'blades' of various sorts (i.e. flakes detached from a core and not worked cores) and they look as though they were imported into Europe from the East; that is to say, south-western Asia.

The latest of the Upper Palaeolithic cultures, the Magdalenian, had complex roots and branches. It is divided (in France) into six phases.

of prehistoric painted art. It was as long ago as 1896 that Emile Rivière (we shall meet him again) was working in the Dordogne, in the Vézère River valley, where in the heroic, pioneer days of the 'sixties of the last century Lartet and Christy discovered the richest prehistoric field in all Europe. Rivière was prospecting in a cave (called La Mouthe) whose filling had just been carted away by the owner, and he noticed on the now bare walls engravings with traces of colour. In August of that same year, while he was clearing out the filling of the Pair-non-Pair grotto opening on to a cliff over the lower reaches of the Dordogne River, Daleau noticed what looked like pictures on the rock-face. He borrowed a sprinkler such as is used to sulphate grape-vines and sprayed the walls—there stood out vigorous engravings of a horse and other animals, all obviously older than the Magdalenian filling which had masked them. Daleau made some sketches of the pictures and these are often reproduced, though the originals are more finished than the copies indicate. It is possible, even probable, that the Pair-non-Pair pictures were originally painted, but unless a cavern is particularly dry, paintings disappear and only deep-cut engravings survive.

As Breuil's great skill as a draughtsman was beginning to be known (when he was in the field he used to take along with him specimens of his work), Rivière suggested that the Abbé go to La Mouthe and set to work on copies of the pictures. Breuil had found an interesting and (very modestly) remunerative job.

But there was much more to come. Between 8th and 15th September 1901 Breuil was with Capitan and Peyrony in the Vézère Valley. In this one week two discoveries of prehistoric caverns were made.

First of all, Les Combarelles.

It is a narrow passage, in parts so low you must bend almost double. The gallery dodges back and forth with hairpin turns and much of the walls is a maze of engravings. Les Combarelles is an exciting place for the specialist, but the layman may find it rather a bore. One man I took to visit it said he could make out no pictures at all, and that despite a raking light which I flashed about this way and that in a laudable effort to convince. However, for its discoverers (the splendid French word is *inventeurs*, the 'inventors' in the Latin sense) Les Combarelles was a revelation of the utmost importance. On 10th September Breuil wrote to Jean Bouyssonie:

'Hurrah! Talking of discoveries, here is one and what a one! An immense engraved grotto more than 300 metres long and on over half of it engraved figures of animals, especially horses, but also antelopes, reindeer, mammoths, ibexes. I still feel as though I had dreamed it all—just to happen on it, quite casually, as you might find a stone on the road. And how we slaved yesterday! I traced eighteen of the beasts—some of them are magnificent . . . all in all I spent ten hours in the grotto; I am half dead, I am aching all over, but I am very well pleased. Extraordinary, eh? As for myself, I am giving thanks to Providence.'

There is a good deal of the essential Breuil in this first of his reports on discoveries: his enthusiasm, his vivid way of writing, his tireless energy, his patience, his friendliness, his sense of the religious in the widest acceptance of the word.

He was twenty-four years of age and had had his first real initiation into the mysteries and magnificence of cave-art, to the study, the publication and the explanation of which he was to devote much of his career. If, however, Les Combarelles was an unsuspected treasure, the nearby Font de Gaume cavern was known to exist, at least its entrance was known, though no one seems to have bothered to explore the long, rather narrow cave, or to have suspected that it concealed in its recesses a wealth of prehistoric paintings. The place seems to have served mostly for the love-making of local boys and girls.

It was Denis Peyrony who left Breuil and Capitan at Les Combarelles and went off alone to see if the Font de Gaume might not also be engraved, or painted, or both. Of the three discoverers, Peyrony was the one who knew this Vézère country-side the best, since he had long lived there and for years had there followed his first profession of schoolmaster (later he was to be a full-time prehistorian, founder of the Les Eyzies Museum and official director of prehistoric antiquities for the Dordogne). The Font de Gaume lies high up above the leafy valley of the Beune, a tributary of the Vézère, and when he had penetrated some considerable distance into the cavern Peyrony began to make out a multitude of paintings of animals in naturalistic style —bison, horse, mammoth, reindeer, aurochs, ibex, bear, wolf, two rhinoceroses, some isolated human figures and a mass of signs. These were the beasts among which men lived towards the end of the last Ice Age, the animals with which our ancestors seem to have felt a relationship we cannot fully understand.

Later on Breuil was to spend long days copying the Font de Gaume pictures, some of which, such as the red rhinoceros and the affronting reindeer, have become familiar from the Abbé's copies which Prince Albert of Monaco published in a fine volume devoted to the grotto.

Both Les Combarelles and the Font de Gaume are rather ill-cared-for and the latter's polychrome paintings have little of the freshness and brilliance of the Lascaux pictures, which, however, were until 1940 completely sealed up for millennia.

The prime importance of the Les Combarelles and Font de Gaume pictures was that they showed without any doubt that prehistoric painting was a fact. But, naturally, as the proofs piled up, the more rabid became the opponents of cave-art. The Les Combarelles engravings were laughed off as mere scratchings by refugees from Napoleon's recruiting sergeants. Numbers, it was affirmed, could be made out as though branded on some horses' rumps. To Breuil himself was attributed the honour of having made the frescoes at the Font de Gaume. Some of the more vociferous critics were men who had faked the cave-fillings at Cro-Magnon and the Grotte de l'Enfer (this latter also near Les Eyzies) so as to bolster up their wrong reading of

the evidence about the order and succession of the late palaeolithic 'industries' and culture-phases. The 'Battle of the Aurignacian' had opened up a second front. The fight was on and no
punches pulled.

In August 1902, however, a delegation of French archaeologists visited La Mouthe and agreed that the pictures were authen-
tically ancient. A photograph of the scene shows, among
others, Emile Rivière, Denis Peyrony, Breuil, Daleau and Emile
Cartailhac. The latter was to play a determining role in Breuil's
career. Cartailhac, who was born well before Boucher de Perthes
died, was brought up in Toulouse, that splendid city in south-
western France which plays such an important part in the history
of prehistorical studies. He was trained as a lawyer, but had
private means (much of which he spent in furthering the cause of
science) and travelled far and wide, visiting archaeological sites
in France, Spain, Portugal, Italy, Greece and Egypt. He had been
at first highly sceptical about prehistoric painting (see p. 60),
though by 1902 he had been much impressed by La Mouthe and
Pair-non-Pair, as well as by Marsoulas, a prehistoric cave then
recently recognized in the Pyrenean foothills. Cartailhac also
admired the young Abbé's drawings of Les Combarelles and
Font de Gaume, and he decided to try out Breuil's talents as a
copyist at Marsoulas. It is near Saliès de Salat in the Haute-
Garonne department, and is a short, low-vaulted grotto whose
walls on both sides are almost covered with prehistoric paintings.
And if we wonder why it took so long to discover cave-art we
not only have to bear in mind the current prejudice that 'no such
things could exist'—obviously Stone Age Man could not paint,
painting had been invented by the Egyptians, for Egypt was in
those days (though ancient Egyptian chronology was very vague)
looked upon as the mother of all the arts, the cradle of civilization
and maybe esoteric wisdom—but in addition to such prejudice
there was a remarkable, though all too common, blindness to
the obvious—when it was not expected. During the years from
1881 to 1884 the Abbé Cau-Durban, a careful and reliable

archaeologist, dug in Marsoulas for months on end and never noticed the pictures staring at him from the walls—strange caricatural human figures, shamans, wizards, magicians wearing bear-masks, and there is a number of engravings on stone slabs, pictures that appear also—on a larger scale—painted on the walls. The palaeolothic artists did then refresh their memories with sketches made outside in the open air.

'After he had seen me at work copying the cave-paintings at Marsoulas', wrote Breuil, 'Cartailhac suggested a trip to Altamira.'

It was as far back as 1868 that a man out looking for small game lost his dog in a hole. Dogs seem to have played quite a part in smelling out prehistoric caverns. It was a dog that in 1940 led some lads down into Lascaux. The sportsman of 1868, in order to extricate his animal, shoved aside some stones around the opening and saw there was a subterranean passage leading away into pitch darkness. Seven years later a local landowner, Marcelino de Sautuola, did penetrate some distance but not far. However, in 1878 he visited the Paris Exhibition and was there struck by the display of prehistoric stone implements, and still more by the carved and engraved small objects in bone, by painted pebbles and by statuettes. Many of these things had been recovered by the archaeological pioneer Edouard Piette and they dated back to the last phase of the Old Stone Age and to the succeeding Mesolithic; say to between 15,000 and 5000 B.C more or less. Might not Sautuola's Altamira hold similar treasures?

Well, it did not, but held something much more marvellous.

Sautuola dug about in the forepart of the cavern, and found traces of human occupancy, but it was his little daughter who wandered off one day and came back shouting '*Toros, toros*', magic words for any Spaniard. She had discovered the world-famous

Bison Ceiling where, in lively confusion, are most vivid and impressive paintings of beasts.

The Bison Chamber is peculiar (or was peculiar, since the floor has now been cut away) in that it was low, so low that a grown man could not stand upright everywhere in it, and the paintings might long have gone undiscovered had it not been for a small child who could walk easily upright under the frescoed vault.

Sautuola made some rough sketches of the polychrome pictures and sent them to Vilanova at Madrid University. He came to Altamira and was convinced that the paintings were very ancient. How old, was anyone's guess. As late as 1912 it was being stated that the pictures dated back, most probably, to 50,000 B.C.— that is to say, they were accorded about four times their real age. In 1880 Vilanova talked about Altamira at an archaeological congress at Lisbon. Among those present were Emile Cartailhac (very sceptical) and John Evans, who had been one of the men to back up Boucher de Perthes (see p. 30). Vilanova proposed a visit to the cave, but did not press his suggestion in the face of general indifference. However, Edouard Harlé, a French civil engineer (and afterwards well known as an archaeologist), did, a little later on, go to Altamira and published an account of his visit. He was unconvinced. He saw no paintings or engravings of reindeer and concluded the pictures could not belong to what was then generally called the 'Reindeer Age' (i.e. the Magdalenian, the last culture-phase in western Europe of the Late Old Stone Age); moreover, he could see no painting with a calcite covering such as he thought must exist in a damp cave if the frescoes were really very ancient. He also noticed paint in the cracks and crevices of the walls and surmised the pictures must have been executed with a brush. He was puzzled, too, that on so low a ceiling there were no traces of torch-smoke. His summing-up was that the paintings had been made between 1875 (the time of Sautuola's first visit) and 1879, when his daughter found the bisons.

Altamira faded from men's memories.

Breuil and Cartailhac did not have much money. Cartailhac wrote to Salomon Reinach[1] and got 500 gold francs out of him; Breuil contributed 400 francs Piette had given him for making drawings: 900 francs altogether ($180 or thirty-six British sovereigns). I do not know whether this was all they had, but I do not think they took much more with them, and they spun out the money for several weeks.

Cartailhac asked Harlé to go with them, but although he could not he gave them a letter of introduction to Pérez de Molina, who had been a friend of Sautuola, by this time long dead.

Pérez de Molina met them at Santillana del Mar—the nearest town to Altamira—and guided them through the mud to the cave. Cartailhac was then nearly sixty years of age and that is old to go scrambling about in a huge, murky cavern with no light but that from candles, and to slither over damp rocks and creep for more than 300 yards, which seem like three miles underground where you soon lose a sense of distance in the bowels of the earth.

Both Cartailhac and Breuil had to lie at full length on straw-stuffed sacks and to engage in all sorts of acrobatics, not only to examine the paintings on the low ceiling but also to scrutinize the engravings in which Altamira is so rich. First of all Breuil made rough sketches, and then from measurements taken on the originals executed his excellent copies: 'Before I went to Altamira I had never worked in pastel, but I had to do so now. The little

[1] It does not seem to be clear whether Reinach paid this money out of his own pocket (he was a wealthy man) or got it from the funds of the Institut de France. Reinach was a distinguished archaeologist, a writer of books popularizing scientific matters and a promoter of research. His career, however, was somewhat overshadowed by two bad mistakes. Early on he had accepted as genuine the fake 'Tiara of Saïtapharnes', for which the Louvre had paid a large sum, and, much later, he was strongly in favour of the authenticity of the crude Glozel frauds, fragments of pottery and 'inscriptions' forged by the Fradins and designed to prove the western origin of later human cultures.

water-colour technique I had learned would have been of no use to me in the damp atmosphere of Altamira.'

In fact, Breuil was, very largely, a self-taught artist and maybe none the worse for that.

'After Altamira I copied many thousands of paintings and engravings. The animal-art of the Cave Age was my main concern during my life as an artist. I used pen, pastel, pencil and water-colour. I put in a secondary place the drawing of worked bone or stone artefacts. For dealing with such things I have trained pupils and taught others. . . . I can readily imagine the artists of the Reindeer Age were like me and did not take measurements. They cast upon the rock-face, as I did upon paper, the inner vision they had of an animal. . . . I had two sets of masters; first of all the living and involuntary models provided by my teachers at the Seminary, and, secondly, the rupestral pictures of the Reindeer Age in France and Spain. . . . What trains the copyist, what makes him produce a real work of art in keeping with the spirit of the original, is the close attention he must pay to the pictures in order to appreciate the various fine differences and nuances of drawing technique. . . .'

On the occasions when it was not pouring with rain the two men would eat their midday meal in the open, facing Old Castile's northern coastal ranges fading away towards an ocean that has covered some of the old Altamirans' hunting-grounds. The photograph opposite p. 64 shows Breuil and Pérez de Molina at luncheon. The white blotches on the Abbé's cassock are candle-drippings, since all the work at Altamira had to be done by candlelight only; one can hardly imagine the fantastic fatigue and strain on the eyes which the wonderful copies of the Bison Ceiling entailed.

The fine polychrome paintings (but not necessarily the engravings or other pictures), which are attributable to Magdalenian Phase III, are datable by Carbon-14 method to about 13,540 B.C.

with a margin of error of 700 years one way or the other. It is, of course, organic matter found 'in association' with the pictures that gives a C-14 dating and it should not be accepted as strictly accurate without a building-up of confirmatory evidence. That is to say, if a C-14 finding is wildly discordant with other indications, then it should be regarded with suspicion (see p. 187). Still, if we think that men were painting pictures at Altamira 150 centuries ago then we shall not be so far out.

On 28th October 1902 Cartailhac and Breuil left Santander. The Abbé had begun his career in the caves: 'With my lamp in the darkness, deciphering, copying, tracing, I have spent more than 700 days in seventy-three different caverns, in the Dordogne, in the Pyrenees, in Cantabria, in the Lot, in south-eastern France, in Castile, in Andalusia in southern Italy.'

By the way, Breuil's Altamira copies when they were published excited the interest of a young Spaniard called Pablo Picasso, who went to admire the Bison Ceiling. There is a thesis to be written on the influence of prehistoric art in Picasso's painting.

In April 1903 Harlé again visited Altamira; this time after having had a look at the Font de Gaume. On the 10th of that month he wrote to Cartailhac and Breuil that he was convinced now the Altamira paintings were genuine: '. . . but it is the Font de Gaume that has made me change my mind. But for that I would still say the Bison Ceiling is a forgery.' Cartailhac was less reserved and made amends for his former incredulity in the article he wrote for *L'Anthropologie* and entitled *Le mea culpa d'un sceptique*.

But there were still hard-hearted sceptics (indeed, the breed is not yet quite extinct), among whom was Adrien de Mortillet, the son of Gabriel, who was not quite up to his father's standard, and, out of ill-judged filial piety maybe, not only perpetuated his father's mistakes but also participated in faking evidence to bolster up the elder Mortillet's errors. Furthermore, although Jesuit-educated, Adrien de Mortillet was a rather vociferous agnostic and proclaimed that the Altamira frescoes had been executed 'by Spanish Jesuits in order to discredit prehistory'.

Since 1902 times have changed indeed and instead of Breuil's admirable reproductions we are often offered colour photographs, which, however, sometimes convey a less accurate and faithful impression than the Abbé's copies, which are not vitiated by untrue perspective due to irregular rock-surfaces. Moreover, for the engravings, drawings are quite indispensable; photographs reveal but a maze of lines—and by far the greater mass of prehistoric pictorial material is in the form of engravings. These may not be so spectacular at a first glance, but they are even more significant than the paintings, as we may note, for instance, at the Trois-Frères (see p. 105).

Shortly after Altamira, Breuil read, at a scientific congress in Périgueux (the capital of the Dordogne and thus near to the prehistoric sites of the Vézère Valley), two papers.

The first was a sketch-chronology of prehistoric art-styles based on data from the painted caverns as then known: first, outlines, then some modelling, flat-wash, and then polychrome; finally, here and there, Azilian figures dating from the Mesolithic. In fact, an art-history extending through more than 20,000 years, though Breuil did not express himself then in datings.

The second paper was on the true position of the Aurignacian.

Meanwhile, Breuil's time was running out. His four years were nearly up. Was he going to be posted to a country parish, there to learn some of the more arduous obligations of the priesthood? No; salvation came just in time. The Abbé Brunhes (who was afterwards Bishop of Montpellier), a fellow-student with Breuil at Issy, got him a job as a *privat-docent*[1] in the Catholic University of Fribourg in Switzerland. Here he had to teach prehistory and ethnology and was provided with a small but useful income. From 1906 to 1910 the Abbé spent a good deal of his time in

[1] A *privat-docent* is a private teacher recognized by the university but not on the salaried staff, though taking fees from his students. Breuil's job in Fribourg was later raised to a professorship.

At Altamira, 1902. Breuil's cassock is spotted with candle-grease

Breuil and the Prince of Monaco, El Castillo, August 1909

Le Ruth, 1908. From left to right: L. Raymond, E. Cartailhac, D. Peyrony, Breuil, Féaux, Delugin, de Fayolle, F. Delage, P. Paris

Switzerland, but beyond mentioning that these years 'finished off his education' he did not, I think, often refer to them.

But the Swiss job did not take up all Breuil's time and whenever he could get away he was in the field—and he was beginning to make a name for himself. When, on his appointment to Fribourg, he went to thank Mgr. Deramecourt and to take leave of him, the worthy Bishop of Soissons blessed him and added, 'You will one day be a professor at the Collège de France.' And he spoke truly enough, though he did not live to see the day that crowned Breuil's academic career.

However, by this time, when his Swiss years began, Breuil had come in contact with a man who was to have a determining effect on his career—Prince Albert of Monaco. Cartailhac knew him and induced him to publish the book on Altamira and there-after the Prince put funds at Breuil's disposal for further explorations in Spanish prehistoric caves. Moreover, by 1906, when the Prehistoric Congress was held in Monaco, and the Prince got to know Breuil personally, Albert had already made up his mind to promote archaeological and prehistoric studies. In addition to deep-sea research, which was his first love, and an interest in the infant art of flying, he was maturing a scheme for the foundation and endowment of an Institute of Human Palaeontology to be devoted to the study of Man's origins, his development, his art, his remains, his implements, his rites, his works. No such institution existed anywhere. Then—to some degree—the last thing to be taught and studied was the story of ourselves and how we came to be what we are. In those days anthropology was a Cinderella of the sciences, while prehistory wandered about, like an unwanted child, between archaeology and geology.

From 1906 Breuil, with the Spaniards Alcalde del Rio and Father Sierra and the German Hugo Obermaier, had been at work in the northern Spanish caves, notably El Castillo, Covalanas and Altamira itself.

In August 1909 Prince Albert, on his yacht, arrived in the northern Spanish harbour of Santander. He had come to see for

E

himself how his money was being spent and what results were being obtained. His visit was awaited by Breuil and Obermaier with some anxiety, since on the Prince's impression depended all the future of Breuil's work in Spain.

Albert in 1909 was sixty-one years of age. He had been twice divorced (he had been married at the age of twenty, and at the command of Napoleon III, to the Emperor's second cousin, the daughter of a Scottish duke) and preferred to female society long cruises on his yacht, manned by young Breton sailors and carrying a complement of men of science, draughtsmen, painters and private friends.

In 1909 world conditions seemed very stable. In France the confusion aroused by the Dreyfus case had died down. In Britain Edward VII was coming to the end of a reign that was to mark—though few suspected it—a change in his country's position from that of the greatest Power on earth. It looked as though one could make plans for a long time ahead. As a matter of fact, the First World War cut right through the Prince's plans and his Institute did not begin to function until 1920. However, Breuil was taken on in the new Institute from the time of its founding in 1910.

At the present time (1963) some thirty prehistoric caverns are known in northern Spain and no doubt there are others as yet unknown, since several new ones have been prospected in quite recent years. The caves stretch from Santimamiñe (near Guernica, of Civil War fame and Picasso's picture) in the east to as far as San Román (near Oviedo) in the west, or a distance of over 100 miles, and they lie, almost all of them, in the Cantabrian Mountains, which are but a prolongation of the Pyrenees. The most important are, after Altamira, Pindal, Covalanas, La Pasiega— with red figures sparkling on ivory-coloured walls—and Santián and El Castillo. Though none of the other caverns is as spectacular as Altamira, El Castillo is on a gigantic scale and burrows into a conical, symmetrical hill (near Puenteviesgo) known as La Peña de Nuestra Señora del Castillo. This eminence must have been a great sanctuary millennia ago because in addition to the El Castillo cave, there are also there La Pasiega and one or two others. The El Castillo paintings include animals in outline, many signs, fine engravings, schematic drawings, symbols and no less than forty-four stencils of human hands. There is an abundance of fossil animal bones, including cave-bear (rare in Spain), horse, deer, goat and wolf—or maybe the latter were dog, by far the earliest animal to be domesticated.

But the uniqueness of El Castillo lay in its cave-fillings (they have now been almost entirely removed), in some places seventy-four feet deep, where was preserved a regular sequence of man-made stone implements from the time of the last (Riss-Würm) Interglacial onwards for maybe 100,000 years in all. And these implements indicate that at El Castillo (as at many other sites) neanderthaloid men were the first users of the cavern before it was taken over—maybe ages later—by men like ourselves.

The full importance of El Castillo as offering a complete sequence of 'industries', and therefore a complete record of Man for some thousand centuries, was not quite clear when the Prince of Monaco in 1909 made his way scrambling along a goat-track round the hill of Our Lady of the Castle, but what was clear was that the prospection of these northern Spanish caves was producing results, and the Prince, who was a man of shrewd judgement, saw that those results were due very largely to the small, dynamic young priest in a cassock spotted with candle-drippings and the tall, burly Bavarian with a big, bushy black beard, Hugo Obermaier—also a priest, though one would hardly have guessed it.

The photograph facing p. 65 shows Albert with the bright-eyed young Abbé at Castillo. When the Prince had been shown the rounds his mind was made up. Henri Breuil had communicated something of his own enthusiasm. He would obviously be a good man to get for that Institute of Human Palaeontology. Meanwhile Albert told Breuil to go ahead, hire local helpers, to prospect still more, to explore other parts of the country, where, as Cartailhac—too old now for the rough and tumble of cave exploration—suggested, it would be worth while to visit some half-forgotten and enigmatic painted and engraved rocks. The Prince would foot the bill. Breuil's career was assured.

Unlike many men who rise to fame and then ignore what they owed to those who gave them a start, Breuil never failed to acknowledge what he owed to Albert of Monaco. It is no exaggeration to say that without Albert's encouragement and financial support, without Breuil's appointment at the new Institute, the Abbé's career would not have been possible.

Earlier on in this same critical year for Breuil's fortunes, on 15th April 1909, Denis Peyrony invited a number of archaeologists—Breuil, Cartailhac and Boule among them—to visit Le Ruth near Le Moustier (the type-site of the neanderthaloid 'Mousterian' industry) in the Vézère Valley and there to examine a succession of well-defined strata showing the Aurignacian lying beneath the Solutrean stone implements, which latter were under the Magdalenian. The evidence was quite decisive and entirely confirmed Breuil's contentions as to the place of the Aurignacian. The 'Battle of the Aurignacian' was won.

The victory had a tragic sequel. Girod, who had been one of the Abbé's most violent opponents (and who had participated in the faking of evidence to bolster up the elder Mortillet's classification), was so chagrined by his defeat that it seriously affected his health to such an extent that a few months later he dropped down dead as he was taking part in a congress at Clermont-Ferrand.

On occasion Breuil would say, with some compunction, 'That was the man I killed.'

Towards the end of his life the Abbé contributed to the British review *Antiquity* an entertaining little paper on some fakes he had known. Of course, a great many forgeries have been made and no doubt still are being made, just for gain, as was the case with the 'Tiara of Saïtapharnes' (see p. 61) and unquestionably many such objects still pass for genuine today. But often genuinely ancient things have been denounced as fakes, such as the 'Note Books of Moses'—as they were pompously called—which Shapira offered for sale in 1883. So embittered was he at his failure to get his treasures recognized as authentic (and sold for the very large sum he demanded, £1,000,000 or $5,000,000), that he shot himself; but his bits of leather were no doubt genuine and came from the same region as the Dead Sea Scrolls. The Piltdown imposture was executed by a provincial solicitor who wished to make a name for himself and receive academic honours—or maybe he just had a cynical sense of humour.

However, it is difficult to understand the mentality of a scientist who deliberately falsifies evidence, not from motive of gain, or for ideological or confessional or religious reasons, but just to support a theory he has adopted and will not let go.

It is hardly surprising that with the memory in his mind of the violent quarrels aroused by the Aurignacian question Breuil should have been, throughout his life, merciless towards anyone he suspected of being less than wholly objective and honest in scientific matters. He himself claimed that he was 'always ready to follow the evidence wherever it may lead'.

By 1912 the Abbé had got his data in order and presented it to the Geneva Prehistoric Congress. His paper 'The Subdivisions of the Upper Palaeolithic and their Significance' and the arrangement he there proposed, have, despite some corrections and additions (most of which he himself supplied later on), held the field and form the classical basis for all work on the Late Old Stone Age. But, as Breuil himself wrote, no one will know 'all the struggles I had to face in order to get [it] accepted'.

However, some time before the end of the 'Battle of the Aurignacian' the Abbé (now Canon) Jean Bouyssonie steps forward. The year is 1908. Very little was then known about the bones of early Man. There was the Pithecanthropus skull-cap from Java (found in 1891)—and this was generally regarded as rather ape than Man—there were some bits and pieces of neanderthaloid-type skulls (including the original cranium found near Düsseldorf in 1859) and that was about all. Where the Neanderthaloids fitted into the time-table was not clear and little was known about their skeletons, other than their skulls. Maybe they were hardly men at all and lived in trees or went on all fours like an ape. To understand what follows perhaps we should bear in mind, first, the strong prejudice then existing that any other sort of man but *Homo sapiens* ever lived on this earth, and, second, that no satisfactory definition of what was and what was not a 'man' was available.

It was on 3rd August 1908 that three priests from the Corrèze department—Jean Bouyssonie, his elder brother (later Mgr.) Amédée Bouyssonie and the Abbé Bardon—found in a cave near La Chapelle-aux-Saints the almost complete skeleton of a neanderthaloid[1] man. He had been intentionally buried in a low grotto that never could have served as a home.

This sensational discovery triggered off, it would seem, a whole series of other finds of a similar sort. It was only a week after the Bouyssonies unearthed the La Chapelle-aux-Saints specimen that one Otto Hauser, a Swiss antique-dealer and unscrupulous excavator, dug out at Le Moustier itself (in the Vézère Valley and the type-station of the 'Mousterian' artefacts) the rather damaged skeleton of an adolescent Neanderthaloid. The discovery, or rather the actual extrication of the bones from the earth, was made in the presence of a whole flock of German scientists (though no French savant was there) and Hauser sold the specimen for 125,000 gold francs (or £5,000 gold) to the Berlin Museum, where the bones were destroyed during the

[1] We are stuck with this ungainly term, which by its very barbaric appearance has done something to maintain the fiction of the Neanderthaloids as little better than brute beasts.

bombardment of the German capital during the Second World War.

It was Hauser's exploits that led to the promulgation of French laws protecting prehistoric sites and objects. The Swiss merchant's memory became so detested in French scientific circles that at least one French prehistorian refused for years to visit an excellent hotel just because it was kept by the son of Hauser's foreman.

Bouyssonie sent the La Chapelle-aux-Saints skeleton to Marcellin Boule, then professor of palaeontology at the Paris Muséum d'Histoire Naturelle, and he, after prolonged study, wrote his report, which became, unfortunately, the classical description of a Neanderthaloid. However, the bones are those of an aged man showing many signs of degenerative changes. Furthermore, the bones (and especially those of the skull) were unskilfully reassembled.

According to Boule, the Neanderthaloids (for he judged all the group from this one specimen) were heavy, clumsy, shambling creatures walking with bent knees and with head lolling forwards. In fact, a man, if you like, but one very different from ourselves. We know now that the Neanderthaloids were our very close relations, that they flourished for many millennia, at least 50,000 years, that they comprised many different types, some almost indistinguishable from *Homo sapiens* and some more rugged and big-boned. The features, moreover, which were thought to mark off the two different sorts of men are largely arbitrary.

Under rather beetling brows the Neanderthaloids had prominent and well-formed noses, not much chin eminence on the lower jaw, it is true, but a brain as large as, if not larger than, that of most modern men—though, of course, brain size is not much of a clue to brain quality.

Not a single neanderthaloid cranium of which we possess the base unmutilated shows anything to suggest the head was held any differently from that of *Homo sapiens*, nor do the pelvis or leg bones indicate anything but a perfectly upright carriage. Yet we all too often still see reproductions of Boule's 'reconstruction' and read descriptions of Neanderthaloids that are completely fantastic and misleading.

Boule, of course, was not alone in his views (which, as he was a very obstinate man, he persisted in until his death). Klaatsch, for instance, one of the Germans present at the Le Moustier exhumation, opined that the Neanderthaloids were so 'gorilla-like' that it was obvious 'they originated in Africa, the home of the gorilla'. But then Klaatsch also stated that 'Aurignacian Man' (i.e. *Homo sapiens*) descended from orang-outangs.

The fact is that could we see living Neanderthaloids today most of them would not appear any more strange, if as strange, as Australian aboriginals.

Since Breuil had a good deal to do with the neanderthaloid problems, here is the present-day view about Man and men:

There have been, as far as we can see, but three sorts of 'hominids' (let us use that word here instead of 'men') i.e.:

(1) The Australopithecines, originating probably in central Africa maybe 2,000,000 years ago.

(2) The Pithecanthropoids, wide-spread by 400,000 years ago in Africa, Europe and Asia.

(3) The Neanderthaloids and *Homo sapiens*.

Boule's study of the La Chapelle-aux-Saints specimen did more, however, than any other of his publications to establish his position as the leading palaeo-anthropologist (i.e. expert on hominid fossils) and to confirm Prince Albert in the conviction that Boule was the obvious man to head the Institut de Paléontologie Humaine—or the I.P.H.

4

Spanish Years

'El mundo es una máscara; el rostro, el trage y la voz, todo es fingido.'

GOYA at San Antonio de la Florida

('The World is a mask, the face, the clothing and the voice, all is feigned.')

'IN THE Sierra Morena and in Andalusia I had to ride for long distances through very wild country, but I had good maps and in the mornings I would ask my guide to point out the place we were making for and to trace out the track we were to follow. Then I would jump on my horse and gallop off until I was a few miles ahead of the men, who, with the pack-mules, followed on foot. When I was quite alone, and far from any sign of man, I would slow down to walking pace—and let myself think.

'I noticed everything around me: the earth and its natural formations, the plants and the flowers, the insects and the birds. Little, I think, escaped my eyes. Yet all the time I was thinking: thinking about my country, about a speech I had to make at a marriage in two months' time, about controversies and various problems I was involved in, about something I had discovered a few days before and its meaning, about scientific or religious questions that occupied my mind. In fact, about everything which made up my real, personal, active life.

'I let my mind wander freely from one subject to another—as loosely as the reins that lay on my horse's neck—and everything simmered inside me, quite quietly, like a stew cooking over a slow fire all day long.'

So Breuil described the way illumination comes when you do not seek it too fiercely. What he did not add was that he smoked nearly all the time. He was a non-smoker until he was about thirty, but after the beginning of his Spanish years he made up for lost time. He used to say that as at first he was handicapped by not knowing the language (and in those days especially it was rare to come across a Spaniard who could, or would, talk anything but Spanish), and felt, when sitting about in cafés, that he had to do something *pour se donner une contenance*—'to keep himself in countenance'—so he took to smoking and never left off. Indeed, he was almost a chain-smoker. He rolled his own sometimes, very loosely, but he would accept a cigarette from anyone and was not fussy about the brand. Towards the end of his life, encouraged maybe by friends who had made a virtue of necessity, or perhaps warned by his doctors, he did leave off smoking for several weeks. Then someone gave him a packet of cigarettes and he never afterwards tried to reform. However, he did not inhale and did not use more than half a cigarette. In his Paris apartment there were so many butts lying about in ashtrays, here, there and everywhere, that the Little Sisters of the Poor would pay him regular visits and carry off bags full of tobacco.

Though he was a heavy smoker for over fifty years, he was of no use as an awful example. He did not develop lung-cancer nor, apparently, was his heart affected. He remained active, would take long walks and climb up rocks until past seventy.

From 1909 until the outbreak of the Spanish Civil War in 1936 hardly a year passed without his spending some time in Spain. By 1910 he had discarded the *soutane* for field-work and had adopted the rig he was to retain for all his explorations—light yellow waterproof knickerbockers, high laced boots (on occasion rubber waders) and a sort of Norfolk jacket with very large pockets—what countrymen in England call 'poacher's pockets'. Underground, or when the sun was not too strong and when in ecclesiastical dress, he would have a beret on his head (when in caves it was stuffed with old newspaper so as to protect him from bumps); but when it was hot he would don any sort of wide-brimmed headgear that came to his hand—whether it was his own or not. In 1950, when an exhibition was arranged at the Museum of Man on 'The Rupestral Art of South Africa', both the Abbé and Pastor Ellenberger chose which of their copies were to be displayed. Then, after greetings all around, Breuil disappeared. It was some little time before they found he had walked off with Ellenberger's hat.

During the 1939–45 war Breuil attracted a good deal of attention in the streets of Lisbon because he went about in a pale blue sun-bonnet. When it was suggested to him that this was a 'female hat' he grumbled, 'That's the first time I've heard that hats have got a sex.' Twenty years ago (and maybe still today) it was for-bidden in Portugal to wear ecclesiastical garb in public. The rule was a hang-over from anti-clerical times and had been maintained, or at least not abrogated, by Salazar. Maybe, however, the pro-hibition did not extend to foreigners, since when I was with him in Portugal in 1941 he wore, I am almost certain, a *soutane* in the anthropological laboratory of the Academy of Science (but this was indoors) and undoubtedly he was cassock-clad when we lunched together (but then he had just come from baptizing the child of a French friend) at the exotically gaudy Hotel Aviz (now demolished), among gilded wrought-iron gates, blue and white tiles and frescoes depicting the glories of Portugal's past.

It was Cartailhac who, when Prince Albert promised further subsidies for prehistoric prospection in Spain, suggested the Abbé should turn his attention to some sites—engraved and painted rocks—which had been discovered long before but since forgotten; such as Las Cabras Pintadas in the wild valley of Las Batuecas, mentioned by the dramatist and poet Calderón de la Barca (who died in 1681); La Piedra Escrita at Fuencaliente in the Sierra Morena, reported to the statesman Floridablanca in 1783; or Las Letreras de Vélez Blanco (in the south-east of the province of Almería), found in 1871.

It is noteworthy that popular imagination had saddled some of these rocks with names implying 'writing', for indeed the stones are covered with designs, symbols, schematized figures of wild and domestic animals, representations of human beings—men and women, often in pairs, and sexual symbols ranging from the semi-naturalistic to the most obscurely schematized. Such engraved and painted rocks are all much later in date than the naturalistic cave-art of the Cantabrian sites such as Altamira or Covalanas. Some of these archaic patterns resemble the tattoo-marking on Algerian and Moroccan women[1] of an older generation, and Breuil was amused when I showed him a sketch of a 'prehistoric' pattern I had copied from the design clipped on a Spanish mule's rump.

Over much of Spain from the Sierra Morena to Andalusia there are these post-palaeolithic pictures in which can be seen a progressive stiffening into schematization. Most of them are in red ochre and represent human figures, some clearly recognizable as such and others identifiable only because there is a series of modifications leading up to the symbol Man's body has become. Animal figures are just as simplified, often in fantastic manner, —ibexes and stags, more rarely sheep, wolves and birds, also oxen, horses and felines—and then dots and circles, zigzags, waves, hands, 'combs' and stars or suns. . . . Man's perpetual preoccupation with symbols.

Maybe these great stones were spirit rocks before which offerings were made.

[1] Or Mr. Somerset Maugham's personal badge which appears on all his books.

The schematic paintings and engravings lasted right through the Spanish Neolithic, but ceased in the Bronze Age.

The Spanish rock-paintings and -engravings fall into three main groups. There are these 'Written Rocks' that are of great interest in showing the growth and development of a schematic, geometric and symbolical art. Then there are the palaeolithic naturalistic cave-paintings of Cantabria—and also of one or two sites right down in southern Spain. Although Breuil would visit the Cantabrian sites from time to time most of the excavation there was done by Hugo Obermaier, Paul Wernert and the Spanish archaeologists. The Abbé liked exploration and discovery more than digging. Finally there are the 'Levantine' rock-paintings of eastern Spain.

These are not in caves but mostly in shallow rock-shelters— some, indeed, on exposed rocks—and it seems certain that these pictures span a long space of time. Breuil's firmly held opinion (shared by Obermaier) that all of the Levantine paintings are of Late Old Stone Age—and therefore roughly contemporaneous with the pictures of Lascaux and Altamira—is probably erroneous. From the first the Spanish archaeologists attributed these paintings to a later epoch, to the Mesolithic—when men in Iberia were still hunters, but, north of the Pyrenees, anyway, do not seem to have done any paintings apart from those on pebbles.

The first of the Levantine pictures (they are small, many of them can be covered with one hand) showing human figures, animals and a certain number of 'scenes' were first identified by Cabré Aguilló, a professional photographer, at Calapata, near Cretas in the province of Teruel. Breuil did not hear of Calapata until 1907. In the next year he copied Calapata and also Cogul, and thereafter did much both to study the pictures and to encourage the search for more. There are now some forty Levantine stations known, with about seventy painted niches.

It may be thought curious that such exposed paintings could survive for millennia, but when there is a sinter[1] deposit, as there often is, it binds them. Nevertheless, when they are watered, as they sometimes are to bring out the design clearly, they tend to fade. Still, many of the pictures are palimpsests and represent a succession of art-styles covering no doubt many centuries. Moreover, some of the paintings show signs of the schematization which was to merge into the designs of Spanish neolithic art.

The human figures in the Levantine pictures are almost all in movement. The static women at Cogul are an exception. Men are shown jumping, leaping like ballet-dancers, running, dancing. As you look at them you feel you are witnessing actors in a shadow-show, actors whose bodies are greatly elongated by the play of light. In some of the figures, though there is always distortion, the general proportions of the human body are respected. In other figures everything is sacrificed to action, action conveyed with a startling and subjective cunning. And some of the pictures are very like African ones. The archers' combat at Morella la Vella can be matched in the Uwenat rocks right down on the borders of Egypt and Libya. There is a leaping bowman at Saltadora in Spain very similar indeed to another at Bogati in Basutoland. Breuil was, later on, to devote a good deal of time and attention to the study of possible reciprocal lines of art-influence between western Europe and Africa.

The animals (mostly in naturalistic style) are not so varied as in the Old Stone Age pictures of Cantabria, and both the animals and men's naked bodies bespeak a mild climate. There is a battue of ibex, there is a whirl of frenzied, possessed women dancing at Cueva de la Vieja (Alpera)—more than seventy figures —there are stag-hunts, there are the striding, lurching warriors of La Mola Remigia: tense, active, alert, alive; head-dresses of feathers, masks; very African. And there are combats; fighting men. When did men begin to fight? Before ever they were men,

[1] A siliceous or calcareous deposit formed by water.

no doubt, but they did not portray their battles before the time of the Levantine Spanish paintings. There is the first battle-scene. And what did men fight for? Food? Women? No; primarily for status. In the line of La Mola Remigia warriors, there is a chief, his head-dress is more elaborate, he takes the initiative. . . . An American scientist [1] has well said:

'Contrary to popular belief fighting in bird and mammalian societies is concerned not primarily with courtship and sex, but with position and status among the males. The view that sexual competition was primary came from erroneous conclusions based on observations of animals in zoos and in highly artificial conditions of restraint. Recent extensive field observations have shown that fights over mates are of secondary importance to those over status.'

Man the cannibal, Man the tool-maker, Man the status-seeker.

Spain is a rock. Most of its barren, stony soil is very ancient. As you fly over it today the country presents the surface—and the colour—of a crocodile-skin suitcase. Spain is a miniature Africa, an old upland surrounded by rather narrow coastal strips.

Breuil was indefatigable on horse- or mule-back, but also on his own feet, trudging up the hot hills, making his way along the *barrancas* beside a trickle of stream edged with oleanders, where you would swear it had never rained for ages. The Spain of Breuil's Spanish years had changed but little from the times of *Ford's Handbook* (1845), or even of Borrow's *Bible in Spain*. If here and there today the diesels, 'motos' and scooters tear along new roads, and new factories and workers' dwellings rise on every hand, there are still huge tracts where nothing has changed for centuries.

[1] Dr. Hudson Hoagland of the Worcester Foundation of Experimental Biology, and president of the American Academy of Arts and Sciences.

The Abbé visited over 250 sites, either alone with his muleteers, or with friends, pupils or colleagues: Willoughby Verner, Burkitt, Henry Field, Dorothy Garrod, Obermaier, Porcar, Cabré. He got about all over the country—Almería, the Sierra Morena, Andalusia, the Batuecas, Estramadura, all the Levantine region. He travelled thousands of miles from Estramadura, 'with its circling cranes', to Santistebán del Puerto, 'where in the winter of 1912–13 the wolves devoured at least twenty cows and full-grown bulls', to the Sierra de Cádiz, to 'the eternal stifling dust of La Mancha' and everywhere 'the heart-rending misery'.

With his muleteers he would as often as not spend the night in a smuggler's smoky hut or share a swineherd's dwelling. 'One halt we made was at the shack of a particularly dirty old swineherd who, with ready courtesy, offered *gazpacho*[1] and what humble fare he had. The man was *sordo como una peña* [as deaf as a post] and refused money, though his eyes lighted up when I offered him a packet of cigarettes.' Again with his muleteers over La Mancha's melancholy, unending plains and feeding 'on *guisos* [meat sauce], oil, saffron, beans and smoke-cured bully-beef'.

Or we can see him down in the Sierra de Cádiz at the Laguna de Janda set amid written rocks. One day the Abbé set off alone to entomologize, collect beetles and butterflies. He always liked to break away when he could and renew his old passion for bugs and moths. With him went his inseparable companion, his 'English' dog called Mider. I do not know what was the race of this intelligent animal to which Breuil was much attached. In continental Europe an 'English' dog often means, alas, a mongrel. Nor do I know how Mider got his name. I thought once it might really have been 'Miler', but apparently it was not. Maybe the Abbé knew Mider was English because of his character, disposition and temperament. Once he and I discussed the delicate subject of nationality in animals. Why are French cats different from English cats? Well, maybe the French drown those animals which in England would be regarded as having a fine, independent

---

[1] A cold soup of bread, olive oil, vinegar, garlic and onions.

attitude towards life. What is allowed in one society is not allowed in another and where in one country one might be congratulated for laying out an insolent fellow, in another land one might hang for the same action.

On this day the Abbé wore his high waterproof boots. He had his double-barrelled shot-gun and his game-bag slung over his shoulder. But before he had done much entomologizing or shot much game a great storm crashed up, whipping the lagoon's surface into high waves. One after another the little islets disappeared. Flocks of white egrets, cranes and marsh-hens flapped and fluttered by in the wind. Breuil took refuge in an old hut, where there was a hammock (maybe he used this on his archaeological prospections) which he soon found useful. The little tarpaulin skiffs broke their moorings and the old wooden decoys bobbed along on the waves towards the shack where the water came oozing up through the planks. Breuil's companions, alarmed at his long absence and at the state of the weather, set out on a rescue expedition. They found him stark naked, lying in the hammock and awaiting the end of the storm. Perhaps he was thinking of swimming his way out.

In olden days the Alpera Gorge and the valley of the Batuecas in the god-forsaken region of the Jurdes was held, even by the wise men of Salamanca University, to be haunted by demons and inhabited by pagans. In 1599 the good Bishop of Coria rejoiced that the discalced Carmelite monks who had set up a monastery in this wilderness 'would kick the devil out of the country'.

Here is our Abbé in the Batuecas: 'Under the burning caress of a June sun the torrent was leaping and dashing its roaring cascades against the rocky bastions, on to the stepped parapets of the savage gorge. From time to time, under a low vault of lentiscus and ilex, a basin of crystal waves revealed a bottom of variegated rockery.' We may note that on occasion Breuil did not mind letting his pen run on into rather luscious prose. When he plunged into this inviting bath his muleteers thought him crazy: 'In that natural bath I enjoyed the divine intoxication of the crystalline

F

coolness and in my gambols I shot up spurts of water which fell
in babbling cascades on to the clear mirror of the pool.' Then,
when he was cool, clean and collected, he went back to his
astonished Spaniards 'who had congealed sweat on their filthy,
rancid skins'.

He liked swimming and Dr. Henry Field, the American
anthropologist, has told of an amusing visit he paid with Breuil to
the Montespan Cavern (where is the celebrated image of a headless bear (see p. 182)): a subterranean river, the Hounatau, runs
through the cave, and at one point you have to plunge into the
stream and swim beneath water for some distance. The Abbé
stripped naked, threw himself in and emerged puffing and blowing, saying, 'That's something, eh?'

After his bath in the Batuecas, Breuil walked up to the local
presbytery—in Spain he enjoyed plenty of hospitality from his
fellow-priests—for a 'frugal dinner' followed by dances. The
local boys and girls twisted and twirled far into the night—and
then on the Sunday morning more dances in traditional costume
at Rio Mal de Abajo; yes, Breuil got to know rural Spain pretty
well.

Colonel Willoughby Cole Verner was a British officer who,
after retiring from the Army, bought a house near Algeciras,
opposite Gibraltar across the Bay. And in this home he spent a
good deal of each year, not only because the climate suited him
but also because the wild, deserted valleys and mountains northwards shelter a rich treasure of bird-life, and Verner was a keen
ornithologist. To this day the way from the sugar-cane-fringed
water-meadows of the lower valleys up to the rock-ringed plateau
of Ronda runs through a country where you see hardly a sign of
human life except for a goat-herd here and there, while swooping
or gliding you may be lucky enough to glimpse the great golden
eagle.

Verner spent a good deal of his time wandering about on mule-back accompanied by a single guide. While he was prospecting one day to the west of Ronda, perched over its precipitous ravine, the guide remarked, 'Over there, near Montjaque and Benoaján, there's a mysterious cave the people call La Pileta.' It seems it was as long ago as 1902 that some peasants seeking guano for fertilizer began to let themselves down with cords into a pit which at its bottom had an opening leading into a cave. As there were mysterious markings on the walls, the cavern got the name of Los Letreros.

Verner, his curiosity aroused by what his guide said, answered, 'Let's go and see.' He had no interest in—or knowledge of— prehistoric matters, but he did explore the cavern (then very difficult of access) and when he returned to England wrote articles (in the *Saturday Review*) entitled 'Letters from Wilder Spain', and these attracted Breuil's attention. The year was 1911.

Twelve months later Breuil, Obermaier and Verner were at La Pileta, which was to reveal some surprising things. The cavern was occupied by Man during long ages, or at any rate for periods over a long lapse of time. There were neolithic and Bronze Age hearths and implements, as well as several human skeletons—one at the bottom of a deep chasm. These look as though they might be the remains of men and women sacrificed, or at any rate allowed to die, as offerings maybe to the spirits of the cave or the waters. The bones show no signs of mutilation, nor were they buried, possibly because the victims were just allowed to starve to death in the recesses of the earth—bloodless sacrifices are suitable to some religious demands.

Later than Breuil's time at La Pileta (i.e. in 1935) was found the so-called 'Venus of Benoaján', a terracotta amulet about two and a half inches high (exactly six centimetres), shaped rather like a 'double-axe' and with two holes at the top (making 'eyes' and also holes for suspending the object), two knobs figuring breasts lower down and at the bottom a mass of dots representing the pubic hair. The thing dates from the Bronze Age—and so is some 3,000 years old—but it is evidence of the 'Eye Goddess' cult (see p. 187).

But the paintings are the chief attraction of La Pileta. A considerable number of them are in the naturalistic style of the northern Spanish prehistoric caves and not at all like the Levantine paintings.

In addition to the animal pictures are an immense mass of signs, some obviously stylized representations of animals, together with an abundance of comb-shaped and other designs which occur also in much later times. The symbolical, schematized art of these later ages has, then, its roots right deep down in palaeolithic ages. Obermaier worked out a series of designs ranging from simple but recognizable forms of men and women right up to the signs on Piette's Azilian pebbles.

La Pileta is now quite easy to reach. A road has been made that leads nearly to the cave's entrance. Since Breuil's time new galleries have been explored, though they do not add very much to the evidence the Abbé gathered, and *La Pileta de Benoaján* (Monaco 1915) by Breuil, Obermaier and Verner is still the best book on the cavern.

Of course, the startling revelation of La Pileta was that right down in the Spanish south there flourished in the Late Old Stone Age a naturalistic art closely related to that of south-western France and northern Spain. Evidently southern and northern Spain and southern France were at some epochs linked together in culture. No doubt the lines of communication lay around the coasts, the coastal plains being then much wider than now.

But Pileta does not stand alone. There are three other prehistoric caves with naturalistic paintings in the province of Málaga; one (of minor importance) called Doña Trinidad de Ardales was discovered in 1918. The marvellous cave of Nerja, however (of which Breuil was able to read reports before he died), discovered in 1959, stands out as the most imposing perhaps of all prehistoric sanctuaries.

The succession of lower halls stretches out for 1,000 yards

and in the last hall the roof soars to a height of nearly 200 feet. On all hands is a rich decoration of fantastic stalagmite formations, mighty columns, pillars, gigantic organ-pipes, cascades, lacy flounces, icicles, a formidable florescence of monstrous plants and figures changing shape and form with every step you take; the colours mostly light, even gay (in electric light, anyway): buff, beige, cream, ivory, fawn, pale grey.

A universe in little. How terrifying when lighted only by flickering torches. Such places full of dread must have powerfully influenced men's religious ideas—in the widest sense of the term.

These lower caves end in a steeply rising slope of what from some distance looks like dark grey dust pierced here and there with jagged stalactite tusks. Above this scree, and reaching to the vault, is a wall of rock and in it, some 130 feet above the cavern's floor, is a hole. It is a mild mountaineering feat to scramble up to this opening, which leads to another succession of passages and halls where are prehistoric naturalistic paintings.

A journey through Nerja by torchlight to the sound of musical stones (some of the stalactite flounces were in remote ages nicked to modify the notes they give out when struck) and echoing chants and up the Mountain of Doubt to the upper galleries must have been an awe-inspiring experience, moulding men's imaginations, conditioning their memories, enriching their speech, packing their minds with erroneous certainties, in dark recesses where time and distance are abolished. Maybe a world of the dead, peopled by inpalpable, invisible, but real creatures.

And scattered about here and there in the lower galleries and halls are men's bones, dark grey as the soil that half-hides them. . . . Interments? Remains of meals? of sacrifices?

By the time of the First World War Breuil could speak Spanish well.

It was, indeed, the only foreign language he really mastered, though his knowledge of English was good enough for the reading of any scientific book, and, in his later years, when in South Africa he had to speak English for much of the time.

Few foreigners had the Abbé's acquaintance with the Spanish countryside, north, east, south and west. He was, then, drafted into the French 'auxiliary services' and posted to the naval attaché's office in Madrid. One of his main jobs was to act as courier carrying secret despatches to and from the Gibraltar naval base. For some time (during 1916) Wilhelm Canaris (afterwards admiral and head of the Nazi *Abwehr* until in 1945 he was shot on Hitler's orders), fitted out with a fake Chilean passport, in addition to being active in hiring agents and supplying submarines and other craft, spent a good deal of time in the Algeciras area watching the movements of Allied and neutral shipping. Breuil had then for part of the time a very efficient German 'opposite number'. The German set-up in Spain was, as a whole, reasonably effective (though it is difficult to get any Spanish machine working in a way Germans think it ought), but then most Spaniards from the King downwards were either pro-German or at least anti-Ally (anti-French from Napoleon's time, anti-British because of Gibraltar and ages of enmity), though some prominent men such as Romanones were shrewd enough to guess, as time wore on, that the Germans were not likely to win. Allied Intelligence in Spain had, then, to face a good deal of passive and even active resistance. There were comic interludes, as when one of the French attachés, carrying most confidential papers from Madrid, lost them after his arrival in Paris. Some of us who had to decode telegrams relating to this misfortune were sure the fellow had not left the papers in a taxi but in some lady's apartment. And we were right; only the lady, as we had not foreseen, was patriotic, although she took some time to find out where to deliver the treasures, since she had no idea of her guest's identity. The hero of this piece of buffoonery has since had a distinguished public career.

Not only did he shuttle back and forth between Madrid and the

Rock, but the Abbé found occasion to prospect on the side. In the summer of 1917 he passed some time, disguised as a sailor, coasting along the eastern shores of the country. He glided past 'the splendid pyramid of Vedran, Ibiza' and dawdled along the coast from Dénia to Calpe 'examining the great pitted [*cariés*] cliffs of the Mediterranean littoral' as he lay on the deck of a felucca amid crabs and onions and gazed down 'through pellucid green waters on to anemones and star-fish'—and from time to time holding his own with pro-German and unco-operative officials.

He also did some lecturing at the French Institute in Madrid, it seems with great success, though the applause he provoked might have been due to the innate courtesy of the Spanish people. However, the laughter that enlivened Breuil's addresses was certainly not only due to his personality and the interesting things he had to say but also to his sallies being couched in highly idiomatic and colloquial Spanish. He had learned the language camping out in the wilds. His teachers had been those resolutely unwashed muleteers, often his sole companions for weeks on end. Fine fellows, all right, but whose language was hardly of the politest.

Breuil had seen Gibraltar for the first time with Willoughby Verner in 1914 and had then come to the conclusion that a good deal more was to be found out there concerning Stone Age Man. A neanderthaloid skull had been discovered on the Rock as long ago as 1848, but not much serious archaeological prospection had ever been undertaken, very largely because Gibraltar was a closely guarded naval base and inquisitive visitors, whether scientists or other, were not welcomed, as Breuil was to realize. On 28th April 1917 he was prospecting along the north face of the Rock, that is to say the part that faces La Linea in Spain (there was not, of course, in those days any airport), and as he was grubbing about near the Devil's Tower a military police-man caught him. The Abbé whipped out his diplomatic passport, but the man insisted on going through Breuil's pockets and con-fiscating the 'rubbish' they contained. He had to leave his specimens behind. It was wartime and even bits of stone and rock were suspicious.

In April 1919, after the war was over, Breuil was back at the Rock and unearthed quite a number of fossil bones—none of Man, however. It would certainly be worth while doing some more digging, perhaps another neanderthaloid skull might turn up. So it was he urged his English student, Miss Dorothy Garrod, to excavate at Gibraltar. She did so and found a second neanderthaloid skull. So we can say that in addition to finding for himself the Porc-Epic (see p. 180) and second Saccopastore skulls (see p. 185) the Abbé was the instigator of the Gibraltar discovery.

Breuil liked Madrid life. He never needed much sleep and was an early riser, though in later life he would have a short nap after luncheon. It must have taken some time for him to fit into the Spanish programme, dinner at ten o'clock at night and then a show. He left some descriptions of his favourite artistes: Adelita Lulu, the witty *diseuse*; Argentinita, the dancer; Raquel Meller, singing 'El Relicario', 'La Violetera' and the other songs that were to bring her world-wide fame; La Bilbainita; María Guerrero, the classical actress; and, above all, Pastora Imperio, about whom he waxed lyrical: . . . 'the sculptural majesty she imparts to a body so marvellously flexible and vigorous . . . her deep-set, jet-black eyes flashing arrogance. . . .'

When on his way backwards and forwards between France and Spain the Abbé would sometimes stop off at the Castel d'Andorte, a private lunatic asylum—not for any studies in psychopathology but just to visit his friend Dr. Lalanne and his prehistoric site of Laussel. From Les Eyzies you pass through the leafy vale of the Beune stream. High up is the entrance to the Font de Gaume. Then you go by Les Combarelles. You swerve on to a highway that leads you past the prehistoric bas-relief of

Cap Blanc, maybe the finest of all palaeolithic sculptures. There are six large horses in high relief. It is probable that originally they were painted in bright colours. The men of the Old Stone Age no more admired stone unadorned by paint than did the ancient Greeks. Facing Cap Blanc is the keep of Commarques and the pepper-pot tower of the Castel de Laussel, five miles upstream from the Beune's confluence with the Vézère. This area really is, as advertised, the 'Capital of Prehistory'. The Great Shelter of Laussel faces nearly due south and it was here that Lalanne found the well-known statuette of a woman holding a horn—one of the finest of the Old Stone Age sculptures. In 1911 Lalanne unearthed at this site a bas-relief representing copulation. Such scenes are not so rare in prehistoric art as is often thought—probably because, like homosexual or very markedly erotic Greek vase-paintings, such things are considered unfit for reproduction in books addressed to the general public. There are the stallion and mare at Le Roc, the bull and cow at the Fourneau du Diable and representations of human coitus—Pech-Merle, La Marche, etc. So we know something of early Man's intimate behaviour. The assumption of the face-to-face posture, with all its implications, comes later. Representations of sexual connection run, however, right through the history of art. You find them in neolithic engravings of the Saharan highlands and you find them (also *a tergo*) in Etruscan tombs—a death-life complex from prehistoric times?

Breuil did not devote any special volume to prehistoric sculpture, though there is now a good deal of it, e.g. at La Penne (Tarn), La Chaire à Calvin and the 'Three Graces' or headless, naturalistic, naked female figures of which the discoverer, Dr. Dorothy Garrod (with Mademoiselle de Saint-Mathurin), has written: 'The grace, the technique, the *attitude* of the sculptors so far revealed, go far to revise our ideas of what sort of a man our Magdalenian ancestor was; and suggest a degree of sensitivity and even sophistication which are hard to visualize even in much later ages.'

Human skeletons have been found buried at the foot of some prehistoric sculpture (e.g. Le Roc, Chancelade)—have we here examples of very early 'grave-stones' or funerary monuments? Or were the places sacred in themselves and so suitable for interments?

In October 1952 Breuil, together with M. Bétirac, a prehistorian of Montauban (see page 193), visited the La Magdaleine grotto at La Penne. It contains remarkable sculptured female figures.

Prehistoric sculpture, unlike the mass of prehistoric painting, is either in the open or near the foreparts of caverns. 'There is,' the Abbé said, 'no "metaphysical reason" for the sculpture being near a cave's entrance.'

'Sculpture needed a considerable time for its execution and in dark caves would have necessitated prolonged illumination by means of fatty or resinous substances. But where there was daylight no artificial lighting was required . . . these female figures if not used for reproduction rites served to charm hunters taking their ease either by day or at night by the flickering flames of torches. Beautiful and suggestive figures to fill the mind with pleasant thoughts. . . .'

> . . . *hominum divomque voluptas*
> *Alma Venus . . .*[1]

When he had time on leave Breuil would go back to Amiens, visit relations and seek for more evidence of the most ancient men who lived by the Somme's banks. Time and again he would dig about in the Saint-Acheul gravel-pits, and no one who ever saw him at work on a site can ever forget it. He was incredibly

[1] The delight of Men and Gods
Fostering Venus . . .

active, darting about, pointing, scraping, picking and choosing, discarding and slipping in his pocket . . . but during the 1914–18 war the short, cassock-clad figure bobbing about, digging and probing, aroused the alarmed suspicions of an old lady who was accustomed to taking her walks abroad near the pits. Having made up her mind that here was quite clearly an enemy agent, disguised as a priest, and probably preparing mine-emplacements, she tackled him and asked what he thought he was doing. 'Madam, I am looking for Saint-Acheul implements' . . . 'Nonsense, we have not lost any, and I should know, for I am Mademoiselle de Saint-Acheul.'

And she was too.

As we have seen, Breuil owed to Prince Albert of Monaco those Spanish years which were to prove among the most fruitful in all his life and it was chance that aroused Albert's interest in archaeology and prehistory, the chance that led to some remarkable discoveries almost on his own doorstep.

The story goes back to 1868, when Albert of Monaco was twenty years of age. Stimulated by the growing popularity of the new gambling casino at Monte Carlo, work was pushed forward on the Genoa–Nice railway along the coast. The tracks kept mostly down almost to sea level, while the main road, the old Roman Via Aurelia, is often high up, some hundreds of feet above the Mediterranean. While the line was being constructed just over the international border between France and Italy, only a matter, indeed, of less than a quarter of a mile into Italy, the workmen disturbed the ground in front of a number of caves pitting the rock-face only some twenty feet above sea level and at the foot of crags known locally as the Baoussé Roussé; that is, Balzi Rossi in classical Italian, or the 'Red Cliffs'.

For the distance of a few hundred yards the face of these cliffs is slightly concave and its russet surface curiously pleated so you

might think it scored with frozen rills. At the base of the cliffs
are six entrances, most of them in shape like an inverted 'V', and
each opening gives into a grotto; once there were seven of them,
but one cave was, a number of years ago, quarried away with
its little headland. The railway passes so close to the cliff-face
that you can lean out of the window and touch the rock with a
walking-stick. The whole site is evocatory. To your left stretches
the shore-line along to the Rock of Monaco. Against the face of
the Red Cliffs is the openwork steel casing of a lift which runs
down between the Via Aurelia above and the level of the caves
beneath—a drop of over 300 feet. High above the constricted and
congested highway is the stone mass of the late Serge Voronoff's
castle-laboratory, where he kept his apes and performed 'monkey-
gland' operations advertised to restore youthful vigour to tired
old men. But Voronoff was a charlatan and his 'cures' illusory.

Although there was never a road (one is being constructed
now to relieve the crush on the Via Aurelia) along the foot of the
cliffs, there has always been a path by the sea's edge and as long
ago as 1846 Prince Florestan of Monaco, Albert's grandfather,
scratched about in the fillings of rock, stone and earth which
blocked the caverns almost to their roofs and projected in
sloping tongues outside. At odd intervals from 1854 to 1868
other amateur archaeologists dug about in the Baoussé Roussé,
but it was not until 1870 that Emile Rivière undertook serious
excavation, and although his methods would be called slapdash
today, he did, during five seasons' work, produce some highly
interesting results. He unearthed the complete skeleton of a tall
man, lying on its left side, the bones stained red and the skull
and other parts adorned with ornaments in pierced shells. These
bones are now in the Museum of Man in Paris. In addition,
Rivière recovered a mass of worked flints, fossil bones of animals
and some prehistoric statuettes of a type fairly well known now:
female figures with featureless faces, prominent breasts, bulging
buttocks and legs ending in a point. Altogether five of these little
figures were found at the Baoussé Roussé. Much ado has been

made about these objects[1] as indicating that Late Old Stone Age populations ('modern men' or *Homo sapiens*, such as ourselves) had figures like Hottentots of today or maybe the women also possessed those pendulous *labia minora* forming what is known as the 'Hottentot apron'.

As a matter of fact, the bulging buttocks of the statuettes, their so-called 'steatopygy', is in most cases not more marked than that to be seen in living women along the Ligurian shores today. Breuil held that of all these Venuses only two were really 'steatopygous' and I have counted ten ladies with behinds relatively as large as those represented in the images of 25,000 years ago and that in one afternoon's walk not more than a few miles from the Baoussé Roussé.

A later excavator at the caves, one Jullian, discovered more statuettes (which Breuil, however, held to be from a cave other than that in which they were found) and also (in 1884) unearthed a complete skeleton also dyed red. But the night after it was found it was smashed to bits by the owner of the grotto, who thought he was not going to get his fair share of the booty. . . .

In the early 'nineties Prince Albert himself did some excavating at the Baoussé Roussé and became so interested in the site's possibilities that he got together a team and started really scientific exploration of the caves, or at least of some of them. A Canon de Villeneuve, another priestly archaeologist, led the dig, and during seven seasons' work the Prince's men unearthed a mass of exciting treasures from three of the four main caverns. Albert also appointed a committee to study the material and to publish a description of the finds. Two of the members of this committee were Emile Cartailhac and Marcellin Boule.

---

[1] The statuettes apparently all belong to earlier phases of the Late Old Stone Age art, and they are the only 'chattel-art' objects common to western and eastern Europe—in fact they have been found as far off as Mal'ta in the Lake Baikal area of Siberia. The most beautiful of these 'Venuses' is the ivory 'Venus of Brassempouy' found by Piette, but others of the statuettes have come from places in France (Lespugues, Sirueil, etc.), Italy (Savignano), Austria (Willendorf), Czechoslovakia, Germany and European Russia.

Here is a passage from Cartailhac regarding the Grotte des
Enfants at the Baoussé Roussé—we must remember that when he
wrote these words, over sixty years ago, the chronology of the
Old Stone Age was still very vague:

'Above, with the passage of time, there spread an earthy layer
resulting from the slow decomposition of the rock and from
material blown in by the wind. For this grotto indeed we cannot
claim the torrential action of water which played such a considerable part, owing to the conformation of the terrain, in the Grotto
du Prince [another of the Baoussé Roussé caves] since natural
causes have contributed more slowly to the formation of the
strata, we must consider that they correspond to a very long lapse
of time—compared with our short historical periods . . . a little
dust on the surface, a few pieces of rock that seemed as though
they became detached only yesterday—and that is all that 2,000
or 3,000 years has brought.'

It was the Baoussé Roussé which decided the Prince to devote
a great deal of money to the furthering of prehistoric research
elsewhere.

Later on Italian archaeologists worked at the Red Cliffs (the
caves are now completely emptied of their contents) and there
is much material from them at the Italian Institute of Human
Palaeontology at Pegli (near Genoa), but the objects found by
the Prince's men are admirably arranged and displayed in the
fine new museum at Monaco. It lies high up and in the so-called
'Exotic Garden' of cacti, fleshy plants and Mexican flora. There
is a magnificent view over Monaco Harbour and the coastline
eastwards. You can see the Red Cliffs themselves beyond the
high-perched old town of Menton.

An hour spent in this little museum affords a good introduction
to the Late Old Stone Age. The exhibits are not so numerous as
to confuse (there are just two large rooms), the explanatory
labels are clear and some of the objects striking enough: the

human skeletons, the implements, the statuettes, the huge, cruel jaws of the cave-bears, the remains of all sorts of beasts . . . but judging from my own experience at the museum most of the visitors to Monaco have other ideas in their heads than any about their own very distant past history. . . . In the 'Exotic Garden' (and therefore on Prince Albert's own territory) is the 'Observatory Cave', now hundreds of feet above sea level—and never at any time near the sea even when the waters rose to their highest—but here no human fossils were found, though the cavern was undoubtedly the home both of neanderthaloid (see p. 71) and our own type of Man.

However, all the Baoussé Roussé grottoes were once under the sea. This much is quite certain since the lowest stratum of their fillings, lying upon the bed-rock, was composed of beach-pebbles; some of the mollusc-shells in these lower layers were of species indicating a Mediterranean a good deal warmer than today. The caves, then, were invaded by the sea during the warm period or 'Interglacial' which preceded the last (or Würm) Ice Age beginning about 70,000 and lasting to about 10,000 years ago.

When the glacial periods or 'Ice Ages' (there were four of them during the time Man developed) were at their peak the ice piled up over Scandinavia, much of Britain and northern Europe, with the Alps as a solid, gigantic ice-land rising up farther south. In North America (although there were no men there until some 25,000 to 30,000 years ago) the ice-face pushed down to about the line of the Ohio and Missouri rivers. There was, then, an immense amount of water locked up on land, and since so much water had been withdrawn from the sea, naturally the general sea level sank, at times to as much as 100 metres—about 325 feet—or even more, below the present surface.

Obviously men could not have used the Baoussé Roussé until the grottoes were dry, that is in the earlier part of the last Ice Age. An Ice Age did not set in suddenly. There were backward and forward movements, oscillations, phases when it was colder and phases when it was warmer. Still, the tendency was for the climate to get harsher and harsher. Even so, there were long periods of warmer weather during the last Ice Age (Würmian), the so-called 'Interstadials'. It is quite possible that we are in an Interstadial now; anyway, there is plenty of ice about on land and in the seas.

Though, during the last Ice Age, there was no great ice-sheet in France, still the central massif was covered with glaciers and much of the country was 'tundra'—like parts of Siberia today—with plenty of snow in winter, dwarf shrubs, mosses and lots of peat forming. Farther south came cold, dry steppes where sand-winds raged, depositing at times fine loam (or loess). An un-pleasant sort of homeland, though some men did live in it. But then, as now, there were local climates. You cannot judge climate by latitude alone. New York is on that of Naples and London on that of Kamchatka. The Baoussé Roussé had one of these local 'microclimates'.

Often, for a considerable distance off stretches of the French and Italian Rivieras, the Mediterranean is remarkably shallow, so shallow, indeed, that it is hoped by off-shore dumping of earth and rock excavated during the construction of the new sub-terranean railway line through Monaco, and by importation of rock from France, to add fifty acres or so to Prince Rainier's realm.

Our remote ancestors had, then, at the Baoussé Roussé, a rather pleasant little homeland sheltered by a mountain-screen from chilly northern blasts and provided with hunting-grounds at the front door.

The caves tell clearly the tale of their inhabitants. The first were Neanderthaloids (see p. 71) who were, at least some of them, not much different from ourselves and whose fossil bones, stone implements, and even the imprints of whose feet, have been found at various places along the western and north-western coasts of Italy. After the Neanderthaloids in western Europe came *Homo sapiens*, and the most ancient European skull of 'modern' Man does not seem to be more than about 40,000 years old. Neanderthaloid Man left none of his bones at the Baoussé

Sierra Morena, 1912

c d'Audoubert, 1912. From left to right: Begouen, H. Begouen, M. Begouen, Breuil, J. Begouen, E. Cartailhac. Twenty-four hours after discovery of clay bisons

Breuil at La Pileta, April 1926

Roussé, but the grottoes served as graves for his successors.[1] About twenty skeletons in all were unearthed, most of them of 'Cro-Magnon' type—fine, upstanding people with longish heads and rather short, square faces. But two of the skeletons found by Prince Albert were of a middle-aged woman and a youth, both have been held to be 'negroid', though not dissimilar types can be seen in Europe (especially in southern Italy) today. In any case we have no reason for supposing that these two were necessarily black-skinned and kinky-haired. We know surprisingly little about the origin of existing 'races' of mankind.

Most of the skeletons were stained red, and as the bones were in what is called 'anatomical association'—that is, they had not been disturbed—it is probable that the corpses were laid in a bed of red ochre or the dyeing was effected by the sprinkling of pigment on to the semi-putrescent bodies so that the mass of rotting flesh served as a bath for the bones. In many cases parts of the skeletons, and notably the heads, were protected by an arrangement of stones, a flat one lying on two uprights. Not only were implements buried with the dead but they were adorned with head-coverings, bracelets, anklets or necklaces of marine shells, fish-bones and deer-teeth. The dead, then, were buried with their finery and weapons.[2] We may deduce from such

[1] A skull found in the Niah Cave in Sarawak (Borneo) seems also to be about 40,000 years old, so there were *Homo sapiens* in south-eastern Asia (Borneo then being joined to the mainland) about the same time as Combe-Capelle Man (the earliest undoubtedly European *Homo sapiens* of modern type) flourished in France. The indications seem to point to somewhere in the eastern African region as having been the 'cradle' of *Homo sapiens*. In any case we can say that Aurignacian-type implements (associated with the European *Homo sapiens* of the later part of the last Ice Age) appear in Libya, in Kurdistan and in Afghanistan towards the end of the Riss-Würm Interglacial; that is to say, many thousands of years before 40,000 B.C. So southwest Asia looks like the focus from which Upper Palaeolithic industries spread.

[2] As illustrating either (1) permanence of tradition of (2) fortuitous convergence of custom, some early Maori burials in New Zealand (and therefore only a few centuries old) very closely resemble in adornment, in gravegear and in position of the skeleton, some of the Baoussé Roussé burials.

G

practices what we will: A belief in a future life? A determination to keep the dead comfortable in death and to prevent them from coming back to plague the living? . . .

And though all the men, women and children at the Baoussé Roussé had been intentionally buried, there was no one single style of laying out the bodies. Some of the skeletons lie on their backs with the hands brought up to touch the lower jaw, some have their arms straight down by their sides, some lie on one side, at least one had the legs crossed and the right arm brought up so that the hand was under the head while the left arm was bent double. Maybe the bodies were left in the positions they had when death occurred.

The caverns were not only tombs; in fact, it is rather that the dead were buried in their homes—a practice which in some places lasted right into historical times—and all about were beasts' bones: those of an ancient sort of hippopotamus, elephant, Merck's rhinoceros (also an antique kind of animal), cave-bear, reindeer, leopard and so forth, animals which indicate a succession of varying climates, cooler and warmer, moister and drier.

5

The Caverns of the Volp

'The primitive is not an irrational being . . . but one who observes very minutely and with extraordinary precision, the world around him; he classifies, he indulges in speculation..."chance" has no place in the thought of "savages", there is scientific thought which, for instance, developed the great discoveries of the neolithic age.'

CLAUDE LÉVI-STRAUSS

NAPOLÉON HENRI BEGOUEN was remarkable for a number of reasons, but first and foremost because his title was perfectly genuine and his right to bear it unimpeachable, whereas, in France, most of those used are either improperly assumed, accorded merely by courtesy or just plain bogus—the latter being far the most numerous. Several of the French 'dukes' indeed have no right to the titles they use. Paradoxically enough, and for reasons related to the peculiar nature of French titles before the 1789 revolution, those conferred by Napoleon and his successors during the nineteenth century are, generally speaking, less suspect than many supposedly more ancient and, maybe, more impressive-sounding. The most embarrassing question one could put to most French 'noblemen' would be: 'When was your title created, by whom, what were the terms of the patent, what is your relationship to the man who first received that title?'

To this searching inquiry, however, Napoléon Henri *Comte* Begouen could reply truthfully, 'My great-grandfather was a manufacturer at Havre and was, for services rendered to the French Navy, created, in 1808, by the Emperor Napoleon, an hereditary *comte* of the French Empire and the title has since then passed from father to son in a direct line to me.'

Secondly, Begouen was remarkable in that, despite a healthy appetite for food, drink and high living generally, he survived until the age of ninety-three. Thirdly, although an active and able prehistorian, he surpassed even Boucher de Perthes in the range and variety of his interests. The earlier French archaeologists may have been also lawyers, doctors, priests, schoolmasters, landed proprietors, business men and what you will, but Begouen was country gentleman, journalist, economist, man-about-town, politician (he stood for parliament three times, only to be defeated, it is said, by 'electoral fraud'), diplomatist, German scholar, railway expert, newspaper proprietor, for fifteen years mayor of his home town, 'Mendelian' poultry-breeder, advocate of 'Christian democracy'—as well as professor of prehistory.

As long ago as 1881 he set off from Toulouse to Paris. He was then a young man with a sparse, silky, square-cut beard, pince-nez, *lavallière* tie and a romantic air; something very different from the portly, elder-statesman-like figure we see opposite p. 112, engaged in helping to compose a letter to the Pope. In Paris Begouen got to know Taine, the positivist philosopher, and Albert Sorel, the historian, who between them found young Begouen a job with the highly conservative and well-informed Paris evening paper the *Journal des Débats* (long since defunct), to which he contributed for a number of years. In addition to studying at the Paris Law School and at that of Political Science, he also took a leap into high life. His uncle Henri Chevreau had been Napoleon III's last Minister of the Interior. The Begouen traditions were also stoutly Bonapartist and Chevreau introduced young Napoléon Henri to the Princess Mathilde Bonaparte, the late Emperor's cousin and a lady whose *salons* both in Paris and at Saint-Gratien, to the north of the city, were meeting-places for men of letters, artists, scientists, some Society people and a number of hangers-on. Proust has left a lively account of the Princess's house in the rue de Berri, and in the Goncourts' *Journal* there is racy comment on her friends and lovers, of whom the chief in her later days was Popelin, the sculptor, who confided that 'he had loved her as a husband and he had loved her as a lover but there was no woman more reticent in love-making' —so different from 'the Queen of Spain' (Isabel II) who was 'very lubricious but with refinement'.

Begouen, after covering the German *Kulturkampf* (contest between Church and State) for his newspaper, put in some years as attaché on the staff of the French Resident-General in Tunisia. Much later on he had a hush-hush job in Switzerland during the First World War and he accompanied, as anthropological expert, an expedition to the Hogger Mountains of the central Sahara at a time when travel in the great desert was a real adventure. About 1892 he married a lady with money, who died young, leaving him with three sons. He then settled in Toulouse, where he ran a rather reactionary newspaper *Le Télégramme*. He had also become possessed of a considerable property near Saint-Girons in the Pyrenean foothills of the Ariège department. I give all these details for reasons that will soon be clear.

Toulouse is not only a magnificent rose-red city full of ancient mansions, a city rich in historical associations, but it is also the seat of a university memorable as being the first in France where a chair of prehistoric archaeology was founded. When Begouen settled in Toulouse this chair was occupied by Emile Carthailhac, with whom Napoléon Henri became friendly, and no one could be long in Cartailhac's company without getting some introduction to prehistory, since the old man, in his gentle way, was an obstinate propagandist.

The two men were extraordinarily unalike. The one a retiring and modest scientist, who to the end of his days would sign himself in Chinese fashion 'the old student'; and the other not averse from blowing his own trumpet and collecting an impressive number of medals and decorations, ranging from the Three

Stars of Latvia, through the Pole Star of Sweden to the Legion of Honour—the *cravate* of which he acquired, by the way, quite a number of years before Breuil, but maybe Begouen kept on the right side of touchy politicians. Furthermore, Begouen was such an admirer of the ladies that the Toulouse wits nicknamed him *le comte courant*.[1] But he was a genial, hospitable man, who when he turned his attention to prehistory became a much better archaeologist than some have made him out to be.[2] Breuil would always speak up in Begouen's defence when anyone referred slightingly to the *comte courant's* scientific standing. The Abbé would snap out: 'Never forget the services he rendered to archaeology. He revealed prehistory to south-western France.' Even the *bon vivant* side of Begouen's character was not too displeasing to Breuil.

Begouen, however, does not really come into the Breuil story until 1912 when the Count was involved in a momentous discovery. It so happens that on his land at Montesquieu-Avantès is a hill through which runs a little river, the Volp. The stream goes underground at the entrance to the Enlène Cavern at one side of the hill and emerges again through an opening known as the Tuc d'Audoubert on the other side. In July 1912 Max, one of the Begouen sons, learned from François Camel, a local man, that if you pushed upstream through the Tuc d'Audoubert you could reach a whole maze of underground passages and galleries until you got to a road-block of stalagmite, in which, however, there was a *chattière*, a small opening, a 'rat-hole'.

Even when the Volp is not in flood one needs a flat-bottomed boat to negotiate the stream; after rounding a few bends you get to a little beach from which a passage about twenty-five yards long leads up to quite dry halls and galleries. Max and his two brothers thereupon explored this Tuc d'Audoubert and found

[1] A pun on the phrase *'compte courant'*, i.e. current account in a bank. *Le comte courant* means the gadabout count, the 'wolf'.

[2] Two at least of his many publications are of general interest: *The Magic Origin of Prehistoric Art* and *De la mentalité spiritualiste des premiers hommes;* 'The Spiritualistic Mentality of the Early Men'.

traces that it had been visited in the eighteenth century. Then they were brought up dead against the shining face of calcite. However, in October of the same year Max and Louis Begouen, with François Camel, set out to hack a way through the road-block and climb a forty-foot-high 'chimney' up to a part of the caves which had not been visited by men for thousands and thousands of years.

After climbing and scrambling along, they reached a hall strewn with fossilized cave-bear bones and then came to a chamber where, leaning against a block of rock fallen from the roof, are two splendidly modelled clay bison, each about two feet long and, except for a crack that runs through them, intact. The male is about to mount the female. There are also traces of another animal—the third bison.

On the right-hand side of a nearby gallery is a low alcove in whose fine clay floor are some forty footprints, or rather heel-prints, deep and distinct, and made, it would seem from the size of the marks, by children (possibly five or six of them) aged from about thirteen to fifteen. There is also a number of phalli in clay on the floor, an engraving of a penis on the wall, and at the entrance to the alcove imprints of two knees as well as a series of holes, made, it is said, by 'children's fingers'. A most remarkable thing about this remarkable alcove is that it is so low even a child of less than five feet tall must bend down to enter it.

Human footprints are not so uncommon in prehistoric caves (though they are generally those of adults). They exist at Niaux, at Cabrerets, at Gantiès-Montespan and at Aldène in France, for instance, but the most exciting are those at the Tana della Basura (The Witch's Cavern) on the Italian Riviera, which are also of adults but not of *Homo sapiens*, they are of Neanderthaloids, and they are also in a part of the cave where a man cannot stand upright; some strange ritual there.

At a quarter past midnight the boys went back to the Château de Pujol and got their father out of bed. The older man found it very hard going to negotiate the hole—he was already portly—

and lost some of his clothing in the process, but he did make it and early the next morning sent off a telegram to Cartailhac at Geneva: 'The Magdalenians also modelled in clay.'

Cartailhac replied: 'I am on my way.' Shortly afterwards he was at Montesquieu-Avantès in time to meet Breuil down from Paris.

The clay bisons aroused as much protest and accusation of forgery as the painted caves. Although the bisons were covered with a coating of calcite, indicating great age, the wildest stories were put about. For some strange reason the sculptor Frémiet was accused of having modelled the beasts, but Frémiet had never even set foot in the cave for the excellent reason he had been in his grave for two years before the Tuc d'Audoubert bisons had been discovered. It is hard to say why Frémiet was picked upon (except that being dead he could not defend himself), since his rather flamboyant style (see the Joan of Arc statue in the Place des Pyramides, Paris) scarcely suggests prehistoric art.

But the Volp was to reveal still greater marvels.

In July 1916 Begouen and his three sons were at home—the young men on leave from the Army. It was François Camel who again put them on the track of discovery. He said there was a blow-hole on the other side of the hill from the Tuc and around this opening the snow never lay in winter. They decided to investigate. Camel went down first, then Max Begouen after him. They made their way through passages and halls until they came out again through the Enlène grotto quite near the blow-hole. No doubt the Tuc d'Audoubert and the Trois-Frères (as the new cavern was baptized) were originally one single cave about 800 yards long.

The way into the Trois-Frères was very arduous (there is a new entrance now with ladders leading down into the main hall)—a low passage sixty yards long through which one had to creep on one's hands and knees; then came a succession of halls, rooms and passages until a large chamber, out of which led a passage guarded by sculptured lions' heads; this gallery led steeply up to a hole on the other side of which was a stalagmite slope (into which steps have now been cut) down to the Sanctuary.

The Sanctuary is indeed a temple, a natural temple in the bowels of the earth, a sanctuary which is a prototype of temples made by hands. On either side of the Sanctuary are niches and over the niches 'panels' covered with engravings. Two of the niches on the left side give access to a small passage winding round the outside of the Sanctuary and upwards until it reaches a 'window' overlooking the chamber and about twelve feet above its floor. This corridor is covered with fine engravings and just inside the 'window' is the small painted and engraved figure of the shaman, wizard or god, as Breuil used to call it.

All around is a maze of engravings: horses, bisons, cattle, men disguised as animals, beasts in men's shape, men playing some musical instrument (flute? or bow?), sexual symbols, an ithy-phallic figure of a sorcerer, a whole sorcerer frieze and a wizard in bison's fell, his penis erect and before him a female reindeer, the vulva very large and very clearly marked. She turns her head as though expecting the male.

Early Man was not the master of the world but integrated into it: the world of plants, sun, moon, stars, rains and storm and animals, animals towards which Man stood in some special relation. That there was some real—or simulated—copulation between men and certain beasts during the Stone Age, as later, seems almost certain. One is reminded of the story Richard Andree told (in 1880) that the Mandans of North Dakota, would, when disguised as bison, simulate, by means of artificial phalli, copulation with women.

Man was for long ages a rather small and insecure animal. Other beasts were his brothers and enemies, not his servants or victims. Men could not hope, with material means alone, to dominate their environment, so they sought to influence it through magic. Furthermore, when Man is perplexed and anxious, chants and ceremonies do give him support, so that he is not quite lost in his world. Rites do help a transition from anxiety to reassurance, they do cushion reactions and restore good balance. And St. Augustine wrote, in another connection, they 'cast anxiety forth from the soul'. And, then, one of the widest-spread and longest-lasting of Man's conceptions has been that it is necessary to maintain, by appropriate ceremony and ritual, by words spoken (*in the right tone of voice*), the apparent order of the universe.

But rites may not be susceptible of precise definition nor of clear explanation. As R. R. Marrett said, 'the rite is danced out, not thought out', and Dr. Arthur Waley has remarked: 'The truth is . . . there is no "real reason" for ritual acts. In any community where the performance of such acts is linked to a general system of thought they will be explained in terms of that system. If the system changes . . . without disturbing these ritual acts, they will be reinterpreted in terms of the new system.' So we should be wary of professed 'explanations' furnished today for some rite, ritual or ceremony. Even if the interpretation be sincere it may not be valid for many other people than the interpreter himself. Still, all this does not mean we are unjustified in noting parallels which seem to exist between the practices of Old Stone Age Man and those of peoples today, even of peoples we think of as highly 'civilized'.

For the ethnologist all philosophies and 'religious' systems are 'ethnographical documents of the first order whose study is indispensable if we would understand the myths of our time'.[1] But where we are at a disadvantage is that whereas we can study any social custom, rite, ceremony or habit in the terms of an existing culture, as a whole (and any custom divorced from its setting may be mistakenly interpreted) we can only, for prehistoric times, present the bare bones of a culture, though these can be made to live.

But if we are inclined to feel we are immeasurably superior to our remote ancestors, who must have reasoned logically enough

[1] From *La Pensée sauvage* by Claude Lévi-Strauss.

from the evidence they had, we may ponder these words of wisdom:[1]

'The facts of physics and physiology show that perception is the end result of a series of physical events, the last of which, a state of activity of the brain of the percipient, differs so completely from the events occurring in the object perceived, that the qualitative features of a percept can have no resemblance to the physical object which it represents. This perceptual world, therefore, if I may use the term to describe the whole realm of our perceptual experience, is a construct of the percipient's brain.'

Of course, Old Stone Age Man would not have put it just like that.

And dominating, commanding, the whole intricate assemblage of the Trois-Frères is the Sorcerer or God, the Dancing Shaman. His figure is about three feet long. He has a human body and legs, a huge penis, a long tail, antlers, cat's ears, a furry, bearded mask with no mouth, but staring, owl-like eyes. His hands are covered by what seem like bear's paws and he is bent forward as though executing the slow movements of some ritual dance. He clearly symbolizes some composite being, Man and Beast.

The body is heavily outlined in red paint and the rest of the figure is deeply (and probably has been repeatedly) engraved. Maybe the body was once covered with real hair or fur . . . the presiding deity wearing a head-dress ancestral to helmet and crown, mask and mitre and clothed in what are, perhaps, the earliest known examples of ritual vestments . . . the magic of masks. And surely enough the shaman of the Trois-Frères does remind us of Siberian shamans of today, such as those of the Samoyedes, but we cannot say our Pyrenean shaman played the same role as those in northern Asia now, though we can note that the climate of Late Pleistocene Pyrenees and that of present-day Siberia could be compared.

[1] From *The Nature of Experience* by Russell Brain.

Breuil was to spend ten months of his life—ten months spread over ten years—in copying and deciphering the Trois-Frères engravings, in arranging them in some chronological order, in interpreting them. When he was working there he would remain in the cavern all day long, and eat his luncheon in what had been a cave-bears' lair. In the evening he would go back to Begouen's house and enjoy the Count's excellent hospitality. The Trois-Frères was, perhaps, the Abbé's favourite cave and his copies of the maze of drawings are among the most valuable and significant of his reproductions.

Both the Tuc d'Audoubert and the Trois-Frères are safe from damage and deterioration. The caves are private property and not accessible to the public, for visitors do injure paintings not only by the damp from their bodies but because for their convenience floodlights bathe the rock-walls. Altamira is fading somewhat, and although the arrangements at Lascaux are good, it will be interesting to see how long it will be before the paintings there also begin to suffer from too much light, too much damp and too much variation in temperature.[1]

---

[1] Since the above was written the damage to the Lascaux pictures has been such that the cave is now shut to the public.

6

Breuil and Religion

'*Malheur à la raison le jour ou elle étouffera la religion.*'
RENAN

('Woe betide reason the day that it stifles religion.')

FEW of Breuil's friends, I think, saw him perform religious ceremonies, though no doubt he did on occasion baptize and officiate at weddings and funerals. I know for a fact that he christened the infant daughter of an old friend at Lisbon in 1941, and also that, about ten years later, he baptized the son of Harper Kelley—who was a Protestant. The Abbé was, indeed, markedly broad-minded in religious matters. When in 1952 he accompanied M. Pierre Champion, now Assistant Director of the Museum of Man, to his father's death-bed[1] the Abbé abruptly asked, as he entered the room, 'By the way, is Champion a Catholic or a Protestant?'—a reasonable question enough, since Madame Champion had been a Protestant from Geneva. But, without waiting for an answer, Breuil hurried on, saying, 'It doesn't make any difference, anyway,' and proceeded to administer the last sacraments. Dr. Léon Pales, who was present, says this was the only time in the course of many years' close association he ever saw the Abbé perform a religious ceremony.

When, out in the African bush, he got news in 1951 of Field

[1] The old gentleman was the Benoît Albert Champion, whose door the Abbé had so nearly bashed in to get his cherished specimen, long years before (see p. 137).

Marshal Smuts's death, Breuil said, on a rocky hill summit, a Mass in his intention—and Smuts was a member of the Dutch Reformed Church. Someone took a photograph of the scene, which Breuil showed to a friend in Paris. When this friend made no comment—he was moved by the display of Christian charity —Breuil, mistaking the silence for mild reprobation, said, with the characteristic slight shrug of the shoulders and half-smile, 'In any case it couldn't have done him any harm.'

In his remarks, indeed, the Abbé often displayed what might be called a medieval mingling of sacred and profane. Once driving by a country-town church he shouted, 'That's where I first attended Mass—in the belly of my mother . . .' the last words in English.

At New College, Oxford, in 1946 he and I were lodged in the same buildings; on Easter morning we met on the stairs, and when we got outside ahead of us were two priestly figures: one tall, upright, paunchy; the pallid, hook-nosed face and short head under an old-fashioned clerical hat. It was the eminent, pompous, humourless Pater Schmidt, ethnologist and philologist and champion of *Urmontheismus*—that Man had originally been monotheistic—who had refused, it is said, for his science's sake, the offer Pius XI made him of the archbishopric of Vienna and a cardinal's hat. Breuil and Schmidt were, let us say, not temperamentally akin. The other figure was of a shortish, rotund, cheerful and complaisant ecclesiastic, the late Father de Jonghe of Louvain.

'Which way are you going?'

'I'm going to follow *them* to church,' and out shot his indicative finger in a gesture familiar to those who ever saw him spotting a specimen in the field. His voice did not sound much more than resigned. 'Where are you going?'

'I'm off to Hall to get some breakfast.'

'Ah, well . . .' and then a quick flash of a smile, 'the Holy Ghost be with you, anyway. . . .'

It is sometimes written that Breuil was a man of deep and

sincere religious faith. This may well have been so. I never put any question to him about religion, though I know one of his French friends who did inquire how the Abbé managed to conciliate the findings of science with the teachings of the Church, and got this reply: 'The two things are separate and distinct. They run parallel. They do not touch.'

He also wrote in a little paper entitled *La science éloigne-t-elle de Dieu?* ('Does science tend to make men Godless?'), 1952: 'Science and religion are two different problems; science observes, ascertains, it does not explain. Creation is a continuous process and it is our duty to submit to the moral laws decreed by God and transmitted by religions.' Note the plural to the last word.

But, as far as I know, he never made the slightest attempt at proselytism—in this unlike Teilhard. His secretary, Miss Mary Boyle, a Scotswoman, was for some time lodged in a South African convent, the superior of which said one day:

'I think it extraordinary that you've been for so long closely associated with the Abbé and yet he has not converted you to Catholicism.'

'Why? I haven't converted him to Protestantism.'

At least on one occasion Breuil, in clerical costume, attended, seated in the front row, a Protestant service on board ship.

He told me, 'I am a Catholic, and I think Catholicism is the best sort of religion, though I am free to confess that I often find myself more in agreement with a Protestant pastor than with another Catholic priest.' What does one say to that? I murmured, 'Yes, the richness of spiritual life, the liturgical splendour . . .' He finished for me: '. . . and the compassion.'

However, Breuil would criticize rather sharply certain aspects of Catholic discipline (as opposed to dogma) and once gave me quite a long dissertation on clerical celibacy. On this delicate matter he spoke, I fancied, with more warmth than if he had been reviewing the subject quite dispassionately.

The celibacy imposed upon the Roman clergy has, of course, no doctrinal or dogmatic significance. In theory permission might be given at any time for a priest to marry, and those Churches of the oriental rites (Uniat Greek, some Armenians and Copts, etc.) where the lower ranks of the secular clergy are not allowed but obliged to marry, retain their customs though in communion with Rome. Breuil thought this obligation to abstain from marriage gave rise to more tension and abuses than were justified by the admitted advantages: economic, social and maybe spiritual. From time to time we hear that the Catholic rule of celibacy may be relaxed, but it is most improbable any such step will ever be taken. And then some may be inclined to agree with Henry de Montherlant, who has said that if we are tempted to think of a priest as *un pauvre diable*—let us say 'a man to be pitied'—at least he has not got a wife.

Since his speciality was prehistory in the widest sense of the term, Breuil did not have to meet a challenge concerning Christian origins, the apparent inconsistencies in the Scriptures or the circumstances in which the canon was composed and adopted as such.

In fact it was not until fairly late in his life that the Abbé thought it worth while to write about the relations between science and religion. However, while he was in South Africa in 1942–5, he received, it seems, a number of letters from fundamentalists and others asking him to 'explain his position with regard to the Holy Scriptures'. Without disparagement we may say that the intellectual atmosphere of Johannesburg is rather different from that of Paris.

So Breuil published a little pamphlet printed in Basutoland and carrying the *imprimatur* of the Catholic authorities in Johannesburg. He gave me a copy of this paper with the remark that maybe I might find it useful one day. Since the article is now almost impossible to come by, perhaps some passages from it may be illuminating:

Breuil at Cambridge, 10th March 1920. Doctor honoris causa. Next to him is
Earl Haig

At Altamira, August 1925. Breuil, Begouen and Obermaier preparing a letter to
Pope Pius XI

Trois Frères, 1927. To the right Dr. Pales

Breuil on Monfreid's boat, 1933

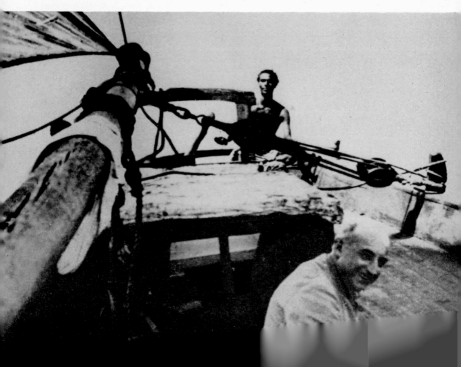

'We consider as faith the belief that the Holy Scriptures contain the Christian revelation (and the pre-Christian) and we Catholics add to these, tradition—the tradition contained in the works of the Fathers of the Church and in the whole of Christian life since its beginning, the tradition to which we ourselves contribute a part as we continue to reinterpret the Bible according to the discoveries of science and the progress of human thought.'

To an objective observer, I think, the Catholic position with regard to tradition must seem a strong one, since it is tradition which vouches that writings composed it is not clear where, by whom and when, relate to events which actually occurred.

Breuil went on:

'A first and fundamental point I have retained from the teaching I received during my ecclesiastical studies, is that although guided by God, the author of a book included in the Bible, was not, therefore, precluded from being a man of his own day, a man speaking and writing according to the customs and the ideas of the circle to which his remarks were addressed. The written book represents a stage in revelation moving forward, and it spoke the language of its time; it was directed first to a contemporary audience, and after that and beyond it, to all believers.

'A second point, no less essential, is that the type of truth in a book is determined by its literary quality. For instance, the kind of truth contained in Proverbs and Ecclesiasticus[1] does not mean that each proverb is a moral truth; the latter book is full of extremely pessimistic and materialistic views. It is a true statement of truth in Salomon's epoch, accurate or undesirable as you choose.

'The Book of Job is a novel in verse about the problem "If God is just why is a righteous man persecuted in this life?"

---

[1] The Book of Ecclesiasticus, which forms part of the Roman Catholic canon, is relegated by the reformed Churches to the Apocrypha.

H

Perhaps Job existed, but the theme is treated according to the poetic fashion of the day. For instance, the seven days and seven nights during which Job's friends kept silence when they found him on his dunghill, the equal number of verses spoken by each in addressing Job, etc. . . . all this springs from the literary conventions obligatory at the time the book was composed and it is designed to lead up to God's reply blaming Job and his friends for their accusations . . . absolving Job, reproaching him only with having wanted to understand what is beyond the comprehension of a human mind . . . the Book of Job . . . is filled with fictions . . . having no connection with historic truth.

'When we open the Book of Genesis . . . we should read as a caption "Great Popular Traditions of the Jewish People". Popular traditions are not history . . . the first chapter, borrowed from a "Yahvist" document, is followed by a second account of the same subject in which the chronology of created things is quite different and betrays another line of thought; the importance, the hierarchy of living beings with regard to Man. This was taken from an "Elohist" source. The compiler who placed the two documents side by side must have known that the two sequences in the creation of things were chronologically irreconcilable.

'Chapter II, verse 4. (1) The earth is bare and deserted. (2) It rains. (3) The origin of irrigation after the creation of Adam *from the earth.* (4) Plants growing out of the earth in the "garden". (5) Adam lives in the garden. (6) A geographical fragment. (7) Man becomes bored with the garden. (8) God models *from the earth* animals to help him. (9) Adam names the animals but finds no companion among them. (10) Adam's mysterious sleep. God makes Woman to come out of Adam's side like a permanent ectoplasm or materialization. (11) Adam recognizes her as his companion. The Elohist document then continues with the account of the Temptation and the Fall.

'In this account, I am personally inclined to lay stress on all *living things*, plants, Man and animals being drawn from the earth by God . . . it, therefore, does not seem to me, judging by the account, that the creation of Man's physical organism differed from that of other beings. They all sprang from the earth.

'It appears to me that all this can be, in a deep, spiritual sense, explained thus: the "earth" and the "garden" mean the physical work necessary to collect food. Food-gathering . . . the animals named by Man . . . mean to the Hebraic mind, natural science . . . all this, then, is philosophy very beautifully presented in pictures . . . the expression of a profound truth in a symbolical, pictorial story. . . .

'To a naturalist it is evident that . . . the more evolved plants living on soil enriched by bacteria can only have existed after millions (or thousands of millions) of years of bacterial weathering of the globe's surface, and that animals living on plants (or those among them living on other animals so fed) cannot have developed until the flora was sufficient for the expansion.

'Palaeontology is the study of the succession of these beings throughout the ages. It aims at establishing their phylogenesis. The oldest organisms in the very ancient deposits (which have been too crumpled and remineralized by orogenic phenomena many times repeated) have been so destroyed that our knowledge of the origin of life on the earth begins only at a late date when there was already a great variety of polyps, asteroids, molluscs, arthropods and inferior vertebrates . . . in the development of forms in each group we note simple, small beings, followed by larger ones, more and more varied and complicated. We then come to gigantic forms which were generally followed by degeneration and sometimes by the total extinction of the group.

'The only method of explanation we have for all this is *evolution*, the only way to understand all things. . . . All that exists derives, at least partially, from what precedes it, and engenders, also at least partially, what follows it. . . .

'Working hypotheses, even if incorrect, are *the* essentials of progress. Only in mathematics and logic can a pure Absolute be attained.

'There are palaeontologists and biologists who recognize that if there happen to be stimulating circumstances, reaction springs from a "psychic force" . . . what is the nature of this inaccessible reality which is so supremely active? But here we are no longer in the domain of science but in that of philosophy.'

Then Breuil gives us the only piece of 'philosophy' I think he published. It is not very much like Teilhard's:

'These forces are . . . outside our comprehension. We are ourselves contained in them . . . the truth is that the cosmos is an indivisible cosmic fact, a single reality, inside which swarm . . . individual beings in their infinite variety. The cosmos is not God. It feels its way as it were with a sort of freedom of adaptation . . . making a thousand experiments of which only some succeed, and some much fewer still (such as human intelligence) modify, locally at least, the setting and framework of things.

'What is this unit, more essential than any one of us? This cosmos of which the dust of life is the blossom, the face of which only one known being, Man, is able to contemplate . . . himself creating art, beauty, imagination, or troubling it, in his humble way, with erratic and excessive passions? . . . For Man, as far as his thought can grasp it, the cosmos is a large body moved and organized by a single law, an Energy beside which all others are as ripples.

'The cosmos and all it contains are the creation of God . . . this omnipresence of God the Creator, in all activity, moral as well as physical, is to me the most profound truth that thought and the human heart can apprehend.

'A long time ago, that great Pope Leo XIII, in one of his encyclicals, wrote that as regards natural science the Holy Scriptures reflect only the knowledge of their times. . . .

'You ask me about biblical chronology . . . I might reply that there is no biblical chronology. . . . the truth is that whereas the Indians and Babylonians did not trouble about the thousands of centuries of humanity's existence, the Jews believed (as a result of their computations) that Man was created between 7000 and 4000 B.C. . . .

'Adam and Eve in Paradise: (a) A period in a country with a sub-tropical climate where fruit ripens all the year round and where lack of clothes is no hardship. A life of food-gathering in a state of nature. (b) Signs of cooler weather. Man grows conscious he is naked . . . the great voice of God peals forth. I am inclined to think this means earthquakes and volcanic eruptions (the flaming sword) chasing Man away from the place where he first developed. The skins in which Man clothed himself mark the dawn of the Hunting Age. Here we have probably memories of the rigorous climatic conditions in the northern hemisphere during the last Glaciation. An epoch of violent seismic disturbances was experienced by Man at a remote period of the Pleistocene and upset the topography of East Africa and Asia Minor . . . all this, though Man witnessed it, took place long ago, before the last Ice Age . . . in such circumstances we might place the date of Adam and Eve in the longest of Old Stone Age (palaeolithic) periods and their names relate to a whole phase, the longest one, in the development of humanity. . . .

'Cain, the agriculturalist. Abel the shepherd.

'They are the representatives of two parallel types of neolithic culture and, from their very natures, always in conflict since nomadic shepherds ever fight with agriculturalists. But the latter, founders of the first villages, and of settled, organized societies, are stronger than the shepherds—hence the death of Abel. But why in the Bible is Abel's role that of a martyr? There are several reasons. One is historical. The Israelites, mostly shepherds . . . had pastoral traditions. Other reasons are of a higher order. Agricultural peoples are usually far more devoted to the lesser gods, ruling fine weather, rain, to the genii of fountains, trees and mountains, to the sun and the moon, etc., and do not pay much homage to the great God of heaven, too high and too far off . . . but the division of work into trades, into stable, well-ordered groups, favours the development of material civilization.

So Cain is the father of those who build fortified villages (Enoch), sound the trumpet (Jubal)—which means military organization —and invent metallurgy (Tubal Cain). Here we have the progress of material civilization which developed in Mesopotamia and Egypt from 7000 to 5000 B.C.

'The pastoral peoples of which Abel was the symbol, had better morals and far higher religious concepts . . . they were given to meditation and the contemplation of the sky and of nature. They had time to look at the heavens and dream. They were the authors of philosophy, of mathematics, of poetry, of astronomy . . . from an amalgam of these two [tendencies] the higher civilization emerged.

'By the way, note the mention in Chapter VI, 1–4, of Genesis, of "children of men" and "giants" which latter the translators agree were not of Adam's line, these latter being called "sons of God".'

The so-called 'Pre-Adamite' theory that there had been men before Adam was launched long ago. As far back as 1655 a French writer, one Isaac de la Peyrère, got himself into a good deal of trouble by suggesting this hypothesis, but Isaac's foundation for his contention was based not upon the Book of Genesis but upon a passage in St. Paul's Epistle to the Romans, Chapter V, verse 14, which runs: 'Nevertheless death reigned from Adam to Moses, even over them that had not sinned after the similitude of Adam's transgression.' And this quotation seems a rather insecure foundation for the 'Pre-Adamite theory', whereas in the Book of Genesis, as Breuil pointed out, there is a clear distinction made between the 'sons of God' and the 'daughters of men' and still more between 'the giants in the earth in those days' and the 'sons of God'.

Breuil went on:

'I can assure you that in the Catholic world, and I think in the Anglican and probably in the Lutheran, such ideas are usual and to mention only the Catholic Church, she has furnished to Prehistory, Geology and Palaeontology many of her clergy whose names are illustrious, such as Teilhard de Chardin, a Jesuit, Dr. Hugo Obermaier, a Bavarian, the Abbé Bouyssonie, a Frenchman, and myself.

'We must not confound religious truths with the symbolical forms by which they are passed on from generation to generation. These forms must be adapted and purified in accordance with the development of the human spirit. On the other hand, scientific truth founded on facts must not be confounded with provisional theories constituting working hypotheses.'

Of course, this able piece of special pleading is as illuminating for what it does not tell as for what it does, since, as Malinowski pointed out a good many years ago, Christian theology is based upon events which are held to have occurred once upon a time in a Mesopotamian garden. And in 1909 the Pontifical Biblical Commission laid down as fundamental truths that Man was specially created, that the first woman was formed from the first man and that the human race constitutes a unity. Moreover in 1950 (and thus six years after Breuil's paper) the Papal Encyclical *Humani generis* proclaimed that 'Original sin is the result of a sin committed in actual historical fact by an individual man named Adam, and it is a quality native to all of us only because it has been handed down by descent from him'.

As a postscript to Breuil on religion there are two quotations which are, I think, illuminating as expressing an admiration for the Catholic Church, and the two passages come from the writings of men who were resolutely agnostic, though admittedly they were born into Catholic communities; two men, moreover, whose ideas and whose ways of life were very different. First of all George Santayana:

'Without this supernatural, environing world . . . spiritual and moral life would be precarious and its forms, while it subsisted, would be innocently and endlessly divergent . . . the *unnaturalness of nature as we find it*, its need of a supernatural complement before we can bear to live in it, is implied in any ascription of dominance to the good.'

And now Paul Valery:

'*Soyons justes: le seul catholicisme a approfondi la vie intérieure, en a fait un sport, un culte, un art et a pu aboutir . . . à organiser, subordonner, diriger les formes mentales à créer des points fixes dans le chaos. . . .*'

('Let us be honest, only Catholicism has plumbed the depths of the interior life and has made of it a sport, a cult, an art, and has succeeded . . . in organizing, in subordinating, in directing mental forms so as to create fixed points in chaos. . . .')

7

The I.P.H.

'Il n'y a pas de première place, il n'y a que des places à part.'
COCTEAU
'There are no first places, there are only individual places.')

THE Founder did not live long to see his Institute working
in its new home. He died in 1922. I am afraid I cannot give
a very satisfactory first-hand impression of the man to
whom Breuil owed so much, for although I saw him several
times, I met him only once. The time was during the First World
War. The circumstances of the meeting, however, are very clear
in my mind, since our host had invited to the same luncheon
party both the Prince of Monaco and Prince Roland Bonaparte.
The latter was what used to be called 'a patron of science' and he
had done something to further research in pre-Columbian
archaeology. But he was no reigning prince, far from it. He was
the son of that Pierre Bonaparte who towards the end of the
Second Empire had created much scandal by murdering a
journalist (called 'Victor Noir')—and getting acquitted. In 1871
Pierre married one of his servants by whom he already had a son
aged thirteen who had up to then borne his mother's name of
Ruflin. Roland Bonaparte then may have had the right to call
himself 'prince' (as was his father) but certainly not 'Imperial
Highness' as he was apt to do. Albert of Monaco and Roland
Bonaparte were on good terms—there was, indeed, a link between
them, for Roland had married one of M. François Blanc's

daughters who died within ten months of marriage and left her widower a nice large slice of the Monte Carlo millions.

So, seating at table was liable to present a problem.

The French, despite what some innocent foreigners may imagine, are a people pervaded with preoccupations concerning class and caste. Not only are those in official or quasi-official positions most fussy about precedence and correct modes of address, but the more prosperous sections of the population are very stuffy and intractable when it comes to places at table, at ceremonies and the like. Even at what must be considered informal family meals a strict precedence will be observed.

The question of seating at this Monaco-Bonaparte luncheon was, therefore, put up to Albert's private secretary. Answer: 'His Serene Highness is always pleased to meet his old friend Prince Roland Bonaparte . . .' No 'Imperial Highness'. Implication: 'Always pleased to meet him when he is in his proper place.' So it was that Albert, on a chair slightly higher than anyone else's, occupied the middle of one side of the table (the place of honour in France) with our host on his right, while Roland sat opposite to Albert. Each could imagine himself the presiding genius—had it not been for that slightly higher chair—but then Bonaparte was a tallish man and Albert short. So everyone was happy.

Conversation, alas, did not concern the sciences, and although I knew little or nothing about prehistory in those days, I had seen and copied (while I was trying to learn to paint in Montparnasse) Breuil's pictures of Altamira, and I did know these had been published by Prince Albert. Talk stayed on a social level, of course, but the two princes did, I remember, converse a good deal about America, which they had both visited several times. On the eve of the First World War Albert had returned from a long hunting trip in the Rockies. In the Monaco Museum you may see a number of excellent little paintings of him riding or stalking or standing by his trophies, and the pictures are near a few stuffed specimens of his bag, a moose and a bear among them—they do not seem so out of place among the Baoussé Roussé relics.

The large portrait on the museum wall is a good likeness of the Maecenas-Prince. He was a short, pale, tired-looking man, of simple and dignified manners. His life had spanned an extraordinary change in his family fortunes. When he was born in 1848 his family was more or less broke. The realm of Monaco consisted then, as it does now, of some 370 acres, mostly barren rock —less than half the area of Central Park in New York. The handful of subjects, not a thousand in all, were housed either in huddled alleys near a rather shabby palace or in shacks by the sea-shore. The ruler was Florestan I, and in that same year, 1848, his suzerain had annexed more than four-fifths of the principality, including the only productive part, the district of Mentone. The Princes of Monaco, who had been hard hit by the French Revolution, did in 1814 get back their patrimony, but on conditions making them the vassals of the House of Savoy, the head of which then bore the now forgotten title of 'King of Sardinia'. The Monaco princes, however, passed most of their time in Paris, and Florestan, the successor of a brother whom his loyal subjects had set eyes on but thrice during a reign of twenty-five years, had, in his younger days, been reduced to playing bit-parts at the Ambigu-Comique Théâtre in Paris at a time when French contempt for actors was still as lively as it had been before the 1789 revolution. This Florestan married a lady about whose origins little is recorded, she had also been on the stage—as a dancer—and was peculiar in that before her marriage, and as an unmarried woman, she bore two quite different surnames.

When Albert was four years old his father, Charles, Florestan's son and heir, was rash enough to indulge in the organization of a spontaneous popular demonstration, at Mentone, of loyalty to the princely House of Monaco, but the crowd recognized him as he was leading the cheers and would have torn him limb from limb had he not been rescued by Sardinian soldiery and clapped into jail, for the Monesgasques used to be rather a truculent lot, as befitted a race living by petty piracy, smuggling and maybe less avowable activities. In the preceding century his subjects had beaten one of the Monaco rulers to death and thrown his corpse into the Mediterranean.

The reference books tell us that Charles's wife was a 'Comtesse Ghislaine de Mérode', but no such person figures in the genealogy of the patrician Belgian family of that name. The name of Mérode, indeed, was best known in the early part of this century as that of a lovely actress who was the intimate friend of Leopold II of Belgium. . . .

When Charles succeeded his father he realized that he must get into business. But what could be made out of Monaco? It had no sort of natural resources and was not even readily accessible except by sea. Monsieur François Blanc came to the rescue. He had had a somewhat chequered early career and at various times had had—as is the case with many great and good men—a few differences of opinion with the police, but in their middle years François and his twin brother Louis-Joseph acquired considerable fortunes running the gambling-tables at Bad Homburg in western Germany. When in the 'fifties of the last century the Blanc brothers saw the Prussian Government was not going to renew their contract, Louis-Joseph decided to pull out, but François was headed for greater things. Mme Blanc, a German who had begun her career as a waitress in a beer-tavern, played a considerable part in urging on her husband's ambitions, and both the daughters of the couple afterwards married princes—of a sort.

In 1856 Blanc got a fifty-year concession to run a gambling casino, and the first unpretentious little den was up on the Rock of Monaco itself, facing the palace. Two years later, however, Blanc was doing so well that his backers were ready with more funds, so the Prince rented him some rising ground called the Colline des Spélugues on which Blanc built his new casino. On 13th May 1858 the ten-year-old Prince Albert performed his first public ceremony. He handled the trowel and slapped the mortar around the Casino's foundation-stone. In the boy's honour

Blanc baptized his new concession Eliseo Alberto or 'Albert's Elysium', and it is by this name that the famous paradise might have been known. But sager counsels prevailed and in 1859 Blanc hit upon the magic words 'MONTE CARLO': everyone knew the name 'Monte Cristo' from the elder Dumas's novel. There was a Count of Monte Cristo, but now there was also a Prince of Monte Carlo.

Charles (or Carlo) got a huge lump sum down plus a yearly tribute and an agreement for further lump sums to be made over every ten years. M. François Blanc died in 1877 worth over 200,000,000 francs gold; that is, $40,000,000 or £8,000,000—multiply by five to get today's value.

Soon Monte Carlo was flourishing and its peak period was during Albert's reign, when on the green baize tables there piled up in glittering mounds hundreds and thousands of golden 100-franc pieces—no chips, no counters, nothing but solid gold, and each coin bearing the effigy of Albert's grave, pouchy, bearded profile and the superscription 'Albert, by the Grace of God, Sovereign Prince of Monaco'—a comforting reminder that part at least of the money lost at play was devoted to furthering the cause of science, subventioning the Institute of Human Palaeontology, and incidentally making Henri Breuil's career possible.

To get to the I.P.H. Breuil would take the Métro (the Paris Underground) to the Jussieu station and then walk up the rue Linné. Many of the streets thereabouts bear names recalling men of science—Geoffroy-Saint-Hilaire, the zoologist, Cuvier, the palaeontologist, great Buffon, the naturalist, himself. Maybe one day they will name a street after Breuil.

This part of Paris has changed a good deal in the last forty years. The exotic minaret and green-tiled roofs of the mosque rise behind the Jardin des Plantes buildings. The old, odorous Halle aux Vins, or Wine Storehouses, has given way to a tall block of university science laboratories, but the quarter still remains old-fashioned (and, strangely for Paris, singularly devoid of decent eating-places) and the rue Mouffetard has still one of the most colourful of the Parisian out-of-doors markets.

Breuil would enter the Jardin des Plantes by the south-west gate and pass the Cedar of Lebanon, whose seed, legend has it, Jussieu (the botanist, who was among those to recognize 'thunder-stones' as man-made) brought in his hat from the Levant. The story is not true and the seed came from Oxford. Over to the left there is Cuvier's house and nearby the laboratory where Henri Becquerel discovered radio-activity (it was no longer ago than 1896). Nearest at hand is the statue of Chevreul, the chemist, the longest-lived of all scientists. He died at the age of 103 in 1889. On the right is the hill where Monsieur le Comte de Buffon received Marie-Antoinette.

Then, maybe, the Abbé would turn into the zoo for an hour or so. Whenever he was near a zoo, and had the time, he would whip a pencil and sketch-book out of his pocket and settle down to draw the animals. He would say he had to keep his hand in, his eye trained by living beasts. He seems to have had one of those 'oriental' visual memories that project real images on to shut eyelids. Like the palaeolithic artists, he could carry away a vision with him and throw it on to a surface when far from his models. He trained himself thus to sketch from very early on. He drew his family and friends, as well as his professors. The drawings of horses facing p. 49 were done from memory in the classrooms at Saint-Sulpice and they are very life-like.

Breuil sketched while he explained, he sketched on a black-board while he lectured, he sketched in his letters. I have a precious one he wrote to me when he was in Africa in 1947. The writing is on six pages (there are a few words I never have been able to decipher) and the margins are covered with fine little thumbnail drawings of prehistoric African wall-paintings.

Strangely enough, the Abbé's talent was confined to portraits of animals. When he ventured to reproduce human figures,

landscapes or buildings his work was not on a higher level than
that of any fairly efficient amateur.

On his way from the Jardin des Plantes to the Institut de
Paléontologie Humaine, the I.P.H., he would pass by the façade
of the zoological museum and out of the gardens by Buffon's
house (where he hardly ever resided) and make for the boulevard
Saint-Marcel.

Prince Albert had founded his I.P.H. in 1910. Some time before
he had explained to Boule what he wanted and asked him to
draw up plans. Building began soon afterwards, and the Institute
should have been opened in 1914 but the First World War held
things up. In the meantime Boule's laboratory had to serve as
temporary quarters. Boule was professor of palaeontology at the
Muséum d'Histoire Naturelle, whose laboratories are grouped
around, in and near the Jardin des Plantes. The Muséum
d'Histoire Naturelle is not a museum in our sense of the word, or
rather it is a number of museums and something more.

In 1794, thus in the middle of the French Revolution, the
old Jardin du Roy, both botanical and zoological, which had
been run by Buffon (who died in 1789 on the very eve of the
Revolution), was renamed Muséum d'Histoire Naturelle and in
succeeding years was to undergo a number of changes until it
became a unique institution of higher learning. There is a
number of chairs, each held by a professor; to each chair is
attached a 'laboratory' in the widest sense of the term, either a
museum or what may be called a living laboratory. Thus to the
chair of zoology are attached the menagerie at the Jardin des
Plantes and that at Vincennes on the eastern fringes of Paris.

To the chair of botany belongs the botanical garden, to the
chair of palaeontology the museum of that science, and so forth.
Although the professors do not have to deal with undergraduates,
and though lecturing does not occupy much of their time, some
of them have a lot of administrative work to do, such as super-
vising the zoo, while the professor of anthropology is also director
of the huge Museum of Man and running that is a full-time job.

The boulevard Saint-Marcel, where Prince Albert chose to build his I.P.H., is a broad, characterless thoroughfare (though under part of it is the oldest Christian necropolis in Paris) on the edge of the fifth and fifteenth arrondissements. You are, as the crow flies, but a few hundred yards from the little world of the Jardin des Plantes, but you are in another country.

The Institute building—adjoining a nursing-home for policemen—is of dull yellowish brick and dirty grey stone, and resembles a prison. Both it and the Oceanographic Institute (in the rue Saint-Jacques and also donated by Prince Albert) are described as being in the 'Monaco style of architecture'—it is difficult to judge. In any case, the I.P.H. was built to last. Its massive walls and stone-flagged floors are those of a fortress.

When in 1920 the building was complete, Boule moved in as director and Breuil as professor of prehistoric ethnology. Obermaier, a former enemy alien, had by this time been dropped and, anyway, was provided for with a chair at the University of Madrid.

At the I.P.H. and during term-time Breuil had to lecture twice a week to a select group of post-graduate students—altogether for five or six hours. The Abbé had both a private room and a laboratory where he spent a good deal of time when he was in Paris.

He did not ask for essays or written matter but made his students do practical work. If anyone put up a problem he would discuss it in masterly fashion, with plenty of his expressive little grunts and interrogative 'ehs', opening up stimulating views and darting from comparison to comparison. He said it took him two days to sum up a student. If one ventured to suggest two days was not very long, he would retort, 'It's enough for me to find out what he can't do.' In this connection he once gave some opinions on education in general:

'My own experience is that like any fairly good pupil I did know the "programme" so that I was never failed in an examination. I was neither a better nor a worse student than any other but as soon as the examination was over I hastened to forget most of what I had learned. I would not say that the cramming was quite useless; something of what I had taken in floated about and in fact still does float about in my subconscious mind and no doubt influences my present thoughts and activities. I know the knowledge exists and that I have only to put out a hand, take a book and refresh ideas which have become vague. Far be it from me to say that all scholastic schedules are useless. They certainly do contribute something towards moulding the minds of students. But what I must say is that the one thing students are never taught is to think.'

And Breuil would not have any students, disciples or followers about him who did not think. He was not deceived by fools with good memories, nor did he take them for persons of independent and creative thought.

Dr. Dorothy Garrod, famed as the discoverer of the second Gibraltar skull (see p. 88), for her excavations at Mount Carmel and at Angles-sur-l'Anglin, has told how the first day she reported at the I.P.H. the Abbé handed her a filing-box full of off-prints and remarked: 'Just take a look at those. If there's anything you don't understand come and ask.' The papers were Commont's notes on the Somme gravels—pretty tough going for a beginner without much geology.

If a student came back bristling with queries Breuil would be delighted and say, 'It was a test; if you'd said you understood it all I'd have taken no more interest in you.'

When no one asked questions he would make no overtures but sit smiling and silently smoking. He had, as a matter of fact, despite his self-confidence in his own powers, standing and knowledge, little or none of the schoolmasterly urge to facile domination. He was not a 'boy among men, a man among boys'. He had no professorial, pedantic pomposity. There was nothing of the fussy usher about him; no, not at all. He would nearly

I

always wait for others to make the overtures. If you sought enlightenment he would go to great pains in explanation. I remember shamefacedly how patient he was in answering some silly questions of mine in earlier days. He would discuss anything scientific, palaeontology, early Man, biology, geology, stone implements, art . . . or anything to do with scholarship. If you did not seek enlightenment, then he would engage in chitchat about his travels, about men and women, about life in general, gossip, the ups and downs of existence, the disciplines of the Church, the manners and customs of Chinese merchants. He was indulgent to his friends but not to the extent of crediting them with more sense than they had. Hence, some people would call him harsh, which he was not. He could, in most cases, do credit to his enemies' wits. I never heard him callous, but there was maybe something a little objective in the way he would refer to the disappearance of old companions and friends. Perhaps this was an attitude to avoid sentimentality, perhaps it came from a clerical training: too much fuss must not be made of transitions. He was marvellously quick at stripping the incidental from the essential, though not in what might be called a inhuman way. He rarely ignored the bonds of our common humanity.

It was Breuil's work at the I.P.H. that led him to devote more of his attention to the problems of the Lower Palaeolithic, especially as they appeared in southern England. As he remarked, 'the days of Lyell, Prestwich and Reid were over. British geologists were taking a rest.' He soon realized the old framework was bursting open. In southern England deposits of 'warm' fauna (i.e. the remains of animals that flourished in a warm climate) were inserted in between a 'cold' fauna and the younger loess formations which had been laid down at the end of a glacial epoch.

Starting off from the observation that in northern France and southern England there was to be noted an alternation of hand-axe and flake industries, the Abbé saw that the old 'Chellean' had to be pushed back to the first or Günz-Mindel Interglacial, while at the same time he established that Chellean and Levalloisian were parallel to but different from Clactonian and Acheulian.

So there lived some sort of Man in the Thames and Somme valleys at the same time as a 'southern elephant' and the so-called 'Etruscan' rhinoceros—long, long ago.

It was Commont's work on the Somme terraces that was Breuil's foundation for his study of Lower Palaeolithic chronology. As long ago as 1904, Breuil, when poking about in the Baltil-Tellier gravel-pit at Amiens, met a small, timid-seeming man who asked if he might examine the Acheulian artefacts the Abbé had just dug out of the red earth of the Somme thirty-metre terrace. The man was Commont, a humble elementary schoolmaster and a self-made scientist. He had tried to make his data fit into the framework Boule had constructed in 1889.

As late as 1908, Boule placed both Magdalenian and Solutrean in post-glacial times (i.e. later than 10,000–8000 B.C.), the Acheulian in the Riss-Würm Interglacial, while the Riss Glaciation Boule held to be Pliocene and not Pleistocene at all. Such an extraordinary jumble of errors (as we know them to be now), coming from a most eminent man of science, serves to pin-point in striking fashion the vast sweep of Breuil's work in constructing the prehistoric chronology which we all use today without maybe giving a thought to the man who established it and what he did to get it adopted.

Commont had found 'Chellean' core-tools (roughly chipped on both sides to an oval shape) in the base gravels of the Somme forty-five-metre terrace at Saint-Acheul, together with Acheulian artefacts and remains of *Elephas antiquus*—a very ancient form of elephant. Commont also devoted much study to the Saint-Acheul thirty-metre terrace, where he found 'evolved' Acheulian.

The first of Commont's researches was that Boule's 'short' chronology could not be accepted and that the most ancient deposits (i.e. those in the highest terrace at Abbeville and

Saint-Acheul) must date from before the deposits containing 'typical' Acheulian implements.

The second result was that a solid framework was provided for some of the most ancient types of stone implements (Clactonian, Levalloisian, Tayacian) which up to then had been left floating up in the air, so to speak.

Breuil's work was so varied and his range of interests so wide that all he did for the classification of artefacts may seem rather tiresome to non-specialists; still, the immense task he accomplished in this field was capital for the stabilizing of prehistory. We may be inclined to think that too much attention was paid to the minutiae of stone-tool manufacture and typology, and nowadays there is some justification for this view, since we have at our disposal dating techniques unthought of even a decade ago. Until about 1950 computations in years were arrived at largely by dead-reckoning and the astonishing thing is that these computations agree fairly well with the datings obtained by Carbon-14 and K/A (potassium argon) methods. There was, it is true, the theory associated with the name of the Yugoslav scientist Milankovitch which attributed the extension of the glaciers to variations in the elliptical orbit of the earth around the sun, the position of the rotary axis in space, variations in the reflections of the sun's rays, etc. For some ages (e.g. the Mindel Glaciation) the 'curve' agrees fairly well with K/A results, but for other ages the 'curve' seems wildly out of line. For instance, the Milankovitch figure for the beginning of the Würm Glaciation is 126,000 years ago, as against 70,000 years now generally accepted.

It is useful to retain the names Günz, Mindel, Riss and Würm for the four Ice Ages of Europe during the Pleistocene Period which began over 2,000,000 years ago and is the only geological age which concerns us for the story of Man. However, as we have noted before, there were colder interludes during the 'Interglacials' and there were warmer phases during the 'Glaciations'. Furthermore, not all geologists agree that there were four distinct Ice Ages, but perhaps only two main ones (in the Pleistocene).

In these matters, as in so many more relating to our history, it is best to acknowledge no immutable rules; theories are fine and hypotheses useful, but must be changed when necessary. This does not, of course, mean there are no fixed points. There are, but flexibility must be used in explanation.

But there is another consideration, and it relates to a matter Breuil was to study much and on which he threw a great deal of light.

Here is the problem.

Why, when the sea level rose with the melting ice of an Interglacial, did not the waters wash away all traces of former beaches?

In addition to the seesawing of icing and de-icing, there was, on the whole, a fall in sea level during the last million years—to take only that space of time so important for the story of Man.

It is possible that some of the fall may have been due to the scooping out of deeper pits in the oceans' beds. It is again possible, though by no means proved, that with each Interglacial less ice may have been melted. It is estimated that at the South Pole alone there are some 7,000,000 cubic miles of ice, but there is reason for thinking that this has not been melted for a very long time, possibly not at any period during the Pleistocene.[1]

It is thought that if all the ice in the world were to melt, the general sea level might rise by as much as 100 metres—over 300 feet—though even then we should not get a sea level as high (with regard to land, of course) as at some times in the past (e.g. the Günz-Mindel Interglacial).

The inescapable conclusion is, then, that the land masses have been all rising during the Pleistocene.

Breuil tackled the problems of ancient shore-lines and sea-beaches in Portugal, in Morocco, in Mozambique, in South Africa and in France and England. Everywhere the old shore-lines are at comparable heights.

[1] One of the most detailed of Breuil's studies on this problem is the book he and Zbyszewski published in 1943: *Les plages anciennes portugaises entre les Caps d'Espichel et Carvoeiro et leurs industries paléolithiques.*

8

Un vieux prêtre rogue *or Breuil at home*

'The only world with reality and significance—that of our
latent consciousness.'

PROUST

"YOU have probably heard the London Geological Society
has awarded me the Prestwich Prize . . . nothing could
give me greater pleasure especially since I regard it as a
counterpart of the gesture Lyell and Prestwich made to Boucher
de Perthes and as an acknowledgement of all I have attempted to
do in unravelling the Quaternary problems in the Somme Valley
and in others, as well as in Portugal and South Africa, and, I may
tell you, without any encouragement in France where this fellow
X, by means of many false reports, is endeavouring to undermine
what, for the past twenty years, I have accomplished by my
studies in quarries and gravel-pits of which he knows nothing. I
said to him one day—when he had just delivered a ridiculous
lecture reducing the antiquity of Man to a matter of 25,000 years
and had had the impudence to ask for my opinion—"You are, as
far as Quaternary terraces and formations are concerned, in a
state of baptismal innocence; maybe you have seen them from a
car but you know nothing about their 'anatomy'—you are like
a street-urchin shoving his nose against a pastry-cook's window
and staring at the sugar-coating on a cake . . . he doesn't know
what is underneath." But this does not prevent him from talking

as pompously as a bogus Pope—a man whose whole information is got out of books.

'The sympathy shown me by the British and their firm backing (he has been sending offensive letters about me to as far afield as Lisbon, saying I am on very bad terms with the British) are a splendid retort to his lies and sham science.'

So Breuil in one of his letters to me.

He was, indeed, all his life grateful for the recognition he received in Britain and I think he was one of the few Frenchmen I have known who really like the British (and especially the Scottish) and American approach and ways of life. Hemingway wrote that one of the nicest things about France is that no one there is ever your friend for an obscure reason. And, of course, when there is a clear reason for a friendship then it is more likely to be genuine and lasting and fruitful than one based upon vague sentiments, and surely the most satisfactory basis is community of intellectual interests—in the widest sense of the term. Breuil's real friendships were with people of his own pursuits. But they must be men and women who were honest—not necessarily of the highest ability, but sincere. He was, to the very end, trenchant in his criticism of anything he felt was pretentious or superficial. As late as 1957—when he was eighty—he wrote in a review about a foreign prehistorian: 'He has never been anything but an astute compiler, a parasite on science and an exploiter of real scientists.' He would write of a book: 'It is just a rehash of my work.' He disliked being plagiarized—though if due acknowledgement were made he was generosity itself in allowing the fullest use to be made of his writings—but I remember him saying to one author who had asked for an opinion on his book, 'And may I remind you my name's Breuil . . . B R E U I L.'

Here is the Abbé on ignorant critics:

'I can understand ignorant people (and of course those who are half-educated, or less, and men who may be highly competent in mathematics or stratigraphical geology), when confronted with facts that are, for them, not only completely novel but unrelated to anything they do know, becoming giddy when they have to face vast expanses of time and dumbfounded by a great art that is from 10,000 to 40,000 years old. What, however, is strange is that by mental sluggishness they are induced (without sufficient knowledge of the evidence which is scattered about over a huge area) to produce "hypothetical" explanations whose ingenuousness is really imbecile. In folklore it was the Devil, or the Saints, or Gargantua who made the megaliths, and all that is poetical enough just as are stories of sprites and hobgoblins. But we are no longer in the age of folklore, though it seems we are still in that of ineptitude when no one, least of all a pseudo-scientist, reminds himself that the worst sin of the spirit is to speak learnedly about that of which one is entirely ignorant.'

Not only was he implacable where false learning was concerned, but he was inclined to be vindictive about the professors thereof. In speaking of someone who had not measured up to his standards he might say, 'We must down him'—*il faut l'abattre*. Yes, it must be admitted he was inclined to bear a grudge—though his anger and ill-will could be appeased if one set about it the right way. Unkind critics tell us that clerics generally are a little apt to be vindictive. In my young days there used to be in France a particularly tough sort of whipcord popularly known as *rancune de prêtre*, 'priest's rancour'. Why? Because you can't wear it out.

Breuil was, in fact, by nature quick-tempered and impatient. Early on in his career he once took some prehistoric object for repair to the technical director of the Saint-Germain Museum—a quietly competent man, the late Benoît Claude Champion. A short while afterwards the Abbé called at Champion's house and not finding him at home could only with difficulty be restrained from bashing down a door to reach his cherished specimen. As time went on, Breuil got his temper under control, but he was never very patient with fools or with waiting (see p. 50).

Not so long after the First World War, a M. Camille Pitollet, who had been with Breuil on the naval attaché's staff in Spain, ran into the Abbé as they were both diving down into the entrance of the Monceau Métro station. Each was surprised to learn the other lived in that part of Paris, since they had never come across each other in the street.

'Now I know who he is!'

'Who?'

'Why, the man they call in the quarter *le vieux prêtre rogue*, the arrogant old priest.'

The Abbé was delighted, changed his mind about taking the Métro and carried Pitollet off to the apartment in the rue Demours which Breuil had occupied for some years. The rue Demours is in a part of Paris—to the north of the Parc Monceau —that was built up after 1860, and it still contains a number of streets that are quiet and almost provincial, where in the 'seventies, 'eighties and 'nineties of the last century a number of rich bourgeois—artists, successful actors and the like—put up some rather pretentious private houses: Edmond Rostand the playwright, the painter Henner and Sarah Bernhardt all lived there. Part of the rue Demours, however, is enlivened by an open-air market such as are to be found all over Paris even in more or less 'exclusive' sections. And in this market Breuil would do his shopping, hence his figure was a familiar one, maybe it was the street-merchants who found him *rogue*.

The apartment was small and not only crammed with books and papers but also with souvenirs of Spain. To the end he kept with him a mass of Spanish objects reminding him of exploration and adventure—a great green and black riding-cloak draped over an armchair, stirrups, wooden spoons, bowls, posters, earthenware water-jugs, saddle-bags, lanterns and everyday objects of an old-fashioned Spain now fast fading into oblivion.[1]

[1] He gave Pitollet the MS. of the *Spanish Diary*, an entertaining account of the incidental adventures of his Spanish years. Breuil's text was published at Cahors in 1925 in a review called *Hispania*, which is quite impossible to

After his father's death, however, between the two world wars, and his inheritance of a share in the family's modest fortune, the Abbé decided to buy an apartment: in those days this was a rather unusual way of getting a lodging in Paris, though now it is about the only one. Breuil argued thus: 'I'll always be sure to have a roof over my head,' though possibly he did not realize that when you own a dwelling (especially in an apartment house) it costs money all the time, nor that matters such as central heating, contributions towards the upkeep of the structure, and so forth, might prove troublesome later on.

He chose an apartment in a large building, 52 avenue de La Motte-Picquet, a stone's throw away from the southern end of the Champ de Mars and right on the top of a Métro station entrance through which he could, without changing, get either to Cluny (station now closed) for the Collège de France, or to Jussieu for the I.P.H. Breuil never owned a car and if he had he certainly would not have been able to drive it. He was, strangely enough, for one who was so admirable a draughtsman, and so adroit at handling implements, on the whole, rather clumsy with his hands.

The south side of this block looks on to a noisy thoroughfare, but to the north the apartments face a very different scene. Breuil's windows overlooked a narrow, quiet street on the farthest side of which was an odd collection of shacks and cabins, relics of an earlier Paris, called the *Village Suisse*, though even now, when it has been furbished up, it bears no resemblance to a Swiss village. Thirty or forty years ago this maze of alleys was a regular flea-market where on occasion you might light on an amusing find. Nowadays the 'villagers' are very sophisticated merchants, past-masters in the arts of soft-sell and camouflage. Still, to the end Breuil could look out and down on to a strange

---

find today. I have consulted it for the chapter on 'Spanish Years'. Breuil, indeed, kept a diary for much of his life, but, as one of his friends has written: 'It is doubtful whether he or anyone else could read it in its entirety'; that is, decipher the writing.

assortment of junk: old bulk-heads, Victorian statues, birdcages, 'native curios', negresses carrying globe lamps, bunting, flags, stone fountains, wrought-iron railings, ancient baby-carriages, sickly yellow and green *art nouveau* objects of 1900, train lanterns, church ornaments, candlesticks, swords, stuffed hussars, church-spire cocks, barrel-organs and very much else. Such was the backdrop against which Breuil sat when you went to visit him . . . 'ethnographical if not prehistorical . . .'

In the same block, but giving on to the noisy avenue, lived the Abbé's closest foreign friend, the late Harper Kelley, a Harvard man who had lived long in France. Though he had a number of American friends, Breuil refused at least one invitation to visit America. There was, he said, nothing for him to do there. When it was suggested he should tour the Maya sites in Mexico and Guatemala he replied, 'The Maya were moderns, the contemporaries of the Romans.'

As Kelley was rather deaf, he did not mind the rumble of the street and he would sit in his living-room listening to records of classical music, of which he had an enormous collection. The phonograph, however, was never turned on when Breuil came in, for he did not like even classical music.

This No. 52 of the avenue de La Motte-Picquet is curiously arranged; from the street you enter a large, roofed-in space rather like a skating-rink. In each of the four corners is a flight of stairs and an elevator. Breuil and Kelley used different lifts, but the place is so built that you can go up to the sixth floor (in France traditionally reserved for servants) and from any of the corners make your way along to any other corner without coming down to the street-floor. For years almost every morning when he was in Paris the Abbé would patter along the narrow passages and end up in Kelley's rooms for breakfast, at which plans and publications were often discussed. Several times a year the two men would visit the Somme gravel-pits in Kelley's car.

You rang at a third-storey door and a little *judas*, as the French call a grated peep-hole, would flick back and a pair of brilliant

eyes peep out. Then the door would open and you were at home
with Breuil.

An apartment of smallish rooms, a little austere maybe, not
that it was bare, far from it. Ashtrays everywhere, smoke in the
air, books, pamphlets, papers piled up on chairs, tables, book-
cases, all in considerable disorder. His desk was set sideways to a
window and was covered with a litter of papers out of which
rose a Romanesque head of Christ. It was a cast. He had had the
original rescued from the ruins of Louvain during the First World
War, but he returned the carving to its home and kept only a
copy.

On the walls some family portraits in oblong or oval frames;
soldiers in Napoleonic uniforms, rather pale but self-possessed
ladies in late eighteenth- or early nineteenth-century dresses; and
each frame with a name neatly inscribed on a tablet; among others,
a Duval de Nanpty and a Millon de Pomeroy, the one a great-
grandmother and the other a grandmother. The former, as the
Abbé was careful to note in his autobiographical jottings, a
native of Rouen and of a family whose members were styled
nobles hommes, 'noble men'; curiously enough, though probably
Breuil did not know it, Normandy in the north and Languedoc,
Guyenne and Béarn in the south were the only provinces in pre-
revolutionary France where *noble homme* really meant 'noble'; that
is, exempt from certain taxes which afflicted the common run of
mankind. Elsewhere in unregenerate France *noble homme* meant no
more than 'gentleman' in Britain today. The Abbé's forbears all
seem to have borne their real, full names, whereas most Frenchmen and women who use a 'de' suppress the real surname. Thus
the Goncourts never called themselves Jules or Edmond *Huot*
de Goncourt, nor did Theodore de Banville call himself Theodore
Faulin de Banville. There are, of course, a few French families
which have no 'surname', so to speak; that is to say they have no
patronymic other than a territorial one, thus the d'Harcourts.

The abundance of these 'X de Y' sort of names stems, in part
at least, from a brisk trade in manors during the eighteenth

century. The pretty names fetched the highest prices, while some ill-sounding or absurd ones found no takers at all. Who wanted to be 'Monsieur de Montcu' or 'Monsieur de Saint-Farfardet' even at cut prices?

But very many of the present-day 'X de Y' people's names do not date back even to the title-jobbing times of the 1700's, they have just been assumed. Their origins are lost, as was said of one noble, indeed almost royal, race, in 'the mists of the nineteenth century'.

Until nearly the last the small bowed figure in a well-worn cassock would dart about, flick over the leaves of portfolios, grab for a book, let out a spurt of talk and then sit and puff his cigarette and grunt 'hum' or 'eh' with a sidelong glance—and leave a good deal to be inferred by the visitor. Then sometimes his voice would drop and become very rapid, as though hardly able to keep pace with his thoughts. In the presence of some people, at the mention of certain subjects, he was discreet, secretive even. His determination to be silent at all costs could be read on his face when his usually brilliant eyes would glaze over and appear almost sightless.

But when he was with trusted friends he would let himself go, cheerfully, laughingly—and then there would be a slight grimace, a movement of the head which showed he would not continue. But he was not mealy-mouthed. Once when I had recounted to him the odd behaviour of a lady scientist, he remarked rather testily as though pitying my obtuseness, 'Give her a year more, the menopause will then be over, tackle her again.' But I do not want to give the impression he was brusque or tetchy. On the contrary, his courtesy was marked.

He was ready to take any amount of trouble with those he found really interested in his subjects and he often helped such people out of his own pocket. He would, with a long letter, acknowledge printed references to his work. For instance (to speak only of my experience), at the time of his third African journey I was able to be of some slight service to him. Not only did he thank me profusely but he sent me a considerable number of his most interesting and significant papers and publications, each one with a note in his own handwriting. Again, when reviewing a book of mine, not only did he use such phrases (I am sure without sarcasm, for he never sneered) as 'Mr. Brodrick agrees with me that . . .' but he sent me a letter referring to the review and saying: 'It does contain some criticism which I hope will not vex you.'

He was fully convinced of his own worth. He was, as one of his old friends has put it, 'at once arrogant and humble', perhaps rather like the Cardinal de Retz, who wrote more or less that when he was alone he was humble but when he was with others he felt very arrogant. Breuil would refer to his position with disarming naturalness, as when in his paper on religion (see p. 119) he wrote: '. . . whose names are illustrious, such as . . . and myself.' Some people used to flatter him, and since he was human, he rather enjoyed this, but since he was Breuil he did not fail to see through the flattery—and he was like that former Duke of Newcastle who 'never remembered his rank unless others forgot it'. Moreover, he was at his best with poorer, humbler folk. He was not patronizing or condescending, and they liked him very much. The people of the rue Demours region who spoke of him as *un vieux prêtre rogue* were either using the term as a sort of compliment or had tried to get the better of him in the market-place!

I think he was pleased with medals and decorations—although he did not have many of them until towards the end of his career. Still, about 1924 he investigated some (not very exciting) palaeolithic sites in Transylvania and the Rumanian Government made him a Commander of the Order of the Crown of Rumania (I never dared to tell him I knew a man who had received this same medal as a young officer and just for running errands)—and when in 'full dress' he would wear this *cravate*, one had rather the impression that the blue and white ribbon of this exotic decoration was a kind of mute protest against his being kept waiting so long for the *cravate* of the Legion of Honour.

Sometimes (as in the letter quoted at the beginning of this chapter) he would express himself as though his work had not been appreciated at its true value in France, but men who enjoy a high reputation abroad often tend to think they are neglected at home. They compare the polite deference accorded to a foreigner with the more down-to-earth treatment we get from our own fellow-countrymen.

Yet he held the highest academic post open to any Frenchman. He was a member of the Institute of France. His career was not of the sort that would have secured him election to the French Academy (also a part of the Institut de France, but with a prestige considerably higher than the other 'academies' making up that body, since members of the French Academy not only have generally accorded to them a high social precedence but, what is more, receive a particularly good rate of pay for their writings). Ecclesiastics are by no means excluded from the French Academy, but the academicians aim rather high and choose their churchmen from the ranks of bishops and cardinals.

Breuil could have expected no signal promotion in the Church, which rarely rewards what may be called sleeping partners; that is men who, although in Holy Orders, follow careers outside the Church.

In extreme old age the Abbé was an impressive, almost an august, figure even for those who did not see him surrounded by, and accepting with becoming grace, considerable deference. But you did not fully appreciate the man until you had enjoyed a fairly long conversation with him. His talk was almost always exciting and you fell quickly under the charm—if he cared to exercise it. I remember on one occasion at his home he brought out of his folders the sketches Brenans made of the Tassili n'Ajjer rock-paintings (see p. 216), of which we now have excellent colour photographs. As he flipped over the sheets he threw out in a hurried, low voice all sorts of illuminating ideas and suggestions on art-traditions, the mystery of the extinction of cultures, of possible relationship between African rock-art and that of Old

Choukoutien, August 1931. Pei, Wong and Breuil

Breuil and Harper Kelley at the Château de Pujol, 1931

Breuil's copy of the White Lady of the Brandberg

Stone Age Europe. Just flying phrases and some daring enough, but in every sentence there was something to retain.

Some of the French newspapers and reviews keep not only *dépisteurs*, men who track down and ferret out the news, but also *pigeurs*, men who have the knack of finding the right explanation with the minimum of evidence. Breuil was a born *pigeur*. Of course, he made mistakes, and, of course, being human, there were some of his mistakes he would never admit as such—but they were few.

He was absorbed in his work and had little time for hobbies other than entomologizing and gardening—he was, in fact, a keen gardener—but curious as it may seem he showed little interest in pictorial art except the prehistoric, his tastes were classical and he attached little or no value to modern painting— and least of all to abstract art. Maybe he took a long view, a very long view, and thought that fashions in art have changed so often throughout the ages that 'modern' painting, so commercialized and so surrounded with suspect publicity, would go the way of many other fashions.

In his middle years he bought himself a small house and a garden at L'Isle-Adam in the Oise Valley he had known from childhood and in the part of France he liked best. It probably meant little to him that this was a favourite field for the Impressionists, and that Van Gogh died at Auvers nearby and Daumier passed his last years at Valmondois in a cottage lent him by Corot.

It was at L'Isle-Adam that the Abbé would spend his summers, and here his sister kept house for him—when he was not on his travels.

We may wonder how Breuil, with a relatively small salary and little private means, managed to get about so much at a time when travel, if not so expensive as now, still demanded a good deal of money.

As Champollion, the first decipherer of Egyptian hieroglyphics, said, 'Archaeology is a beautiful girl but she has no dowry'.

K

Well, first of all the Abbé had no family to worry about, then his earlier explorations were financed by the Prince of Monaco and his later ones either by those who invited him or by the French Government. There are in France funds at the disposal of various government departments allowing of them according *ordres de mission* or instructions for a 'special mission' with allowances for expenses. Breuil's later trips to southern Africa were paid for by the South African Government and his living expenses while he was there were covered by his salary as a visiting professor. Moreover, he had a host of friends and acquaintances in various parts of the world and they were always glad for him to stay with them. This does not mean, of course, that Breuil never paid his way—he often did so—but his salary at the I.P.H. or even the Collège de France was not such as to permit him long travels in China or tours in Africa. After all, he was, wherever he went, giving good value for the money.

The house at L'Isle-Adam was ill-arranged, but he got it for the garden, where he would spend long hours and where with his broad-brimmed straw hat he seemed like a figure out of a Simenon novel. He used to say that his greatest success was with growing poppies, great clumps of the red ones were dotted about all over the place!

'So, when I am in France and on free days and holidays I tend my flowers and prune my plants. These are quite exterior occupations and leave the mind free to wander at its own sweet will. Yet, one day, one moment, when you least expect it there opens up for you a perspective you had never dreamed of, you hit upon some unexpected formula. Intuition has been at work and produced results much in the same way as it is with those problems you take to bed with you—on awakening you have a solution you searched for in vain during your waking hours the day before . . . the answer springs up at dawn like a lovely night-blossoming flower . . . this is the secret mechanism of almost all great discoveries. But in order that this secret source of our highest inspiration may one day produce ideas, achievements that are lasting, work and unceasing observation must contribute to fill the empty shelves of our hidden and subconscious life— just as in a hive there piles up honey the bees have gathered from a thousand flowers.'

9

Finding 'Acheulian Man'

'God-appointed Berkeley that proved all things a dream,
That this pragmatical, preposterous pig of a world, its
    farrow so solid seen
Must vanish on the instant if the mind but change its
    theme.'

YEATS

THE Abbé was all his life attracted by the prehistory of Africa. Maybe the stories of Livingstone in that old travel-book had aroused his curiosity for good. But there was more to it than that. Though excited enough by the discoveries at Choukoutien (see p. 167) in China, his usual intuition told him that the Far East was a marginal area as far as very early Man was concerned. The secrets of Man's origins and those of his cultural life were to be sought in the continent which was almost unknown when he was a boy but from which came, during his later years, one confirmation after another of his guesses.

As long ago as 1911, in a review of a book on the geology and archaeology of the Orange River region, Breuil gave a good sketch of the country he was to explore fifteen years later.

'Both in the valley of the Orange and in that of the Vaal, the river deposits form gravel terraces . . . the whole country is covered with a layer of limestone only a few feet thick and above this lies, just as unbroken, a deposit of red-brown, wind-blown sand . . . in connection with these deposits was developed the southern African Stone Age whose vestiges belong partly to the end of a period of great humidity and partly to a later epoch . . . there are two very different facies[1] corresponding to two phases of the country's climatic history.'

He was already concerned with prehistoric art in southern Africa:

'The rock engravings and the rupestral paintings are scattered about all over the Orange; the former are found in the open air and on the tops of kopjes, while the latter are exclusively in rock-shelters. The figures are depicted generally only in outline, the rock engravings, larger than the frescoes, usually represent isolated figures and not scenes, whereas the pictures often depict hunting scenes, or those of war, or of folklore . . . all these pictures, even those which appear very fresh, are of a certain age and must not be confused with those which are the work of Kaffirs . . . we may conclude from these facts that separate phases must certainly be recognized in this art which seem to have extended over an immense period of time, maybe as long as our Upper Palaeolithic and all the centuries which have elapsed since its close.'

In 1925 the British Association for the Advancement of Science held its annual meeting at Cape Town. The idea of inviting the Abbé came from Mr. Miles Burkitt, Breuil's first foreign pupil and a man untiring in advertising in Britain the Abbé's achievements.

Some time before the First World War Breuil and W. J. Sollas had spent a few weeks prospecting in southern Welsh caves, but beyond a few parallel lines and blobs painted in red on cavern walls no signs of prehistoric art were discovered. Later Old

[1] That is, 'sets' or 'complexes'.

Stone Age Man does not seem to have been very artistically minded in Britain, but the climate was trying, and, then, limestone caves are rather rare south of the Thames, the Mendips and south Devon being about the only areas where such caverns are at all common.

It was during this same visit to England that Breuil met Burkitt, who was interested in prehistory. The Abbé suggested he come over to the I.P.H., 'since no one in England knows much about the subject'. And Burkitt not only became Breuil's first foreign disciple but also a life-long friend. Within a few weeks after his arrival in France the Abbé carried off his new follower to Spain, where they dug with Obermaier and later spent a good deal of time in the Laguna de Janda region, where Breuil swung naked in his hammock over the waters (see p. 81).

Burkitt and the British Association secured for Breuil an invitation from General Hertzog, then South African Prime Minister, while the French Government and the I.P.H. provided funds for expenses.

Breuil sailed with his American friends Mr. and Mrs. Harper Kelley and visited Cape Province, the eastern part of Bechuanaland, the Orange Free State, Basutoland, the Transvaal, Southern Rhodesia and the Victoria Falls. Besides examining some twenty important private collections of prehistoric objects, he travelled, with the Kelleys, a thousand miles in the Vaal, Modder, Riet and Caledon valleys. The earliest chipped-stone industry ('pebble-tools') of the Vaal left him rather sceptical. These pebble-tools— just pebbles crudely chipped at one end—seem to have originated in central Africa and to have spread over a great part of the continent. They—or some of them—were no doubt made by Australopithecines (see p. 211), but nothing was as yet known of these 'ape-men' of a million years ago.

'Artefacts in chipped stone are very ancient in South Africa . . . the gravel terraces of the Vaal River have proved incredibly rich.'

In Johannesburg Museum he saw Maack's sketch of the White

Lady of Brandberg. The White Lady was to play a great part in Breuil's later years.

After a three months' stay, and before he left South Africa, the Abbé addressed a report to General Hertzog. In this Breuil stressed the importance of South Africa for prehistory and the desirability of establishing an archaeological survey in the Union. The Abbé also put forward Van Riet Lowe's name for the directorship. It was not, however, until six years later that the survey was set up and Lowe got the job. He was to remain (with the exception of a temporary difference of opinion much later on) a firm friend of the Abbé and a supporter of his African explorations.

Breuil and the Kelleys brought back with them fifty-four cases (weighing 3,800 kilos) of prehistoric artefacts, for whose examination and classification a good deal of space was needed. Not unnaturally the Abbé thought he would have this at the I.P.H.

Boule and Breuil never got on particularly well together. Maybe the older man was a little jealous of the younger, especially since the Abbé had demolished some of Boule's hypotheses and theories. Maybe Boule's prejudices were a little anti-clerical. Anyway, there is no hatred, Sir John Myres, the British anthropologist, used to say, like the *odium anthropologicum*—not even the *odium theologicum*!—and certainly anthropologists do seem to be rather a testy lot. Well, their subject cuts very close to the bone, comes very near home to each one of us. It is hard to be as objective as we can so easily be when studying dinosaurs or astrophysics.

Still, in the Boule-Breuil relationship we cannot, in all justice, lay the blame entirely on Boule. He was, as director, responsible for the book-keeping and the financial arrangements of the I.P.H. and he was a methodical and orderly manager. Breuil almost drove him to despair over the expense accounts. The Abbé was no man of business and would never turn in what Boule found satisfactory indications as to how the money was spent. 'I don't expect,' he would say, 'receipts signed by illiterate mule-teers, but just put down how much went to paying them, how much you employed for this, that and the other.' This was just the sort of language that infuriated Breuil. He would flare up and ask if it were suggested that he was putting money in his own pockets or handing it out for improper objects. For the Abbé results alone counted. He got the advance, and his report on his discoveries and finds was, or should have been, amply sufficient as an expense statement.

Breuil had, indeed, but the haziest idea about 'economy' in general; that is, financial arrangements; and about what was and was not usual in business practice. Though he was integrity itself, and the very opposite of money-grubbing or stingy, towards the end of his life, and maybe under some outside influences, he did manœuvre himself into complications which might have proved to be troublesome.

However, there is no denying that Boule was a difficult man to get along with, and fifty-four cases of 'stones' were just what he did not want at the I.P.H. Moreover, he was a possessive and somewhat secretive individual. Paul Rivet used to say that Boule would keep specimens 'hidden under his bed' and he did not give up anything readily, whether it was a fossil bone, a theory or house-room. He was, indeed, of sturdy peasant stock from the mountains of south central France and could be very unco-operative. He would not have anything to do with the fifty-four cases of stones. Paul Rivet came to the rescue. He was then professor of anthropology at the Muséum d'Histoire Naturelle, a doctor of medicine and an authority on pre-Columbian American archaeology. He later engaged in Leftist politics, though despite having been for some years a member of parliament he never went far. He was, however, able to render one signal service to science. It was largely owing to his pull with the 'People's Front' government of Léon Blum that funds were forthcoming to create the Musée de l'Homme, the Museum of Man, in 1937.

Rivet put at Breuil's disposal a large, dusty room on the ground floor at the rue de Buffon anthropological laboratory and Harper Kelley fitted this up, at his own expense, with show-cases, drawers and cabinets. These were removed in 1937 to the Museum of Man at the Trocadéro at the other end of Paris. Kelley was appointed keeper of the prehistoric section at the museum, although he was an American citizen (he was paid from the funds of the National Scientific Research Centre), and the collection and cases remained his property. They were, at his death in 1962, valued at 10,000,000 francs, or some $20,000 (roughly £7,500).

In 1928 Breuil was together with Boule at the Baoussé Roussé examining the results of the Italians' excavations at the Barma Grande grotto, where some of the fossils were left *in situ*, making it the most exciting of the caves for the general visitor. Un-fortunately, during the Second World War the cave was partially destroyed in order to block the railway line and what remains in the little museum down by the sea's edge is rather disappointing.

By 1929 a chair of prehistory was at last founded at the Collège de France and Breuil was the obvious choice as first professor. But he very nearly did not occupy his chair, since early in the year he had gone with Begouen, Paul Wernert and Léon Pales to visit the latter's excavations in the Malarnaud Cavern (part of which is on his property and where in 1889 was found the second neanderthaloid jaw in France) near Castelnau in the Pyrenean foothills. In this cave is a pit nearly forty feet deep down which you get by means of a rope-ladder. Wernert, a heavy man, went down first, followed by Pales's farmer. When Breuil's turn came he said, 'Maybe the ladder's a bit strained, you'd better tie a rope around me in case . . .' and sure enough the Abbé had not dropped more than a few feet when the ladder snapped and left him dangling, but Pales and his workmen managed to hold on, and Breuil was slowly hauled up twisting round and round over the abyss. Begouen cut off a piece of the rope-ladder and put it in his private museum at Pujol—since hangmen's ropes are said to bring good luck if an intended victim is not killed.

Thirty years later, when Pales was pleading for funds to carry on work at Malarnaud, Breuil, sitting as a member of the National Scientific Research Centre's council, strongly supported the application . . . 'for I remember that Malarnaud's a very dangerous cave indeed'.

If you walk eastward from the boulevard Saint-Michel along past the façade of the Sorbonne to your right, and to your left a little garden with a statue of Montaigne carved, apparently, out of cheese, that backs on the Gothic gravity of the Cluny Museum (the only building in Paris which suggests what the old colleges looked like when, in the Middle Ages, this part of the city resembled Oxford or Cambridge), and if you keep on along the rue des Ecoles, on the next corner to your right is a fairly modern building with a quite modern tall extension, housing laboratories. It is the Collège de France.

A peculiar institution, surviving since the time of François I, the amorous and enlightened monarch who lost 'everything but honour' on the field of Pavia in 1525. The Collège de France is, indeed, the only French educational organization to have weathered the revolutionary storms when the old system was swept away and a new one set up by Napoleon. Though the Sorbonne and some of the provincial universities may be, by a polite fiction, regarded as the heirs of the medieval foundations, the Collège de France, which the King founded after much hesitation and a great deal of opposition from the ultra-conservative academic pundits of the time, has remained what it always has been: an institution of higher learning, of new knowledge—a little republic of science. The professors elect their fellows subject only to formal government approval. Moreover, the Collège de France is open to all comers. There is no need to put one's name down, though the professors address themselves first and foremost to post-graduates and deliver a course of lectures which takes up but thirty hours of their time each year. For the rest, the professors are free to engage in research, to write, to travel. No examination papers to be corrected, no prospective doctors to be heard, no more or less interesting undergraduates to be coped with. It is a fine job and only the highest ranking specialists get elected to the Collège de France, and once they are there they are at the top of the academic tree.

But members of this republic have their prejudices. They would not like too many colleagues of foreign origin, too many who were Jewish, nor too many priests, for instance. Just what 'too many' means, is, of course, not always easy to determine. Some years ago one distinguished scientist was blackballed, perhaps because he is Jewish—yet not long afterwards he was elected. Maybe it was thought the retirement of some other professor had left the way free to bring up the numbers of his co-religionists to some mysterious maximum.

It is often stated that Teilhard de Chardin would have succeeded Breuil after his retirement on reaching the age-limit of seventy in 1947. But this is by no means certain. We are told the Society of Jesus prevented Teilhard from putting his name forward. This may well be true, but the Collège de France might not have liked to have had a priest follow a priest, especially in the chair of prehistory, a science lending itself to tendentious interpretations—which Breuil always avoided. Then Teilhard was not, as archaeologist, ethnologist or prehistorian, in the Breuil class.

'As late as 1932', wrote the Abbé, 'we were still quite ignorant of the skull of the innumerable human generations which, during two Interglacials and two Glacials, chipped the Chellean, Acheulian and Levalloisian artefacts in the Somme and Thames valleys.'

In August 1932 Breuil was guided by some of his British

friends to the Swanscombe gravel-pits near Dartford, about ten miles east of London and in the Thames 100-foot terrace. It was here that in 1935 and 1936 were found two fragments of a human skull: the occipital (back and part of base) and the left parietal (forming part of the roof). The two pieces fitted together perfectly, but were unearthed some twenty-five feet apart, though in the same gravel layer. In 1955 the right parietal was recovered.

Quite close to the skull fragments were many Acheulian hand-axes, together with the fossil bones of warmth-loving animals. The deposit, in fact, dates back to the Mindel-Riss Interglacial. During this very long interval of time, maybe 200,000 years, southern England (and northern France) did not enjoy one unchanging climate. There were at least two, if not three, cooler phases, but there were periods when southern England had a very warm climate. We need not imagine, however, that even if hippopotamuses wallowed about in the mud on which London is built the landscape was like that of the Congo today. When the Dutch settled in the Cape Province of South Africa, three centuries ago, there were hippopotamuses in the rivers and it often freezes there in winter. When we think of a lion we imagine him sleeping under a bush or creeping to make a kill at nightfall in tropical Africa, but there were lions in Greece in historical times when the climate was much what it is today.

In 1936 Breuil was again at the Barnfield Pit (Swanscombe) and himself dug out Chellean, Clactonian and Acheulian arte-facts with the fossils of warmth-loving animals. Clearly, then, the Swanscombe skull was that of 'Acheulian Man' and there is reason to suppose that people with the same sort of skulls flourished contemporaneously in the Somme Valley.

Here, then, was the answer to Boucher de Perthes's queries. And here also is a surprise. The Swanscombe skull (except that its bones are rather thick) does not differ from that of *Homo sapiens*; that is to say, of the people who live near Dartford today. And how would Boucher de Perthes's Moulin-Quignon jaw fit the Swanscombe skull? Possibly quite well. But, as we have seen, the tests applied to the Moulin-Quignon specimen reveal conclusively that it is modern.

It is true that we have not the forehead and face-bones of the Swanscombe lady, they may have been rather heavier than is usual with us, and, then again, they may not have been so. The significant fact is that, perhaps as much as a quarter of a million years ago, there lived in northern Europe men rather like ourselves, and they chipped and used Achelian implements. It is true they are what is called 'Mid-Acheulian'; that is to say, more 'evolved' and more finished in technique than the older Acheulian.

And here is a further surprise. In 1952–3 M. Camille Arambourg, a professor at the Muséum d'Histoire Naturelle in Paris, discovered in a gravel-pit near the village of Ternifine in Algeria three lower jaws of a type of man which is certainly pithecanthropoid—like the ancient men of Peking and Java—and very unlike any sort of man living today. And with these Ternifine mandibles were found plenty of Acheulian implements—it is true of a coarser sort than those of the Swanscombe gravels. So here we have, on the one hand, Acheulian implements with what looks like *Homo sapiens*, and also, on the other hand, Acheulian implements with something very unlike *Homo sapiens*. Obviously it would be rash to deduce the existence of any one definite type of man from the presence of any one type of tool, though it is true that whenever artefacts have been found with 'typical' Neanderthaloids (see p. 71) they have always been Mousterian.

Furthermore, it does look as though *in Africa* pebble-tools were made and used by Australopithecines—in the widest sense of that word.

However, let us assume that the Swanscombe skull is not quite *sapiens*.[1] There is a skull from Fontéchevade in France and it dates from the Riss-Würm Interglacial (say, 100,000 to 120,000 years ago) and it is apparently quite *Homo sapiens*.

---

[1] If the Swanscombe skull were complete it might perhaps resemble the Ehringsdorf cranium which dates from the Riss-Würm Interglacial, say about 130,000 years ago.

Therefore there were, it seems, 'modern'-type men in Europe long ages before *Homo sapiens* (of the sort found at the Baoussé Roussé or at Cro-Magnon) made his appearance, say, 40,000 years ago on our continent. The conclusion seems to be that our sort of man kept away from western Europe, anyway when the weather was cold, until he braved the chill during a warmish Interstadial of the Würm Glaciation.

The sum of the matter is something like this: during the Great Interglacial (the time of Swanscombe Man), when Acheulian implements were made and used, Man—some sort of man—had spread over most of continental Africa, southern Asia (from Syria to Indonesia), south-west Europe, southern England and eastwards at least as far as the Elbe.

And it is probable that during this Great Interglacial (the Mindel-Riss) there was in Europe a wide range of human types, some almost (if not quite) *sapiens* and Neanderthaloids of various sorts . . . different 'tribes' (but in all not numerous) more or less isolated by climate and natural barriers and evolving separately.

Breuil devoted much of his time to the unravelling of the complicated evidence presented by man-made tools. For instance, it would appear that from very early times in northern Europe both flake and core (i.e. hand-axe) implements were made and used at the same time. Basing himself on the evidence for a succession of cooler and warmer climatic phases, the Abbé painted a picture of human migrations following the movements of game to the south and east. His conclusions were that at one time central Europe was inhabited by flake-makers who later on invaded western Europe, where hand-axes dominated. Farther southwards is a jumble of industries indicating settlements of migrating tribes.

But this general picture he did not cease to revise, though he never suggested that flake-makers and hand-axe makers were necessarily different sorts of men.

In one of his papers when he was developing his ideas on the Lower Palaeolithic he said:

'Such are the facts which allow me to regard in rather a new light the geological classification of Lower Palaeolithic industries in western Europe and to conclude that they lasted for a long succession of millennia during a series of climatic and geological revolutions. We must, then, suppose that hundreds of thousands of years were necessary for the development of these industries.'

This was written well over thirty years ago.
Then in 1944 he said:

'The final end of the last Ice Age is fairly generally fixed at 8000–10,000 B.C. The agricultural and pastoral life of the European neolithic peoples began only some 5,000 years ago. The mesolithic stage—with no domesticated animal but the dog —came immediately after the retreat of the ice and lasted from about 10,000 to 5000 B.C. The period known as the "Reindeer Age", with an evolved type of humanity, was in the second half of the last Glaciation that ended about 10,000 B.C. The beginning of the last Ice Age (Würm) may perhaps be set at about 120,000 B.C. It witnessed the extinction of the last men of the Neanderthal race; mammoth hunters and authors of the Mousterian culture. These men arrived in Europe during the last Interglacial (Riss-Würm) and supplanted other races of whom we know much less . . . their implements are found *in situ*—or displaced—in deposits left by the third Glaciation (Riss), in those of the second Interglacial (Mindel-Riss) and perhaps earlier still. All this adds up to a good many thousands of centuries whose length may be between 500,000 and 1,000,000 years.'

This general picture still holds good, though some of the figures would have to be revised today. For instance, the beginning of the last (Würm) Ice Age would be 70,000 rather than 120,000 years ago. But Breuil had at his disposal none of the new dating techniques we possess today and his calculations were based on

Teilhard de Chardin and Breuil at the Ming Tombs, April 1935

Portion of a letter written by Breuil to the author describing rock-paintings of the Ero geological data (thickness and succession of deposits, etc.), on the evidence of man-made implements and of the fossil animal bones found with them.

What we may call the 'general order of magnitude' for the dating of the Pleistocene is now fairly satisfactorily fixed. For dates up to 70,000 years ago we have the radio-carbon (or Carbon-14) method by which can be measured the amount of radio-carbon remaining in organic substances. As this radio-carbon disintegrates at a regular known rate after death, the method gives what are, in the main, reliable figures for the date of cessation of life in any specimen not more than 70,000 years old. The still more recently elaborated K/A (or potassium/argon) technique is valid for dating some volcanic rocks of much greater age and gives us figures for the Lower Pleistocene, e.g. the Mindel Glaciation (and much earlier too).

The Middle and Upper Pleistocene (that is to say, what up to a few years ago were termed the Lower, Middle and Upper Pleistocene) lasted about 600,000 years, while the Lower Pleistocene (formerly known as the 'Villafranchian' or final phase of the Pliocene Period) was well over 1,000,000 years in length.

But although we know much more about the prehistory of western Europe than about that of any other part of the world:

'None of the civilizations which developed in our western Europe can be called autochthonous in the full sense of the term. All have their roots in neighbouring continents where their earlier stages underwent an evolution that is often unknown. Prehistoric studies have still immense fields to explore, but the knowledge hitherto gained allows us to see that it is in the caverns, the alluvial deposits and in the loess formations of these vast expanses that there lies the solution to all the problems we cannot solve in Europe, that little peninsula joined on to Asia and Africa.'

L

10

China 400,000 Years Ago

'Philosophy is an unusually ingenious attempt to think
fallaciously.'

BERTRAND RUSSELL

O NE day in 1909 Boule introduced to Breuil a young
Jesuit novice who was living in England, where some of
the French Jesuits had taken refuge after the expulsion
of the religious congregations from France in 1904. The young
man's name was Teilhard de Chardin and he was to see a good
deal of Breuil during the next forty years.

There is now a Teilhard legend forming, and since Breuil and
the Jesuit were on friendly terms and, on occasion, in Spain,
China and Abyssinia worked together, some words about
Teilhard belong to the Breuil story. The two men's names are,
indeed, often coupled, as though they had much in common,
whereas, except that they were both priests interested in prehistory and anthropology, there was as little resemblance
between them in character as in appearance.

Pierre Teilhard de Chardin was born in 1881 near Clermont-
Ferrand (in the Auvergne) where his father had a country house.[1]
The most interesting thing about his forbears was that Pierre's
mother was descended from one of Voltaire's sisters. There were

---

[1] Teilhard's grandfather is said to have had his 'nobility' 'confirmed'
(this is often a euphemism for 'conferred') under Louis XVIII—that is,
between 1815 and 1824.

163

eleven children in the family and every evening the father conducted family prayers, while it was the mother's habit to rise in the morning at four o'clock in order to pray. Pierre came, then, from a pious family and was brought up in an atmosphere different from that of the Abbé's home. In fact, Pierre Teilhard's mother had marked him out, from his infancy, for the priesthood.

Teilhard was thin, rather angular and fairly tall for a Frenchman. In profile he resembled an intelligent Savonarola. His appearance was in such striking contrast to Breuil's that one irreverent onlooker, seeing the two men together, remarked, 'There go Don Quixote and Sancho Panza.' It is true that if Teilhard had not quite the *triste figura* of Cervantes' hero, and although his manners were courteous, he did sometimes convey the impression that if he had not a chip on his shoulder one might very readily alight there. Maybe, however, this is my feeling, since on the occasions I met him he had already become a somewhat frustrated man.

After some early experience in teaching geology and natural science in Cairo[1] Teilhard served with distinction in the 1914–18 war, received a number of decorations for bravery, saved young Max Begouen's life at Douaumont, converted him and became a welcome guest at Montesquieu-Avantès, where with the Begouens and Breuil he explored the caverns of the Volp. Later Teilhard took a doctorate in natural science and studied palaeontology with Boule at the I.P.H. By 1924, however, Teilhard's philosophical speculations had exposed him to difficulties. His superiors in the Society of Jesus forbade him to teach and shipped him off to China where his most significant scientific work was to be done. With Father Licent, s.j., he established proof of earlier Old Stone Age Man's presence in China. In fact, apart from whatever standing his philosophical writings may have secured for him, he did a great deal of first-class palaeontological and geological work and his insight was sometimes remarkable. For

[1] And, in 1913, finding at Piltdown the second tooth of the 'Eoanthropus' fake.

instance, in his later years, when he was in South Africa, not only did he attribute pebble-tools to the Australopithecines (see p. 211) but also suggested the wide-spread distribution of these arte-facts showed that the Australopithecines (still then by many people regarded as apes) were once scattered over wide areas of Africa.

However, now that he is no longer living (he died in New York on 11th April 1955) his reputation stands considerably higher than it did during his lifetime, when he was not generally known at all outside the narrow circle of scientists. His posthumous fame has been forged very largely by those who have an ideological axe to grind. And, as Jean-François Revel has put it, 'in the state of philosophical thought today . . . a doctrine is valued before everything else for its faculty of pleasing, of putting into a state of euphoria sensibilities which have been formed by a certain academic tradition or in a certain religious atmosphere'.

There is an association known as *Les Amis de Pierre Teilhard de Chardin*, though we need not suppose all its members are qualified to judge whether or not Teilhard effected a conciliation between the findings of science and the dogmas of religion.

Teilhard, who was forbidden by his superiors to publish any books—other than on scientific subjects—left a mass of MSS., some of which have already been issued in book form.[1] Both in translation (into no less than twenty different languages, it is claimed) and in the original French these books have been best-sellers. *Le Milieu Divin* by 1962 had sold more than 100,000 copies in France, an enormous number for that country, and Teilhard's literary executor has the matter for at least six more books, in addition to those already published.

Some years before Teilhard died the Abbé discussed him with me. We were talking about the trouble the Jesuit had run into and of his decision to leave France, settle in the United States and there work with the Wenner-Gren Foundation.

---

[1] Although, towards the end of his life, some of his writings did circulate (roneotyped) in France and more or less surreptitiously.

'After all, you can hardly compare us. He is a Jesuit. I am a secular priest. Besides, Teilhard has stuck his neck out (*a prêté le flanc*) with all his philosophical speculations. I have never indulged in such things.'

Breuil meant, no doubt, that he had never published or sought to publish any 'philosophical speculations', though he admitted in an obituary notice on Teilhard that they did, on occasion, indulge in philosophical discussions. Anyway, Breuil's broadcast reviewing *Le Phenomène humain* (on 21st November 1955, and thus seven months after Teilhard's death) is a masterpiece of cautious appreciation.

'And,' the Abbé went on about Teilhard, '*je suis une gloire de l'Eglise*'—could the implication have been that the Jesuit was not a 'glory' of the Church?

In 1962 a *monitum* or 'warning' was issued from Rome that Teilhard's works present 'manifestly ambiguities and even grave errors in philosophical and theological matters and to the extent of damaging Catholic doctrine'.

The fact is that the odd terminology invented by Teilhard seems more poetical than philosophical. The comparison of his 'noö-sphere' with the atmosphere and biosphere is little better than unintelligible . . . and then 'the supernatural is the supremely real', 'the Omega point of total synthesis' . . . 'souls breaking away and carrying upwards their incommunicable load of consciousness' and so on. The professional philosophers appear to be hard on Teilhard. But, then, those of us who stand without the charmed circle may feel that Wittgenstein hit the mark when he wrote: 'Philosophy is a system of language concerned only with the meaning of non-philosophical statements and not with their truth'; though we may think a British scientist rather severe when he referred to the 'tipsy, euphoristic prose-piety . . . the extra-ordinary, pretentious, anti-scientific mumbo-jumbo of a French priest, the late Father Teilhard de Chardin'.

Maybe all philosophy is necessarily anti-scientific if we take as basic assumptions in science that nature is understandable, that all nature is subject to the same natural laws, that the simple explanation is probably correct and that measurable causes underlie all phenomena. But, as P. W. Bridgman of Harvard has told us:

'The structure of nature may eventually be such that our processes of thought do not correspond to it sufficiently to permit us to think about it at all . . . the world fades out and eludes us. . . . We are confronted with something truly ineffable. We have reached the limit of the vision of the great pioneers of science, the vision, namely, that we live in a sympathetic world that is comprehensible by our minds.'

Teilhard was certainly a scientist with a poetical imagination—and maybe he was none the worse for that—but the 'proofs' he adduced for the existence of God, of the soul and so forth will convince only those already convinced, but who, nevertheless, are tireless in seeking reasons for being confirmed in their convictions.

In these circumstances it is hardly surprising that the Society of Jesus clamped down on Father Pierre Teilhard de Chardin.

It was Teilhard's great good fortune to have been in China when the startling discoveries of Peking Man were made. But highly inaccurate accounts still appear concerning the part played by Teilhard in these finds. He did not 'discover 30 miles from Peking, a gallery 100 metres long, 50 metres high and 30 metres wide'. He did not unearth any of the fossils of Peking Man, he did not identify 'the implements chipped by the *Sinanthropus* who lived 300,000 years ago'.

The site of Choukoutien in the Western Hills at the edge of the high plateau, some thirty-five miles from Peking, had been prospected as long ago as 1921 by the Swedish geologist Gunnar

Anderson. However, despite bits of worked quartz found at the site, it was looked upon as purely palaeontological (that is, containing animal but no human fossils) until in 1927 Dr. Birger Bohlin, another Swede, recovered a large hominid tooth which Davidson Black, the Canadian director of the Chinese Geological Survey, identified as belonging to an unknown type of man he dubbed *Sinanthropus*. It is now recognized that Peking Man is a Pithecanthropoid of more or less the same type as the original 'Pithecanthropus' discovered by Eugen Dubois in Java as long ago as 1891. In 1927, of course, the later and quite numerous pithecanthropoid Java finds had not been made.

Discussion about the Pithecanthropoids raged for a long time. They were men with low, long, flat heads, constricted foreheads, beetling brows and projecting, snouty faces of rather ape-like appearance, but they walked perfectly upright. In fact, the upright position and the freeing of the fore-limbs came long before reduction of the face to what we may call 'human' proportions. The Pithecanthropoids also made tools, they knew the use of fire (in China, anyway) and they were cannibals. Obviously they were men. And they flourished in Asia, Africa and Europe (as far as we can see as yet) from about 600,000 to perhaps 300,000 years ago.

During the summer of 1928 Dr. W. C. Pei, then in charge of the excavations, found fragments of a skull, two pieces of lower jaws and a number of teeth. In the following year he exhumed a well-preserved skull that was clearly of a Pithecanthropoid. Later, with the aid of funds from the Rockefeller Foundation, Pei carried on his work and found many other fossil bones. Their condition—some split, some skulls gouged out at the base— make it fairly certain that Peking Man's remains are those of cannibal feasts. In all up to the time of the Japanese invasion the remains of some forty-five individuals were recovered, though some of these were represented by a few teeth only.

But all the fossils disappeared mysteriously in December 1941 after Pearl Harbor and none has ever been found again.

Teilhard's visit to Breuil's laboratory led to the Abbé being invited to China in October 1931. The trip was arranged by Davidson Black, W. H. Wong and the Rockefeller Foundation, the latter paying the expenses of the journey. The photograph opposite p. 144 shows Pei, Wong and Breuil, who is wearing an imposing Mongolian fur bonnet which he also used later on in European caves: it had plenty of room for old newspapers as stuffing and also for iron rations, a candle and matches. Facing p. 144 is a view of the Abbé and Harper Kelley sitting on the steps of Begouen's Château de Pujol. Breuil is still sporting his Mongolian bonnet.

By the time of Breuil's arrival at Choukoutien, Pei had already recognized ashes and charcoal at the site. Indeed, from bottom to top of these old cave-fillings there is evidence of man-made fire, so Breuil's diagnosis was confirmed. The Abbé studied particularly the Choukoutien industry. It is mostly of rather crude chopping-tools and chipped pebbles. There is nothing like the early Acheulian tools made by the Pithecanthropoids of Algeria (see p. 158). So Breuil's diagnosis of the bit of stag's horn brought to him by Teilhard de Chardin was right even to the sort of tool employed in working the bone. There can be no reasonable doubt that the Choukoutien implements were made and used by 'Sinanthropus', though it has been suggested he was killed and eaten by some other sort of man, though of that man there is not the slightest trace.

No doubt the Peking men ate one another. Cannibalism is the most ancient specifically human social habit we know of. The remains of the Australopithecines (those proto-men who flourished in Africa 1,000,000 years ago and more—see p. 211) look like those of meals. Protein was scarce, hunting luck precarious; enemies' bodies, those of the family who had died, more or less naturally, or had been disposed of because they were becoming a nuisance, all furnished a welcome addition to early Man's diet. Fontéchevade Man appears to have died from a tremendous bash on the head, while the Steinheim skull (of the same type as the

Ehringsdorf, see p. 158) belonged to an individual who got a blow which smashed in a quarter of his face.

All sorts and kinds of men have eaten other men right up to the present time and more or less plausible explanations have been provided to account for the habit. Basically, however, it was, no doubt, a utilitarian habit around which during the ages accumulated a mass of beliefs and rites and ceremonies. A complex in which are mingled cannibalism, skull-cults, human sacrifice, and participation in it, runs right through our history.

Little by little, something was revealed of the life of Peking Man. He lived some 400,000 years ago. He not only ate meat but some sorts of fruit (e.g. the berries of the *Celtis*) and probably other plants.

Teilhard de Chardin was not in China during Breuil's first visit to the country and was crossing Asia with the 'Yellow Cruise' (*La Croisière Jaune*), an expedition fitted out by the Citroën motor firm. However, when in 1935 Breuil was again at Choukoutien, Teilhard was with him. Together they went up as far north as Harbin in Manchuria and there unearthed Late Old Stone Age implements, and the Abbé spent much time at the Peking Man site, which he got to know well. In fact, Breuil was, together with Professor Hallam Movius of Harvard, the westerner who was best acquainted with the lair of *Sinanthropus*.

Breuil and Teilhard explored the thirteen tombs of the Ming emperors, forty miles south-west of Peking, and the photograph opposite page 160 shows the two of them beside one of the colossal statues lining the avenue of approach to the imperial mausolea. Here it was that in 1957 was opened the tomb of the Wan-li emperor buried in 1620 in a scarlet coffin next to his two consorts in a gorgeous, vaulted, palatial resting-place under a great tumulus.

One wonders if the ladies died natural deaths or whether the

custom did not still linger on into seventeenth-century China of
sending companions to accompany at least Sons of Heaven on
their last journey. The fact that the consorts were buried in the
same tomb as their lord and master suggests that either they
passed away very opportunely at the same time as the Emperor,
or that they were helped on their way—not slaughtered, of
course, nothing so crude, but maybe a potion . . . Red has been
a funerary colour throughout the ages, at least from the time of
the ruddy skeletons of the Baoussé Roussé. The death-pits of the
Chinese Shang rulers, 3,500 years ago, had red funeral chambers
and not only did human sacrifice still flourish in those days (and
for a good deal longer in China) but a considerable number of
slain retainers and murdered women helped these sovereigns to
face the dark future. In ancient Egypt, however, it seems that
retainers and servitors were no longer slaughtered on their
masters' death after about 2500 B.C. (end of Second Dynasty.)

Breuil, in his writings on skull-magic and skull-cults (see p. 183),
stressed the significance of the use of red ochre throughout the
history of Late Old Stone Age Man—and afterwards. St. Ambrose
related of the martyrs St. Gervase and St. Protais (whose remains
he found in A.D. 386 and deposited beneath the altar of his new
basilica in Milan) that the red colour of the bones 'proclaimed
their martyrdom'—the skeletons came, no doubt, from a prehistoric burial.

When, a few years ago, they opened the splendid sarcophagus
of a priest-ruler at Palenque in Mexico there was revealed not
only a dazzling display of green jade ornaments but also a skeleton
stained scarlet. Yet it would be rash indeed to conclude that it
was similar motives, beliefs and hopes which induced the Baoussé
Roussé men to stain their dead red, and led the Maya 250 centuries
later (more or less) to colour the corpse of their king.

Breuil got on well with the Chinese, liked their sense of humour,
their immense ingenuity, their down-to-earth philosophy of
living, their common sense—and their food—as well as their art,
though he probably did not see much of the seamy side of the old

China: the cruelty, the corpses shovelled up into the dust-carts and a misery greater (or let us say on a greater scale) than anything he had met with in Spain.

Though the Abbé was not what could be called an art-collector (except of prehistoric objects), he did bring back from China a whole lot of jades, snuff-bottles, porcelains and paintings, and he would need but little encouragement to display his treasures in his Paris apartment. Maybe he was rather inclined to over-estimate their value (both aesthetic and commercial), but many of them were very attractive and certainly appreciated a good deal in worth after the time he acquired them.

Teilhard, who of course knew China and the Chinese better than Breuil, does not seem, throughout his long sojourn in the country, to have come to terms with the Chinese spirit. In one of his letters there is a disabused passage describing the 'same old China'— 'blue skies, yellow roofs like circumflex accents, peach-trees and pink lilac, the cry of pigeons on the wing'—and he found, as his friend Father Leroy, s.j., the biologist, put it to me, that Chinese conversation (he meant what one hears in the market-place, in buses, in the streets) was dull: 'on a very commonplace level, all about food and money'—but, then, a good deal of conversation in other countries runs along similar lines.

Anyway, Teilhard was objective enough to have grave doubts about the results of Christian missionary effort in the Middle Realm. There is, indeed, distressingly little to show for generations of heroic—and expensive—evangelization. Teilhard, more-over, took little interest in comparative religion; not that there is much religiosity, or what we should call 'religious feeling', in China, whose people's attitude is still more or less that of the old aphorism: 'If you think there are Gods, then there are Gods, if you do not think there are Gods, then there are no Gods.'

For mystical philosopher-poets, even if they are also able scientists, the Chinese are a hard nut to crack. I do not know if any of Teilhard's philosophical works have been translated into Chin-ese, but if they have they must read rather oddly. The language is so alien to our conventional habits of thought (conditioned by our western tongues) that it most wonderfully transforms all fed to it. The Buddhist scriptures, written originally in a language as chock-full of abstract terms as our own, produced in Chinese a doctrine different from that of farther west. Our language pivots on nouns and their predicates and so produces a mirage of abstractions. The classical Chinese approach is to present instances and let the generalizations take care of themselves—in fact, to show a world made visible in change. There is little trace of our spurious 'reality' composed of 'things' which are constant. Of course, it may be that under the influence of the Party Line the Chinese are getting conditioned to some abstractions, but it is going to take a long time to alter the genius of the language and therefore of the thought of the people who use it.

It is characteristic of the Abbé that one of his few remarks about the Chinese as different from ourselves is an anatomical observation: 'With the Chinese the pallium does not cover the cerebellum as with the men of Europe.'¹ There is the instance, it is for us to make the deduction—if any be justified.

Teilhard was highly contemptuous of ideas about 'racial equality' (and he was in great measure justified—if we could define the word 'racial', maybe) and there is a curious remark in one of his letters. He is writing of the Abyssinians: 'Unlike the Chinese, they are well worth looking at, they all have copper-coloured bodies so that they really blend with landscape and fauna.' One might think Teilhard had never seen one of the many elegant and beautiful Chinese women—though one can hardly say they 'blend with the fauna'.

---

¹ *Chez le Chinois le pallium ne recouvre pas le cervelet comme chez les hommes de l'Europe*. The 'pallium' or 'cerebrum' is the fore-brain and the 'cerebellum' the greater part of the hind-brain.

11

The Horn of Africa

IN HIS younger days, anyway, Breuil was quite a good shot and he liked to be armed when on his distant travels, though latterly, and in southern Africa, he preferred to a gun an imposing Congolese javelin. This fearsome object he would use as a staff, the blade topping his bowed figure as he tramped along. The weapon, he declared, would keep a lion at bay.

However, in 1932, when he was planning an expedition to Abyssinia, he still trusted to guns and had a rather curious one prepared for him. It was a Mauser pistol fitted with a twisted wire butt, in fact a kind of carbine. What sort of a kick it would have delivered is anyone's guess. He also acquired a piece of equipment, said to be of British origin, consisting of a tropical-cloth shirt fitted down the middle of the back with a thick sausage of some patent material guaranteed to protect the spinal column from the effects of the sun's rays.

It was in 1922 that Teilhard, on his way back from China, met Henry de Monfreid, the 'Red Sea rover' who came aboard at Jibuti. Monfreid, who must now be getting on for eighty, is a French Catalan, a man from the Roussillon and the son of that Daniel de Monfreid who, during Gauguin's last years, acted as the artist's representative in Europe. The younger Monfreid has led an adventurous life, knows Abyssinia, maybe, better than any other European, has written some excellent books about his exploits and is (or was) a stoutly anti-British Frenchman. Though he returned to France some time ago, in 1959 he was off to find the fabulous treasure said to have been hidden by Olivier Le Vasseur, surnamed *La Buse* (the Buzzard), who just before he was hanged for piracy in July 1730, at the Île Bourbon (now La Réunion) in the Indian Ocean, threw a cryptogram message into the crowd as he bawled out, 'My treasure's for the man who understands that.' Up to now no one has. In 1962 Monfreid was off to Abyssinia once more . . . the lure of Africa.

At Monfreid's suggestion Teilhard spent from November 1928 to January 1929 prospecting the region around Obok, the Harrar plateau, the shores of Tanjura and the neighbourhood of Diré-Dawa. From what he saw Teilhard concluded that in French Somaliland and in Abyssinia a stone 'point' industry (Mousterian) had existed for a very long period; roughly during the last Ice Age in Europe and maybe both before and after. Near Diré-Daoua Teilhard explored the high-perched and almost inaccessible Porc-Epic or Porcupine grotto where he noticed schematic pictures painted on the walls.

In Paris Teilhard introduced Monfreid to Breuil and by 1933 the Abbé had accepted the Red Sea rover's invitation to act as guide on a prehistoric prospection through wildest Abyssinia. All arrangements had been made when Monfreid's wife telephoned to say the trip was off since she must remain for her children's education in France. Breuil, as usual, had his mind made up and replied, 'It's now or never.' So in February 1933 he sailed with Paul Wernert and Teilhard.

The port of call was Jibuti. It stinks, it is almost always scorching hot, it is composed of shacks, tumbledown huts, dusty roads and a few peeling public buildings. The town is surrounded by sinister, dark hills and parched plains. About the most pleasing objects to meet the eye are dazzling white pyramids of sea-salt on the outskirts of the town.

As a gateway to Africa Jibuti is sobering. You have landed on an ancient well-worn continent (most of Africa has been dry land for hundreds of millions of years), in the main hostile to Man, riddled with disease, empty, with soils so poor that well over a third of the continent is unfit for Man's abode, though it is true that once the Sahara blossomed like the rose and the Kalahari was rich grassland. Moreover, the desert tends to gain on surrounding country. The African populations are mostly ill-nourished and starved of protein, and so rather apathetic, while, even when more or less well fed, the native Africans are sagaciously work-shy.

A century ago most of the continent was unknown and this is a fact we may bear in mind when we come to judge of its prehistory and of the pioneer work Breuil did in Africa. A hundred years ago it was known that Egypt had had in the past a high civilization, but most of the continent was mystery, still a reservoir of slave-labour in vague realms where divine kings ruled merely by existing. Guesses were indeed made that Man might have originated in the Dark Continent, somewhere in the tropical forests, maybe, 'since our nearest relations, the gorillas and chimpanzees, survived there', as some zoologists said. And, in fact, it does look now as though Man did become Man in Africa —but the best thing he did for himself was to get out of it.

At Jibuti Monfreid put his three travellers on to his dhow and headed for Obok. They coasted by the Jebel Jinn, and explored the strange gulf known as the Gubet Karah, whose shores are a hallucinating landscape of craters emerging from masses of scoriae and lava, black basalt and ruddy vitreous rhyolites. Breuil, Wernert, Teilhard and Monfreid trudged across the dark sandy beach leading to the Assal Depression, 600 feet below sea level and stifling hot. The lake itself, surrounded by volcanic hills, is bordered with a fringe of salt sparkling as snow. You can float in Assal's waters as comfortably as in those of the Great Salt Lake or the Dead Sea. There is no green plant, no bird, no insect, no living things, only desiccated weeds jutting up from between basalt blocks. A suffocating silence.

Nights were spent staring at the stars from the deck of Monfreid's boat. The photograph opposite page 113 shows a very relaxed sort of Breuil; he did not seem much to mind changes of climate, he was as well in one place as in another and took the

M

rough with the smooth. Although he was quite light-skinned, he tanned readily and did not burn red or peel.

Near Obok they discovered, in stepped terraces, large flakes and primitive hand-axes, all certainly palaeolithic. What sort of man made them? After a few days' cruising Monfreid and his guests set off for Diré-Dawa on the Harrar plateau of Abyssinia; all around a typically African scene of spiky trees all trunk and branches and sparse, harsh foliage. Wernert, clad only in shorts (thirty years ago not so commonly worn as now), settled into the Porc-Epic grotto which he shared with a baboon family. Since he browned very rapidly, his skin-change much excited the Abyssinians' imagination. 'For,' they argued, 'if this man can put on colour so easily it is clear he must also know how to take it off as readily. What about us? Maybe he'll tell us the secret.' Impeccable logic. The prestige of a white skin in wildest Abyssinia a generation ago when nothing had as yet been heard of Africa for the Africans.

At the end of February Breuil was at the great painted rock of Sourré by Ganda-Biftu. Three storeys of scaffolding were necessary to reach the pictures, which stretch out for more than 300 yards over a very deep, wooded ravine. Up climbed the Abbé and set to work on his copying, while perilously perched high up on the rock-face. Rather a change from the damp recesses of European painted caverns or the written rocks of the Spanish deserts.

The Sourré pictures are of cattle—bulls, cows and calves—of the great African buffalo, some felines, antelopes, figures of pastoralists and hunters. The Abbé even said he thought he could make out a bull-fight, but he was not sure!

'There were in North Africa wild oxen with very wide horns (*Bos opistonomus*). I do not know whether the domesticated herds were bred from these wild oxen, but I do know that on the painted rocks of Harrar (at Ganda Biftu among other sites) there are depicted herds of black oxen with long horns and slender bodies . . . peacefully grazing together with buffaloes (*Bubalus caffer*) which, like the black oxen, have their calves beside them. All this means that we can touch here on the origin of the "Bovidian" culture extending from Abyssinia to Nubia and the Hoggar, a sufficient time having elapsed to allow for the production of speckled coats [which indicate domestication] as also for the amelioration of the pictorial art in the direction of the Spanish Levantine style, the improvement, indeed, being due to an impulse from the Spanish Levant. By what route could this influence have travelled? Obviously by sea. A battle represented on the Minateda rock [see p. 227] in the province of Albacete, Spain, shows, as aggressors, warriors armed with large reflex bows (with three curves) and this weapon stamps them clearly as foreigners. The reflex bow, of Asiatic origin, was, it would seem, an importation into Nilotic Africa. There was then contact between the peoples of Mediterranean Iberia and those of northern Africa who were doubtless already pre-neolithic in culture.'

Here we have Breuil already following the track of prehistoric European influence in African art, a subject that was much to preoccupy him in later years.

After he had made copies of the Sourré frescoes Breuil went back to Diré-Dawa. It was only in the Harrar region that he found schematic paintings and in this same Harrar countryside the Abbé discovered quasi-Mousterian artefacts (probably indicating the former presence there of Neanderthaloid Man) and one Abbevillian basalt hand-axe.

By 14th March Breuil was at the Porc-Epic grotto and made ready to copy the schematic paintings, sealed under calcite concretions. There are some twenty human figures (which he compared with some of the line-drawings at Levantine Spanish sites), together with elephants, a lion, antelopes, bovines and, very curiously, a stag, a most un-African beast. One is almost inclined to wonder if it is quite certain these pictures were made by *Homo sapiens* since Breuil's exploration of the Porcupine grotto was marked by a surprising and important discovery.

The first time he entered the cave he noticed, to his right, a breccia incrustation on what seemed to be a natural ledge of rock. This aroused his curiosity, so he whipped out of his pocket one of those curved scrapers he always carried, whittled away at the breccia, and in a few minutes pulled out a human lower jaw in a fine state of preservation. It was the mandible of a Neander-thaloid. Breuil put the specimen in his soap-box and thus carried it back to Paris. It is worth while insisting that the Abbé alone found the fossil, because, for some reason or another, the discovery is generally attributed to Paul Wernert.

In 1933 no neanderthaloid fossil was known from Africa (for the skull of Rhodesian Man was not recognized as such), now there is the Saldanha skull from Cape Province (40,000 to 45,000 years old?), the Broken Hill or Rhodesia skull would be about 30,000 years old—but it may be that Saldanha is also not much older than this. Neanderthaloids, then, may have lingered on in southern Africa, and maybe East Africa, after they disappeared as a distinct type in Europe.

Breuil brought back with him from Abyssinia a whole lot of ethnographical material, Christian Abyssinian paintings, utensils, MSS. and weapons (after all, he was an ethnologist) which he deposited later in the Museum of Man. On his way back to France he stopped off for a few days in Egypt and then visited the Holy Places of Palestine.

The next year the Abbé was in Syria and went down to Mount Carmel, where his former student, Dr. Dorothy Garrod, was discovering remarkable evidence about early Man. In the Mount Carmel caves were unearthed two different types of man, that known as Tabūn (represented by one skeleton of a woman) and fully neanderthaloid, and another type called Skhūl (six skeletons), showing variations ranging from the more or less neander-thaloid to the more or less wholly *sapiens*. Much ado has been made about this evidence as showing: (1) Neanderthaloids developing into *sapiens* or (2) interbreeding between Neanderthaloids and *Homo sapiens*. However, it now appears probable that the Tabūn specimen is anything up to 11,000 years older than any of the Skhūl skeletons.

This, of course, does not mean there was no interbreeding between the two types of man who must have lived at the same periods in some parts of the world.[1]

A little later on, in Italy, Breuil himself was to make another neanderthaloid discovery.

Italy is surprisingly poor both in prehistoric art and in the fossil remains of ancient Man. There are the enigmatic paintings of Romanelli (see p. 228) and there are the Levanzo and Addaura engravings—and hardly any other Old Stone Age pictorial art at all.

However, there is plenty of evidence that Neanderthaloids lived in the peninsula. At the Tana della Basura, where were found the imprints of neanderthaloid feet under a ledge so low that the man who made the marks must have been bent double, there is also evidence of some sort of game or ordeal.

All the inner cave of the Tana della Basura (that was until 1950 sealed off by a thick wall of calcite) was Neanderthaloids' realm. There is nothing to suggest it was ever used by *Homo sapiens*. There are no fossil human bones, no implements, but the imprint of cave-bears' feet on the clayey soil and a stream of cave-bears' bones in a trench. There are small mounds of charcoal. There are traces of soot. There is the imprint of a sooty hand. There are marks of men's fingers on the ground—and stuck against some of the walls are rounded clay pellets. At the foot of one wall is a stalactite formation rather resembling some sort of animal—a 'sphinx', the late A. C. Blanc called it. Above this 'animal' and on

[1] The south-western Asiatic Neanderthaloids (Mount Carmel, the Galilee skull, the skeletons from Shanidar in northern Iraq, etc.) have C-14 datings ranging from about 52,000 to 35,000 years ago, the oldest being the Galilee specimen, and the oldest Shanidar about 50,000 years.

to it pellets were thrown. Was there a human target? Probably, since at the foot of this wall are the imprints of seven human heels, maybe those of one or two individuals standing up, for some time, backed against the rock-face.

The pellets are undoubtedly intentionally rolled, since they are of nearly uniform size and had they not originally been round they would not have flattened in just the way they did. Magic? In a cavern the flickering light of torches reflected from stalagmite to stalactite, the bone-strewn floor, the cave-bears' den, the crouching dance . . . in Sardinia to this day boys and girls chuck pellets against a wall. If they stick the thrower's wish is granted. . . .

Neanderthaloid Man also practised some sort of bear-cult. At the Drachenloch site were cave-bears' skulls arranged in some definite order, while at Petershöhle it was deer's antlers that were set out. A bear-cult must have been a very ancient rite. Men seem always to have felt some relationship with this dying and resurrected animal (hibernation and awakening), one that is so amiable in appearance, so ruthless, so strong—though the cave-bear may well have been less fierce than he looked.

Homo sapiens, too, has left evidence of his bear-cults. In a far chamber of the Pyrenean Montespan-Gantiès Cavern, and surrounded by models of animals, all pitted with marks of spears, there is a platform with a clay model of a bear, headless. Then it was discovered there lay between the forefeet the skull of a young bear, no doubt the figure was covered with a bear's skin with a real head. . . . In Greece the bear was sacred to Artemis and at the Artemisium in Cyrenaica the servants of the goddess wore bear-skins. At the Attic shrine of Artemis Brauronia young girls draped in bear-skins (later saffron-coloured robes) were called *arktoi* (bears) and their sacred dance the *arkteia*. Was the goddess originally a bear to whom human sacrifices were offered? The sacred killing of a pampered bear by the Ainu of Japan has survived to this day. Some long, dark thread here, that is part of the warp of our ancient spiritual clothing.

And the Neanderthaloids were, of course, cannibals—they were fully human—and not only cannibals but they practised a skull-cult.

Farther down the Italian coast from Saccopastore, south of Rome and of Anzio, A. C. Blanc found in 1939 a very well-preserved neanderthaloid skull in the last of a succession of three caves, in a hall roughly circular. Not only had the base of the skull been in part cut away—to extract the titbit brain—but the cranium had been placed on the cavern's floor and surrounded by a ring of little stones, a sort of protecting Stonehenge; one or two small bones of animals under the skull: a setting for some magico-religious rite.

In his old age, when his reputation was world-wide, the Abbé was often solicited to write for 'religious' publications, or those issued under ecclesiastical patronage, articles on 'prehistoric religion'. He did not always refuse, since, after all, he was a priest, but he was guarded in his language and did not afford much support for the propounders of 'primitive monotheism' or for those who will read too much into the evidence. He did write a paper entitled *Comment il me paraît que naquit la croyance en Dieu dans l'homme primitif* ('How it seems to me that the belief in God arose in primitive Man'), whose title appears, indeed, rather question-begging, but even in this article Breuil was circumspect.

However, in a paper published in 1951, and entitled *The Religious Practices of Quarternary Man*, he stressed what he considered was one of the most important, if not the most important, of all the ancient rites of Man, a rite that reflected beliefs and induced them—the cult of skulls.

Without denying that a great many of the fossil human skulls we have prove the cannibalism of our forbears, he pointed out that not only the survival of skulls (as against the comparative rarity of other fossil human bones) may be due in part to the use made of them as vessels (Man's big brain has some use, for his big brain-pan holds a good deal more water than that of any other animal with a manageably sized head), but that the evidence was impressive for a most ancient skull-cult.

The Abbé thought the Peking Man skulls and jaws were brought to Choukoutien from some distance away, and pointed out that freshly severed heads have the cervical vertebrae attached, whereas nearly all the fossil hominid skulls have no such bones by them.

When he came to the Neanderthaloids he found a mass of evidence for skull-cults (and here the red ochre plays a part, for skulls often contain some) and he considered the Steinheim (second Interglacial), the Weimar (third Interglacial), as well as the undoubted neanderthaloid skulls of the La Quina child, the Pech de l'Aze child and the Ngandoeng crania from Java, were all used in skull-magic. In some neanderthaloid burials the skeletons were provided with protecting stones over the heads (Breuil said there was evidence at La Ferrassie of 'real burial rites') and at this site one skeleton was headless and the skull some two feet off—separate burial of the head is, moreover, a custom noted for many different lands and ages.

'For hundreds of thousands of years early Man in Europe did not live in caves; did not inhabit grottoes until about 120,000 years ago. Intentional burial goes back some 70,000 years.'

We may note that Breuil says 'early Man in Europe', which does not exclude earlier cave-dwelling in other continents.

The Later Old Stone Age burials, such as those at the Baoussé Roussé (where we may remember were arrangements of stones to protect the head), present a complete skeleton, or one that is nearly so, but skulls found alone almost always lack the lower jaw, which, of course, becomes detached as soon as the flesh rots away, but human mandibles are often used as charms and ornaments. For instance, the Önges of the Little Andaman (a negrito people about four feet tall) bury their dead under the communal hut, but seven days after burial the lower jaw is broken off, painted red with ochre and worn as a charm on a necklace.

The custom of burying corpses under dwellings lasted from

Stone Age times right into those of civilized communities. At Jericho, 9,000 years ago, maybe, there were tombs under houses and there also some sort of skull-magic was practised, since there have been found numerous crania (all minus the lower jaws) but with a face modelled in clay, and one Jericho tomb (by radio-carbon about 3260 B.C.) had no less than 113 skulls arranged around the edge of the chamber, while in the centre was a heap of burned bones—apparently bodies were first exposed until the flesh disintegrated and then the skulls were collected and the remainder of the body burned.

Among the Masai of East Africa a chief treasures his father's skull as a charm, and all over the world, from Labrador to the west coast of Africa, skulls on poles (not necessarily human skulls nowadays) signify sacred places and are emblems of majesty.

No doubt Breuil was right in thinking that if we could get to the root and origin of the skull-cult we should come near to understanding something of the 'beliefs' very ancient Man expressed and created by his 'religious practices'.

But clearly of all parts of the body the head is the most magical, for it speaks; maybe the skull also speaks in some mysterious manner and perhaps foretells, and no yearning is more funda-mental than that to know what cannot be known—the future.

The second neanderthaloid discovery made by Breuil was in 1936 at the Saccopastore gravel-pit in the valley of the Aniene stream (the ancient Anio), and here in 1929 had been unearthed the greater part of a human skull. It was twenty feet below the surface of the ground. The specimen was that of a Neander-thaloid of the less rugged sort.

Where all is now sea between the western Italian shores and those of northern Sicily, eastern Sardinia and Corsica, there was until fairly late Tertiary times (say 4,000,000 or 5,000,000 years ago) a land mass the geologists call 'Tyrrhenis'. It sank when the earth's crust crumpled to push up the Apennines, and on the eastern border of this ancient land mass there sprouted a number of volcanoes whose lake-filled craters still dot the landscape of Latium, but the fire-mountains were still active when Man lived in these parts, both before the last glaciation and during it.

In 1936 the Abbé and the late A. C. Blanc were prospecting in Saccopastore, primarily for mollusc-shells—good indicators of climate, as we have seen at the Baoussé Roussé.

Saccopastore is quite near to the Ponte Nomentano and some two miles from the Roman Porta Pia (the ancient Porta Collina) near which was the *Campus sceleratus* (the 'Polluted Field') where, in an underground chamber, unchaste vestals were buried alive. No blood must be shed. They had infringed the taboo. They had imperilled the City. They must die in expiation. And the Via Nomentana from the Colline Gate led up to Nomentum in the Sabine Hills, where Atticus, Cicero's friend, had a farm, Seneca a country house and Martial a cottage . . . classical ground.

The photograph opposite page 192 shows the Abbé and A. C. Blanc at Saccopastore. Breuil has just unearthed a fine Mousterian point. Blanc is saying, 'Hurrah; now we're on the track of the Neanderthaloids, perhaps their very bones; after all, one skull was dug out of here only seven years ago.' Breuil is holding up a warning hand while his raised eyebrows and compressed lips recommend caution.

Then, only a few minutes later, Breuil put out his hand and pointed. His extraordinarily acute eyes had spotted something. When he was in the field he would generally shoot out a fore-finger and indicate an implement before anyone else had seen it. This time he plied his little scraper and in a few minutes held in his hand the greater part of another neanderthaloid skull—of the same type as the first found at the site. Both of them would be round about 50,000 or 60,000 years old.

The Abbé had repeated his feat at the Porc-Epic Cavern three years earlier, and maybe his neanderthaloid bag would have been three had not that officious military policeman cracked down on him in 1917 and prevented him from scraping about on the Rock.

In this same year, 1936, Breuil put in a few weeks attempting a reinterpretation of the engravings on Bronze Age monuments (from about 2000 B.C.) in Brittany, Britain and Ireland. In fact, for a short time he was back at the old job d'Ault du Mesnil had recommended to him a generation before. What he was mainly concerned with was tracing in these engravings influences from the Mediterranean later sources of religion and culture.

There was a wide-spread cult of a Mother-Goddess as Life-Giver, Food-Giver and Protectress. This divinity probably originated in Mesopotamia. In the form of what has been called the 'Eye-Goddess' (for her representations, though often highly stylized, always show eyes) the Mother-Goddess cults spread from Syria to the Aegean and thence to Italy, the Iberian Peninsula, Brittany and the British Isles. The 'Venus' of La Pileta (see p. 84) is no doubt a talisman of the Mother-Goddess.

By the way, recent radio-carbon datings for Irish passage-graves (Bronze Age) give a figure of about 2000 B.C., whereas they have generally been set from about 1400 B.C. Of course radio-carbon datings are not infallible, although for a dating so comparatively recent there should hardly be a margin of error of 600 years. Radio-carbon tests also indicate that the western European Neolithic began before 3000 B.C.

However, this excursion into the Bronze Age was just a diversion for Breuil, he was soon back again with ancient Man and his works of art.

12

Lascaux

DURING the winter of 1939–40 Breuil delivered his Collège de France lectures at Bordeaux and put in a good deal of time revisiting Dordogne sites. Soon after the war had broken out, Van Riet Lowe had cabled the Abbé to come to South Africa, but, for some reason or other, the censor did not allow the message to be delivered. However, before the German break-through in 1940 Breuil had gone down to stay with Bouyssonie at Brive and while there nearly lost the sight of one eye, injured by a thorn-scratch while he was climbing through some bushes.

He was still at Brive when a young man he had known from childhood, a M. Maurice Thaon, brought some sketches he had made, a day or two before, of paintings in a cave discovered on 12th September by some lads from Montignac, a small town on the Vézère about fifteen miles upstream from Les Eyzies. On 21st of the month a Dr. Cheynier of Terrasson (a town near Brive) drove the Abbé and Bouyssonie to Lascaux—there was, of course, in those days no petrol available for ordinary cars. Then, in Breuil's words:

'After having informed the Prefect of the Dordogne, the Director of Prehistoric Antiquities of the province, M. Peyrony, and the owners of the site, the Comte and Comtesse Emmanuel de La Rochefoucauld, I was again at Lascaux, with them, on 27th and 28th September. Then, on 14th October, I took up my quarters at the country house of M. de Montardy, quite near the cave in which I spent most of every day.'

The entrance to Lascaux was then not much more than a fox-hole:

'It gave on to a steep slope, slippery and slimey . . . under the limestone covering the floor of the cavern was a reddish, semi-liquid mass of clay . . . with flakes of worked flint of poor quality, but palaeolithic, some fragments of reindeer horns and many pieces of conifer charcoal . . . the remains of the grotto's lighting system.'

Breuil had the *gours*; that is, the ridges of calcareous matter which run across the floor, pierced when 'thousands of litres of water rushed down a deep funnel making a great noise which indicated the collapse of a considerable amount of loose material suspended in the "chimney" and also a penetration into lower and inaccessible galleries. The next day we wanted to walk about in the axial passage leading out of the main hall—and on a slightly lower level—but the earth gave way under our feet and sank to a depth of more than a metre [say, about four feet] and then I understood why, in this corridor, almost all the figures are on the roof or high up on the walls in places difficult to reach by climbing. When the pictures were executed these places were easily accessible. It was the ground that, later on, had sunk.

'In the middle of the "nave" (to which you get by a passage out from the right of the main hall) was another drain, but long since blocked up, and this explains why the frieze of small horses and the fine fresco of stags' heads are now right up on cornices out of a man's reach, since here also the floor has sunk by several metres since the pictures were painted.'

It is not, therefore, necessary to imagine some sort of pre-historic scaffolding (most improbable) as some have done to account for the position of the pictures.

'The walls of the great entrance hall were covered by a thin but very hard coating of calcite crystals . . . it would have been impossible to engrave on this, but on to it were painted the finest and best-preserved pictures in the whole grotto.'

And here is an interesting note on the preservation of pre-historic paintings, for not a few visitors to the decorated caverns are astounded that pictures could last 20,000 years—or more.

'The usual cause of deterioration . . . is an exchange of air with the exterior. In summer cold air from a grotto moves out and warm air from without moves in. In winter the process is reversed but causes no damage whereas in summer the outside air, with a high degree of humidity, deposes on the cold cavern-walls a "dew" that is corrosive owing to its high carbonic acid content. Furthermore, the corrosion is favoured by micro-organisms which contribute still further to the destruction of the painted wall-face. . . . Lascaux is very cold in winter but quite agreeable in summer. Most of the prehistoric grottoes, on the contrary, have a pleasant winter temperature and a disagreeably high one in summer.

'The reindeer and its "cold" companions came down to south-western France only from November to February—hence the almost total absence of this animal—and of the mammoth—from the Lascaux pictures. The mass of the Lascaux pictures is Peri-gordian—though a few may date from the early Magdalenian. The Lascaux fauna is, indeed, typically Perigordian—and that was rather a warm phase.

'At Lascaux, as at other sites, we are confronted with pictures related to reproduction-magic (pregnant females, stallion follow-ing mare) and to hunting-magic (arrows directed towards or fixed in the bodies of animals).

'The exceptional freshness of the Lascaux paintings in the first hall may astound and baffle visitors who have not seen Altamira, Niaux, Cabrerets, Le Portel, etc. Such freshness is due in some cases (e.g. Niaux) to the distance from the entrance—far beyond any possible condensation—elsewhere, as at Altamira, Marsoulas, Gargas and Le Portel, there is a roof, not very thick, but impermeable—as at Lascaux. Other caverns have been hermetically sealed up by the collapse of a roof or by masses of fallen earth which completely blocked all access by the outside air.'

Lascaux is now the most visited of all the prehistoric caverns, but there are two of its features which are highly enigmatic. First of all there is the odd 'composite' animal on the left-hand side of the main hall, but such mythical hybrids are not uncommon in the prehistoric caverns, as at Isturitz and the Laugerie Basse, while at the recently discovered cave at Cougnac (not very far from Lascaux) there is a 'scene' and these are very rare in the French and northern Spanish cave-paintings There is what appears to be the figure of a man touched with projectiles and also a 'sorcerer' with an animal's head. Maybe this is a representation of a putting to death, of a human sacrifice. Possibly the 'hybrids' do represent shamans or wizards.

But at Lascaux there is also a 'scene', though it is not shown to visitors. To get to it you must slip through a hole in the wall and climb down a rope-ladder. Then, in a narrow but fairly high passage that becomes more constricted farther on until it disappears as a crack in the rock, there is, to the right, on a rounded projection of the wall-surface, a 'composition', a picture telling some story. There is a wounded bison, its guts sagging to the ground—maybe it has been ripped open by a rhinoceros that is stalking away to the left. In the foreground is a pole surmounted by a bird, and before the bison the schematic, though readily recognizable, figure of a man lying prostrate, a propulsor near him. His head is covered by a bird-mask. His penis is in erection. His neck has been broken.

'I consider the Dead Man, though exceptional, since it is a scene, is not magical but commemorative or mythical. The bird-

At Saccopastore with A. C. Blanc, 1936

Dart, Broom, Breuil, Lowe

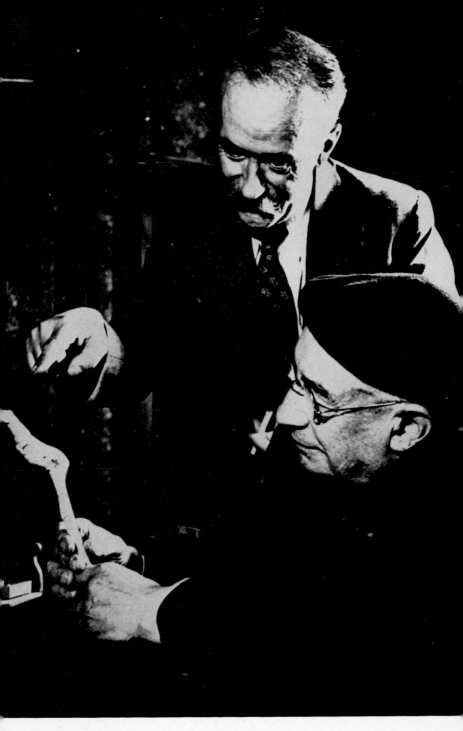
At Montauban with M. Bétirac, 29th October 1952

face of the man may be compared with not only dozens but hundreds of human figures—with animal or grotesque heads—depicted on grotto-walls, on stone slabs or on engraved bone. The "totemic" pole alone is novel. Each grotto brings additional facts to those we already know. . . .'

The Abbé told me that he thought it possible a man might lie buried in the passage floor at the foot of the picture, but excavation there produced only some 'assegais' and 'lamps' (i.e. concave stones) with charcoal. The radio-carbon dating obtained from this charcoal was 15,516 years (with, as usual, a margin of error before and after of a few hundred years). Breuil did not like this finding, since it would mean either (1) that the Gravettian (Perigordian) culture-phase was more recent that had been supposed, or (2) that the Lascaux pictures are mainly Magdalenian and not Aurignacian-Perigordian.

But Lascaux, as the Abbé wrote, *pose plus de questions que je n'en puis résoudre*—'poses more questions than I can answer'.

Breuil did not feel able to make copies of the paintings and engravings since his eye was still troubling him, and later on he was, until too old for such work, occupied with his African explorations. The local photographer took excellent pictures (which Breuil used in his great book *400 Centuries of Cave Art*).[1]

Breuil recommended the Abbé Glory of Strasbourg for the work of deciphering and copying the mass of Lascaux engravings, and he is still studying them. Here, as at most of the sites where there is engraving as well as painting, it is the former which, though less spectacular, is the more illuminating as regards the manners and customs of Man two hundred centuries ago.

News of the discovery spread, and despite transportation difficulties plenty of people arrived to look, but two of the

[1] Though not, I think, so admirable as those by M. Maurice Thaon, published as illustrations to my *Lascaux, a Commentary*.

N

discoverers kept them at bay while Breuil would emerge from the chill cave every now and again and give an extempore lecture in the open air on the grass-grown hillside set with scattered trees.

In April 1941 the Portuguese Government invited Breuil to accept a visiting professorship at Lisbon University, and after some delay over his passport the Abbé set out for Portugal. He was delighted to find a haven in time of troubles, since he was determined he would not go back (as all civil servants had been ordered) and resume his job. He therefore burned his boats and forfeited his salary.

He was in Madrid in May where he gave a few lectures—and spoke of Lascaux. He still had old friends dating from 1914–18 days. He was also able to get out and examine the prehistoric cave at Casares in the province of Guadalajara, to the east of Madrid. Casares is of considerable interest since it is (with the exception of two grottoes in the province of Burgos) the only site with palaeolithic naturalistic paintings between Cantabria in the north and La Pileta, Ardales and Nerja right down in the province of Málaga.

In July Breuil left Lisbon for Morocco and put in several weeks working with Neuville and Ruhlmann in the dune-deposits near Casablanca where there are four ancient raised beaches and a fine series of artefacts ranging from pebble-tools (australopithecine, most probably) and chopping-tools through Chelleo-Acheulian to Acheulian. In view of the discovery in 1955 of portions of a pithecanthropoid jaw in the Abderrahmane gravel-pits (Casablanca), the 'Chelleo-Acheulian' implements were probably used by Pithecanthropoids in Morocco as in Algeria (see p. 158).

The shore-terraces in this part of Morocco afford useful evidence of varying sea levels and also of the fact that most of Africa has not much changed its outline for countless ages.

On his way back from Casablanca to Lisbon the Abbé spent a few days in Tangier, where I was doing a job, and he gave me a complete set of the Lascaux photographs. These were if not the first to get out of France at least the first to arrive in Britain. I can remember that one day as we walked from the old American Legation (then still hidden away in the maze of alleys off the *Zoco chico* in the Moorish town) to his hotel at the far end of the rue du Statut—maybe two miles or more—how we talked of everything and anything except the one subject that filled our minds—the war and our chances. . . .

After his return to Lisbon he and Zbyszewski (a Pole by origin but I think naturalized Portuguese) did a considerable amount of work on the raised beaches of the Portuguese coast—but Breuil was not thinking of remaining long in Portugal and soon after he got back from North Africa he wrote to Van Riet Lowe saying he wanted to visit South Africa again. Ever since 1929 the Abbé had been intrigued by African prehistoric paintings and their relationship with those of western Europe and especially Spain.

At Breuil's request Van Riet Lowe approached Field Marshal Smuts, who agreed to Breuil's going to South Africa, but would not promise a trip to the Brandberg to see the White Lady—there was a war on. A good deal of time was wasted in communications and it was not until 28th October 1942 that the Abbé landed in South Africa to take up his job as visiting professor at Witwatersrand University (Johannesburg) and begin his collaboration with Lowe on the archaeological survey. He remained in South Africa for thirty-two months and although he did manage to break away fairly often, still he had to spend more time in lecture-room and laboratory than he liked. In all, he left Johannesburg on twenty-four 'tours'—some of which lasted only a few hours, while others took several weeks. He went all over the place: the Orange Free State, the southern shores, the mountains of Basutoland and Mozambique. He got to know pretty well the bare, yellow landscapes of the veldt and the shores from Cape

Town to Port Elizabeth, the valley of the Vaal and its tributaries.
He worked on raised beaches—still the problems of rise and fall
of sea levels—on the succession of industries in the river valleys,
he copied rock-paintings, he excavated . . . in all he was 370 days
away from Johannesburg, so he really could not have complained
of being too much cooped up.

As he always rose early, he not only wrote up his diary but in
1944 be began to draw, with greasy crayons he had brought from
Portugal and on odd bits of paper, a series of sketches which were
shown to Smuts. These represented scenes from the life of early
Man, the Sinanthropus at home, the banks of the Vaal in African
Old Stone Age times, the Cap Blanc, the Trois-Frères shaman
and so forth: thirty-one of them in all. Smuts found a British
publisher, contributed a foreword and the book was issued as
Beyond the Bounds of History (1949). This was the only book of
Breuil's in which he let his fancy roam and the little volume has
been too severely criticized, especially in France, where all
Breuil's opponents gave tongue, proclaiming it was 'absurd' and
'non-scientific'. The Abbé was duly chastened and contrite,
though the book sold quite well and found imitators in Britain,
the United States, South Africa and . . . Japan. As a matter of fact
it is a rather amusing and instructive little introduction to prehistory and might well be reissued.[1]

Breuil was a sturdily patriotic Frenchman, despite his cosmo-
politan tastes, and in addition to lecturing on prehistory during
this long sojourn in South Africa he preached three sermons on
Joan of Arc (I do not know how he treated the English or even
the Church) and he published an article 'The Heritage of Joan of
Arc'. He also felt called upon to write a letter to Smuts in which
he urged that 'Germany must be annihilated'. Breuil added that
he did not expect a reply, but he got one when he next visited the
Prime Minister: 'Though you have the appearance of a man of

---

[1] Although this was the only book of 'reconstructions' he ever published,
Breuil often amused himself with such sketches and sometimes gave them
to his friends.

peace, you are really a brigand.' The Abbé seems to have taken
this as a compliment. Perhaps he was at heart a man of the
maquis.

From 16th August to 1st September 1944 Breuil was in Portuguese East Africa inspecting river-terraces. When they were on
their way to the Limpopo the members of the party drove in
two cars, the leading one fitted with a radio. The Abbé was in the
second. Suddenly the leading car blared out the 'Marseillaise'.
Breuil took off his hat under the tropical sun and was ready to
weep. Paris was freed.

They crossed the Limpopo on a ferry and as they rowed the
ferrymen sang high and low, in great cadences.

'What are they saying?' asked the Abbé of a Swiss doctor in the
party.

'They are saying, "We are ferrying great personages." '

Breuil raised his head. The natives of those parts were men of
considerable discernment.

Then the tone changed and became grave, mournful.

'What are they saying now?'

' "Weep my mother, weep, for that sort of people will give us
nothing." '

Two days later they were back on the other bank of the river:
Breuil, Van Riet Lowe, Dr. Malan, the Swiss doctor, Mrs. Malan
and Miss Boyle. The same ferrymen, but this time a high-pitched
interrogative, puzzled chant.

'What are they singing now?'

' "Four men and only two women. How will they make out?" '

In November 1945 the Abbé got back to France well pleased
with his work on the coastal areas, marine transgressions (i.e.
rises in sea level), ancient beaches and their industries. He summed
up thus his opinion on South Africa's place in prehistory:

'Its numerous and astounding fossil pre-hominids, the geology
of the Vaal River and its terraces, the well-proven succession
of worked-stone cultures (lasting nearly a million years), the

splendour of its painted and engraved rocks, attract the attention of prehistorians all over the world.'

Breuil was at Oxford during the Easter vacation of 1946 and there took part in the conference held to prepare the first post-war Congress of Anthropological and Ethnological Sciences. He received the Huxley Medal from the Royal Anthropological Institute in London, and then in September he was down at Arcy-sur-Cure in the Yonne department, some 125 miles south of Paris and only a short distance from the famed Benedictine Abbey of Vézelay. The Arcy caves give on to a fairly narrow terrace beside the river and are noted as being where the first fossil bone of a Neanderthaloid was found in France as long ago as 1859. In recent years the caverns have been carefully explored and a large fragment of a further neanderthaloid jaw recovered.[1]

Also, one of the caves has prehistoric engravings, situated farther north than any other palaeolithic pictures in the country. To get to the engravings, after a fairly easy passage for about forty yards with an average height of over three feet, there comes a very low passage, what the French call a *laminoir* or 'rolling-mill', some seventeen or eighteen yards long. Here Breuil (then aged sixty-nine) got stuck and it took a good many minutes of pulling and shoving to move him along, but he did get through and made his way on to where the roof rises and you can stand upright, and where are the two small chambers with the mammoths, the head of a bison, 'an awful horse'—as the Abbé called it—a reindeer, a whole bison and some other figures.

The interest of Arcy lies in its having been a neanderthaloid refuge, and maybe shrine, and also in its position so far north— evidently the mammoths' sanctuary was a poor sort of missionary outpost in the dreary tundra of Ice Age France.

[1] Under the direction of Professor Leroi-Gourhan of the Sorbonne.

13

The White Lady of the Tsisab

'Anthropology should not only be the study of the customs of primitives in the light of our mentality and of our culture but also the study of our mentality seen from the remote perspectives which we have learned of the Man of the Stone Age.'

MALINOWSKI in *Myth and Primitive Psychology*

EARLY MAN lived by lake- and river-sides. He had to be as near to water as possible. He had no vessels but skulls, men's skulls often, and possibly gourds, though these would be tiresome to clean out with rough stone tools. Ostrich-eggs were in some places—some few places where the great birds existed, and later on—also employed. So there accumulated at Olduvai a vast quantity of both implements and fossil bones.

Olduvai is in the Serengeti National Park (Tanganyika) and it was during the ages, with a succession of wet periods (Pluvials) and dry ones (Arids), turn and turn about a lake and dust-bowl. Since there is a little canyon cut through the old lake-bed, the successive deposits are revealed on the ravine's sides like layers of a *millefeuille* pastry.

Breuil had flown to Nairobi in January 1947 and there presided over the first Pan African Prehistorical Congress. After it was finished he visited the Acheulian living-site at Orgesaille in Kenya and then spent six days in Tanganyika, mostly at Olduvai.

Though some of the most striking discoveries of early Man at Olduvai were made after the Abbe's visit, it was clear even in 1947 that the site was of prime importance for Man's story.

It was during the years 1959, 1960 and 1961 that members of the Leakey family unearthed a number of hominid remains which throw a good deal of light upon the human past of Africa. In 'Bed I' (the lowest and resting upon a lava base), and with a dating of more than 1,000,000 years, were recovered the 'Zinjanthropus' (this is clearly a large form of Australopithacine) with pebble-tools; and then in 1961 part of the skull of a child (aged probably about eleven years) 'considerably older' than the 'Zinjanthropus' but also of general Australopithecine type.[1]

In 'Bed II', considerably later in date than 'Bed I'—and possibly of an order of antiquity of 350,000 to 400,000 years—the Leakeys recovered the greater part of a hominid skull, together with coarse hand-axes of 'Chellean' type. This skull is uncommonly like those of the Far Eastern Pithecanthropoids (particularly those of Peking, see p. 168) and is, no doubt, an African specimen of this once wide-spread type of man who flourished in Libya, in Algeria and in Morocco at certain periods.

So here is our Chellean Man. Or, at least, one sort of 'Chellean Man', who used and made implements like those d'Ault du Mesnil and Commont and one the British archaeologists and Breuil himself found in such abundance in the Somme and Thames gravels.

Can we say that the 'Chellean' people of those valleys were certainly Pithecanthropoids? No, we cannot. No tools at all have been found with any of the Java Pithecanthropoids. Among the tools of Peking Man there is nothing resembling a 'Chellean' hand-axe. The European pithecanthropoid Mauer jaw was accompanied by no artefacts, while the implements Arambourg

---

[1] Killed, so thinks Leakey, by a bash on the head—and so advertised as evidence of the earliest murder—though this reading of the bones has not been accepted by all.

found with his Ternifine pithecanthropoid jaws are not, strictly speaking, 'Chellean'. They are of rather more advanced technique —'Chelleo-Acheulian'—and the pithecanthropoid remains unearthed at Casablanca (Morocco) were associated with a rather coarse 'Mid-Acheulian' type of hand-axe.

So here again is proof, were any needed, that we cannot tie up any peculiar type of tool to any one type of man exclusively, and this, if we come to think of it, is just common sense.

Still, it is a fact that whenever remains of what is clearly recognizable as a Neanderthaloid have been recovered if there are any implements they are Mousterian. But this remark applies to a relatively short period (compared with the long millennia that Pithecanthropoids flourished in various parts of the world) —a matter of 40,000 or 50,000 years. Furthermore, it is highly probable that the 'pebble-tools' now recognized in many parts of Africa were made and used by hominids of the general 'Australopithecine' type.

The news of the discovery of 'Chellean Man' reached Breuil several months before he died and gave him, if not a clear answer, at least a strong hint, to the question of what sort of man lived once in Picardy and its extension northwards; that is, southern England; for certainly Pithecanthropoids lived some 400,000 years ago not far from the Rhine, of which the Thames was once a tributary.[1]

After Kenya and Tanganyika the Abbé flew on to Johannesburg.

He was to remain in Africa until April 1949, and during these two years he travelled all over southern Africa, visited the Rhodesias, the Belgian Congo, Angola and South West Africa. But the centre on which he pivoted was the Brandberg and in the

[1] There is a potassium/argon dating of 325,000 years for the 'Chellean Man' at Olduvai and of 400,000 for the Torre di Pietra (Rome) site.

Brandberg is the Tsisab or Leopard Ravine that encloses the White Lady.

On 21st March 1948 Breuil wrote to me:

'We are leaving for a great African tour on 31st of this month: first of all Southern Rhodesia (Fort Victoria), the Victoria Falls and neighbourhood, Elisabethville and the surrounding country, Kasai (Angola) and then two months in South West Africa where we spent a few days last August, occupied in copying some extraordinary painted rocks, already mentioned, but very unsatisfactorily reproduced by Frobenius and Hugo Obermaier (from material supplied by the discoverer Maack). These copies of mine will, I think, arouse a good deal of discussion in Europe when they are made known. There is a *white woman*, Diana?—Isis? astounding, and a whole procession around her. Some Rhodesian rock-paintings are somewhat similar, but less spectacular.'

The Brandberg is a great granite mountain mass lying some seventy miles inland from Cape Cross, where in 1485, on his second voyage of discovery, the Portuguese navigator Diogo Cão (or Cam) set up the fourth and most southerly (21°50′S.) of his stone pillars or *padrãos*. He made no attempt to explore the interior of this godforsaken land and he saw no signs of human beings. The Brandberg, in fact, rises from a desert plateau, with no permanent water-holes at all, but through whose rocks run veins of gold and copper. The Brandberg is cleft with ravines, the chief of which is the Tsisab, in which during the rainy season runs a torrent and where there are some permanent water-holes, the only ones for fifty miles around.

As long ago as 1920 a Lieutenant Jochmann found several rock-paintings in the Brandberg (that Maack visited again in 1920), but did not see the White Lady which is hidden in an alcove

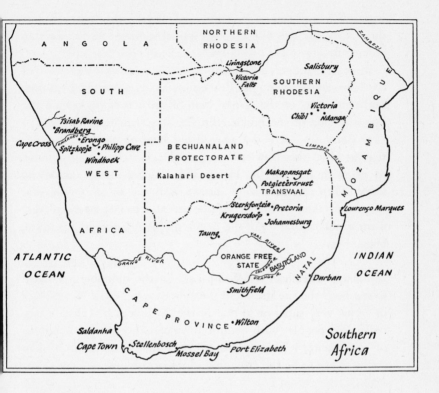

Southern Africa

—where the sun never strikes the painted surface—high up above the ravine and on a terrace access to which is had through a narrow passage.

South West Africa was, until the end of the First World War, a German colonial possession and a considerable proportion of its white inhabitants are still of German origin. In 1917, when the war was drawing to its close (though few knew it), a German topographer called Maack, while working among the sun-scorched, arid rocks of the Brandberg, found, when he was half dead with hunger, thirst and exposure, a great fresco of figures, among which was the White Lady. He managed to draw some sketches in his notebook and these it was which Breuil saw in 1929. As he put it, they 'betray the deplorable conditions in which they were made and cannot be compared with those that I, in conditions of the greatest comfort possible, took fifteen days to execute in 1947. And I went back to the site in 1948 and in 1950.'

In 1928, however, a Fräulein Weyersberg, at the suggestion of the German archaeologist Frobenius, made copies of the White Lady and also of the 'Girls' School' in a rock-shelter on the opposite side of the ravine. But she stayed in the Brandberg a very short time. It is not an inviting kind of place. At Breuil's request Mrs. Alice Bowler Kelley got Dr. E. Scherz of Windhoek to go with her to the Tsisab and to photograph the White Lady. These pictures were shown to Breuil in 1937—the year they were taken—while in 1942 he was able to inspect an enlargement in the laboratory of the Archaeological Survey at Johannesburg.

'Maack's sketch of the White Lady of the Brandberg revealed to me both the site itself and the existence in South West Africa of an art very superior to that of the Bushmen. It is the art of a red-haired people (with Semitic profiles) who painted hundreds of rock-shelters. The picture of the White Lady of the Tsisab seems to me to be the crowning glory of this art.'

While he was engaged on copying this great fresco, the Abbé camped at the foot of the painted rock while lions prowled around. Despite 'the conditions of the greatest comfort possible', it was a hard life for a man over seventy. The heat, the glare, the climbing, the bending, the fatigue of long hours examining and copying. He had with him in addition to Miss Boyle, Dr. Scherz and Mr. Strey, the two latter to photograph and prospect.

Breuil thought that on the White Lady rock there were eleven successive levels of painting. The eleventh—and last—is a polychrome, symbolical, ceremonial procession. There are animals: eland, oryx, springbok, an antelope with man's arms and legs, an oryx with human hind quarters, a hartebeest with human hind legs, a man with a crocodile's head, a person with a jackal's head, a white man disguised as a baboon; there are twenty-eight human figures, including the crocodile-man, musicians and others, steatopygous women—the procession is led by two youths who, like the crocodile-man, are infibulated.

The White Lady herself is striding along towards the left. She holds up to her face either a cup or a large white flower, in her left hand stretched out behind her she has a strung bow and arrows, and a sheaf of three more. From waist to feet she is rosy-white, while from waist to neck she is covered in some dark-coloured, clinging garment, with short sleeves and embroidered with several bands of beads. The face is very delicately painted and is, Breuil considered, of 'Mediterranean' type; in any case it is not negro or 'African' at all.

Behind her is an uncanny figure, dark in colour, the tallest of all. On his dusky face is painted in white a lower jaw complete with teeth and also an eye-socket; in fact his head is a skull. He is infibulated . . . and then after him are two red-haired young people running . . . and still more figures.

Of the many problems raised by this most enigmatic of the African rock-paintings the Abbé wrote:

'We cannot explain this mixture of races except by a column, or better still, a ship's company, of foreigners, settling in the country for some time, or returning on several trips, and camping among the rocks near the fresh-water spring. My opinion is that a mixed group of foreigners, mixed when they were recruited, in the course of their journeyings added to their company negro servants, also foreign to the region, and that they brought with them beliefs such as are found in Egypt and Crete . . . the Lady's costume is obviously Cretan.

'The Brandberg Rock on which is to be seen the cortège of the White Lady, was the sacred rock of a people who at many other sites painted their daily occupations of hunting, occasional warfare and social and religious life. . . . Among the granite rocks of the Brandberg, the Erongo and the Spitzkoppen there are scattered the sheets of the most beautiful "album of the rocks" to be found anywhere.'

After his 'great African Tour'—and therefore about November 1948, though the letter is undated—Breuil wrote to me describing his adventures:

'I have devoted six months of this year to my great southern tour; first of all in south-eastern Rhodesia. I wanted to see, and to copy, the pictures in Impey's cave, alias Dandabari, near the Ndanga reserve, sixty miles from Fort Victoria. . . . I also visited, and partially copied, two other rock-shelters with similar personages—different from the southern races (*races australes*) . . . an unfortunate occurrence (social unrest) prevented my finishing my copies of a third and a fourth site, both of them important—and this makes me furious. All I have is indifferent photographs. The presence of these "foreigners" is undoubted. One type, white with straight nose and reddish hair; the other bronze-coloured with Semitic nose and of tall stature . . . what do these facts signify?

'After a month in the Upper Congo and then some time in north-eastern Angola, I got back to Windhoek, and with the aid and assistance of various local persons, ex-German, I went again to the Brandberg and the Tsisab Ravine where I copied about fifteen other sites, during a period of three weeks. I camped out among the rocks; then I was two weeks in the Erongo massif —which is much more extensive than the Brandberg—where I copied about thirty paintings while leaving on one side others that are third-rate. As my companions and I explored only a small part of this vast mountain I think one could find there ten times as many paintings. From the Erongo I went off to do the same sort of work in various smaller mountain masses, called the "Spitzkoppen"—two fairly big and eight small ones, and I did the same thing with about ten other sites. None of them, however, is as splendid as the shelter of the White Lady . . . although most of them are in the same art-style and were the work of the same people with the reddish hair, a Semitic people, often depicted with a white or light-coloured visage. One can see this people engaged in all the occupations of their daily life: hunting, sometimes war (with the Bushmen), sport, trading, dancing, camping, courting, travelling, quarrelling, pleading with the chieftain, family ceremonies, scenes of homage or adoration, rain-making, etc. etc. Note the existence of Nilotic-type bows . . . and in the war-scene, use of the lance. No shields, no quivers, but poisoned arrows with fixed points, and, almost certainly, helmets (probably not of metal), sometimes with many plumes or with crests pendant behind . . . mythical figurations of imaginary creatures . . . and I have forgotten the common employment of the water-bag made of antelope-skin with head and feet cut off, such as those I used in Somaliland among the Danakali. The Bushmen employed ostrich-eggs.

'These imaginary creatures seem to have some connection with the other world: in the funerary scene, the "package" containing the body (probably in a leather sack) is between the feet of a quadruped with human legs, a sort of sphinx-griffin, which I take to be the protector of the dead. There is a considerable number of figures, generally in pairs, male and female. The form of the head varies a good deal, sometimes animal, sometimes semi-human, the most complicated is like this.[1] Others have little horns. One of the scenes from the Brandberg (reproduced by Obermaier and Kühn from a sketch by Maack) shows a human being holding an armful of bodies and two other figures (skeletons with prominent pelvis) are taking these bodies from the first personage. One of the skeletons, with crocodile-jaws, seems to be devouring the bodies. No domestic animals.

'There are, moreover, Bushman paintings dating from *before*, *during* and *after* these I am telling you about, and to these, *towards the end*, belong, at one site, cattle, of very wild appearance, and only one animal—that is undoubtedly a sheep—of Hottentot type. But, on three or four rocks, I found partially effaced pictures of

[1] There is a small sketch in the margin of the letter (see opposite page 161).

large animals, but in another *art-style*, much more ancient, and very probably Palaeolithic (Quaternary). Very big bovines (one was between six and seven metres long and was four in height) in outline and looking as though traced with fingers . . . and also the great Saharan *Bubalus* (buffalo)—these latter engraved—they recall somewhat the rather large animal figures of Southern Rhodesia which I have mentioned as being older than the rest of the Southern Rhodesian art as a whole. In the art of the red-haired people there are representations of clouds dropping rain and a few pictures of snakes, often with ears.

'Although I did no digging, I examined the industry at the foot of the rocks—no pottery (except some Hottentot, recent) and some worked stone points. The implements, in quartz and indurated shale, are of advanced Middle Stone Age type . . . a similar industry but without paintings exists in Kenya but in neither the Congo-Angola nor in the Rhodesias. You must go as far south as the Orange Free State to meet it again.

'My supposition is that a population of Nilotic-Mediterranean origin came south through Kenya in a *rapid* migration. Perhaps if they had cattle these died by the way. This population must have lived in South West Africa for a considerable time and have been in contact with Bushmen. However, one day, this people, disgusted by the progressive desiccation of the land, emigrated eastwards, south-eastwards, carrying with them the Smithfield industry, the art of polychrome paintings and an *academic* art-tradition that contrasts with the "human art of action"—though without depiction of volume—of the Bushmen. Battiss has just published his book, it is a handsome volume but, from many points of view, not satisfactory. . . .

'In the south-east, both in Southern Rhodesia and on the two sides of the Drakensberg, other foreigners come by sea, penetrated into the country . . . these foreigners are a mixed lot, the most ancient of them recall, by their costumes, the Sumerians. They have enormous quivers—which the Bushmen do not use—that I have been able to discover again only in Mesopotamia.

photo: Dr. E. Ripoll Perello

Breuil at Burg Wartenstein near Wiener-Neustadt, August 1960. One of the
last pictures taken of him

photo:

Breuil in later years

'The whole business is being worked out. In any case we are at last out of the rut of Bushman paintings which are only a few hundred years old. Paintings and engravings in southern Africa begin at the end of the Middle Stone Age and they developed during the last 10,000 years . . . so southern and eastern African art began when there was still Pleistocene art flourishing in Europe.

'I have had the satisfaction of seeing—after quite enough opposition—I have succeeded in getting this new proposition accepted, namely that in ancient times foreigners were responsible for much of the southern African art.

'But of course, it is now the South Africans who have discovered all this! That is only normal!

'I must apologize for sending you so long a letter to decipher. I shall stay here at least until March, and if my work is not finished until later. All my best wishes for a Merry Christmas. . . .'

On 2nd April 1949 he wrote to me from Johannesburg:

'I shall leave (D.V.) Johannesburg on 25th April and I shall be in Paris the next day—I suppose in time for luncheon. I am now slaving away writing up the captions for my 150 sheets of drawings from South West Africa.'

The Abbé was to modify a good deal his ideas about the origins of the South West African rock-paintings, but his dating for the White Lady remained more or less fixed. He thought she was executed about 1500 B.C.

The scene is laid under a blazing African sun in one of the driest and warmest parts of the continent. Breuil and an aged German were on their way to visit a prehistoric cave called after the old man 'Philipp Cave'. And as the two advanced they were

o

accompanied by a crowd of Africans bawling out at the tops of their voices, and in German, canticles, hymns, songs and poetry. And when they got to the Philipp Cave it was to a bellow of *Stille Nacht, heilige Nacht* (appropriate to the Abbé's sacerdotal character) shouted by grinning negroes that Breuil settled down to work in a huge prehistoric grotto some 170 feet long. The walls are covered with paintings of men and animals, the implements recovered were of African Middle Stone Age and charcoal from the site gave a dating (by radio-carbon tests in the U.S.A.) of about 1500 B.C.—then roughly about as old as the White Lady.

Old Philipp had arranged for the musical welcome in order to show his gratitude for something which had happened to him sixty years before. He and another lad decided they wanted to see France and they did, but when they got back to the Franco-German border there was nowhere for them to sleep, not a room in any inn or lodging-house, but the local *commissaire de police* (police chief) agreed to let the boys sleep in the jail-house where there were lots of empty cells, but he never came back to see how the lads were getting on and they soon became hungry; however, later, another stranded traveller, a Frenchman this time, turned up and on learning the two Germans had nothing to eat went out and returned with an armful of provisions.

Philipp afterwards emigrated to the United States where he made money in hogs but did not like the life, so he sailed for South West Africa (then a German colony) and went in for raising caracul sheep for their fur—a staple industry in the country. Philipp was a genial individual, made friends with his neighbours, and after work and on holidays would teach his men German songs to the accompaniment of tomtoms and flutes.

Philipp said that all his life he had been looking for an opportunity to show his thanks for what an unknown Frenchman had done for him many, many years before. It was at the Philipp Cave that Breuil got word of Smuts's death and celebrated a Mass for him (see p. 109).

This was the Abbé's fourth and last southern African journey.

He had left Paris in a Sabena aeroplane on 20th April 1950 for Johannesburg. He again visited some of the Southern Rhodesian sites and studied the fine paintings in the Mupuwire Cave (Chibi reserve), he was at Dandabari and other painted rocks. In July he was back in South West Africa. The White Lady rock was now protected. Breuil particularly wanted to copy some figures he had left out when he dealt with the 'Girls' School' (see p. 204), but he could not climb up to the site. He was seventy-three and no longer as active as he had been until only a year or so before.

One day during his 1942-5 sojourn in South Africa the Abbé wanted to buy a birthday present and went into Mr. Silberg's jewellery store at Johannesburg. Breuil's small, compact, bustling, black-robed figure was already fairly well known, even in so large a city as the goldfields capital. He had delivered public lectures and his doings were reported in the local Press. Mr. Silberg recognized his customer, and after the Abbé had selected his present, conversation became general. Breuil was always communicative with all sorts and conditions of chance acquaintances. Then the jeweller asked if the Abbé would like to see a box of fossils from the Australopithecine sites out to the west of the city near Krugersdorp. Breuil, of course, said yes, maybe hoping there might be a bit or piece of an Australopithecine among the bones.

We may remember that nearly twenty years ago the Australopithecine material was neither so abundant, so well classified nor so well dated, as now. The Taung discovery of a juvenile skull of the 'ape-man' was made in 1924. The first Sterkfontein (near Krugersdorp) specimen was unearthed twelve years later, while by 1941 a good many bones of a sort of Australopithecine called *Paranthropus* had been recovered. It is, in fact, clear now—though it was not when Breuil visited Mr. Silberg—that the ape-like hominids, whether in South Africa or elsewhere in the continent (and their bones have been found in East Africa, right up on the Sahara's southern fringes, and even in Palestine), fall into two main classes (each one of which includes a number of variations) —that of the *Australopithecus* (the first to be found and named) and that of *Paranthropus*, while in South Africa—but not necessarily elsewhere—the former group flourished a long time before the latter.

Mr. Silberg brought forth his magic box. The Abbé rummaged through it.

'All from the same site?'

'Yes.'

Then the Abbé spotted a well-preserved fossil hyena-jaw. It struck him as being an antique type of hyena to be present in a deposit the South African anthropologists were then inclined to date back to about 500,000 years only. As all the South African Australopithecines were then generally regarded as having been more or less contemporary, this date of half a million years meant that little hominids were living in southern Africa when much more developed types such as Pithecanthropoids were also flourishing—not, of course, that there is anything improbable in various sorts of hominids having lived on this earth at the same time.

The only dating evidence then available for fossils so ancient as those of the Australopithecines was (1) geological and (2) palaeontological; that is to say, from the nature of the deposits as indicating climate, and from the accompanying fossil animal bones as indicating ancient or less ancient types of other animals.

Breuil saw at once that so ancient a type of hyena could hardly be dated to a period so recent (geologically speaking) as half a million years ago. Silberg, noting how interested the Abbé was, made him a present of the specimen which he took to the late Dr. Robert Broom (died 1951) in Pretoria who was the prime promoter of Australopithecine discovery. Broom confirmed that the hyena was of a late Tertiary (Pliocene) type known as

Lycyaena, whose presence in the Sterkfontein deposit set it back to Villafranchian times and therefore the Australopithecine *Plesianthropus* (at least) must have flourished quite a million years ago. It was not until some years later that the Villafranchian (last phase of the Pliocene) was counted into the Pleistocene (which was thus prolonged by at least a million years and probably more). In fact, the Australopithecines qualify well enough for the position of 'Tertiary Man', the elusive creature which had for so long excited discussion. Not that this 'Tertiary Man' was very 'human' looking about the face, though he stood upright and his limbs much resembled those of later sorts of men. He had not a large brain, and his face was snouty and ape-like. Still his teeth were more like ours than those of any ape living or extinct.

Breuil left the *Lycyaena* with Broom, who, in exchange, gave the Abbé casts of parts of the Kromdraai *Plesianthropus*.

This story is apparently not well known, but Breuil told it to me himself in 1946 and it serves as another example of his perceptiveness and rapidity of deduction from almost any sort of evidence presented to him.

On his way back from his last visit to the Brandberg in 1950 Breuil stopped off at Taung in Bechuanaland, the limestone quarry where the first Australopithecine fossil was found. There is now nothing much to see at Taung, the actual spot where the skull was discovered is protected but it is a mere speck lost in a huge quarry. The Abbé had already, soon after his arrival on this last trip, examined the latest (1947) fossils from Swartkrans which were in the Pretoria Museum. On 24th October he was in Dart's laboratory at Johannesburg and there studied the Australopithecine bones from Makapansgat (some 125 miles north of Pretoria) which belonged to a type of Australopithecine Dart had baptized *prometheus* since he thought the site showed signs of hearths. It does not. The black stains are of manganese and the Abbé pronounced definitely that there were no traces of fire. Then on 16th November he was back in Broom's laboratory with

Professor Raymond Dart and Van Riet Lowe. The photograph opposite p. 192 shows the four men examining the skull of *Paranthropus crassidens* from Swartkrans, whose jaw is so big that Breuil could fit it over his own. As he looked at himself in a mirror, the Abbé murmured: '*Mon pauvre vieux, tu a manqué l'aiguillage*'—'My poor old fellow, you ran on beyond the points' —that is, 'you missed the right turning'.

Our present view of the Australopithecine problems is about this: Most of the South African types were small. But they walked upright, that is the prime characteristic that marks them off from any sort of ape. Our remote forerunners walked as we do long before their brains became much bigger than those of some apes, but the upright posture left the hands free to make things, to chip stones, and it was by making things that our forbears developed their intelligence.

The Australopithecines, both in South Africa, where they were flourishing a million years ago, and in East Africa, where they were living maybe 2,000,000 years ago, are, as we have seen, divided into two groups—the Australopithecus group and the Paranthropus group—of which the latter is much the more recent and probably survived in the South African blind alley—cut off by a greater Kalahari Desert—until at least 500,000 years ago, if not until later, and were therefore contemporaries of the Pithe-canthropoids and, indeed, neighbours of them, if as seems prob-able the *Telanthropus* (from Swartkrans, a *Paranthropus* site) was a sort of Pithecanthropoid.

Tool-making originated, it would seem, somewhere in eastern Africa possibly over 2,000,000 years ago and the pebble-tool makers spread to Morocco, the Sahara, Algeria and Palestine and fairly early on to southern Africa. It is possible that climatic conditions, then as always, determined migration. In any case, there was a large Australopithecine form (the *Meganthropus*) in Java about 600,000 years ago.

However, despite all the evidence pointing to Africa as mankind's cradle the earliest 'man' (as distinguished from the

Australopithecines which may be called 'proto-men') we know of is still the Java Modjokerto Pithecanthropus dating back to over 500,000 years.

Breuil left Johannesburg on 23rd January 1951 after having delivered a few lectures on South African prehistory. On 2nd March, at Cape Town, he embarked on the *Edinburgh Castle*. He had with him 500 sheets of copies he had made of prehistoric paintings and a copious collection of pebble-tool artefacts (the work of Australopithecines) and also stone implements of the southern African Middle and Late Stone Ages. The pebble-tools (from the high terraces of the Vaal River) were similar to those he had been doubtful about on his first visit to South Africa in 1929.

Breuil landed at Havre on 17th March 1951, and got to his apartment, 52 avenue de La Motte-Picquet, 'in time for luncheon'. It must have been exactly twelve o'clock.

The Abbé was now seventy-four years old and had aged a good deal since he had got back to France in 1945. There were to be no more distant travels for him. He had suffered what the French popularly call *un coup de vieux*, a sudden appearance of ageing which may be noted in men of mature years when they have undergone some (often ignored or apparently trivial) shock or trauma. And the *coup de vieux* is a warning to go slow. Maybe the African climate had exacted its toll and perhaps we can date the Abbé's definite entrance into old age from that day in the Brandberg ravine when he found his legs fail him and he was no longer able to scale the rocks up to the fresco of the 'Girls' School'.

Although he now moved more slowly than before, and although his figure became a little more bowed each year, his lively conversation and his wit continued unabated. I remember meeting him in the early 'fifties. I was staying at the Cro-Magnon Hotel,

Les Eyzies, and did not know he was anywhere about, but he came in with a number of South African archaeologists, they had spent the morning exploring prehistoric caves: Lascaux, Font de Gaume and so forth. Breuil was in fine form and did ample justice to a copious meal. What was astonishing was that he should have remained so active until his middle seventies. The youth whose health had been so bad he had had to give up all work for a year, the young man his family looked on as unlikely to make old bones, grew to be a man unwearied in travel, in exploration; a man who could ride for days on end through the wildest country; who could spend long hours crouching in damp caverns, perched on ladders or grovelling on the ground while, by the glare of acetylene lamps, he copied timelessly and deciphered patiently endless paintings and engravings, often palimpsests with painting and repainting, engraving and re-engraving on the same surface. But then, as Lloyd George said (though I hasten to add there was no sort of resemblance between the private life of Breuil and that of the British politician), when asked how he managed to retain so much vigour until late in life, 'I never wasted my strength in games and sports.' The Abbé could have said the same thing.

Still, even in 1951 Breuil had not quite bade farewell to Africa. In the next year he was able to view some of the North African *Hajra Mektuba*, or 'Written Rocks'as they are called in Arabic, and these written rocks were to elicit from him some penetrating observations on art-currents, on borrowings and reciprocal influences and on the mysterious problems of extinction of arts and cultures.

He did not know much of North Africa at first hand and he was never far out into the Sahara; he did in 1932 do a tour of Algeria in company with Reygasse and in 1941, as we have seen, he was with Neuville and Ruhlmann working on the geology of the coastal formations in Morocco. He had wanted to pay at least a flying visit to the Tassili n'Ajjer highlands of the Sahara when Lhote and his teams were in 1956 and 1957 copying the rock-paintings Colonel Brenans had sketched long years before. But the Abbé was too old—eighty.

However, in 1952 he attended the Pan African Congress in Algiers and did manage to get out into the south of Oran province and examine some of the rock-engravings. These, in northern Africa, extend over a vast area but are most common in the southern *Oranais*, the central Saharan highlands and in the Fezzan (south-western Libya). The pictures are for the most part of animals including the long-extinct *Bubalus antiquus*—a water-loving beast—and the pictures are mainly interesting as proving that there existed millennia ago a Sahara flowing with milk and honey, where cattle grazed, where great rivers were the homes of hippopotamus and crocodile, where herds of giraffe, zebra and antelope roamed over what are now wind-swept sand-dunes or bitter, murderous, stony plains. Another climate-shift, in its way, as momentous as that in western Europe at the end of the Old Stone Age.

Some of these engravings are neolithic, say 5,000 years old, others may be as early as the last African Pluvial more or less contemporary with the last glaciation in Europe.

As Breuil said:

'I do not think the Saharan neolithic art originated in Egypt. but, on the contrary, that Egyptian civilization was the finest product, the flowering from a neolithic substratum . . . I do not think the engravings with spherical objects owed their origin to the Egyptian uraeus, rather the contrary is probable. I am inclined to think the engravings with the large *Bubalus* (buffalo)— wild in the Fezzan but domesticated in the Oran region—must be dated back to the last African Pluvial (since this animal cannot flourish without a good deal of water); that is to say to at least about 10,000 B.C. . . . the art of the Tassili, Hoggar, Fezzan and Libyan oases was the work of oxherds . . . the absence of *Bubalus* and of the large pachyderms prevents me from considering them as old as the rock-engravings of *Bubalus*. . . .

'An examination of the copies made by Brenans at the Tassili reveals a very mixed population . . . there are tall Libyans, foreigners of aristocratic Mediterranean type, tall Negroes and what seem to be pygmies . . . was it this shepherd-art that crossed the vast spaces extending as far as the north of Tanganyika (where the more southern African painted rocks begin) and where there is also a naturalistic art—but the work of hunters? During the Nairobi Congress of 1947 I visited, with Dr. Leakey, several of the Tanganyika painted rocks where can be seen several superposed pictorial levels. The first five of these (very archaic) recall the line-drawings . . . of French mid-Aurignacian art. Beyond Rhodesia such a style is either very rare or completely wanting-Such absence is not very favourable to the theory of a southern African origin for this art, for had this been the case, the art would have spread northwards . . . in Tanganyika it is only in the sixth level that scenes with human figures (in the "Rhodesian" style) are discernible.'

As an example of Breuil's dating from geological evidence, here is his chronology of the later phases of the African Stone Age:

'The geological dating of the Middle Stone Age is as follows: an archaic facies of it is water-worn in a twenty-five- to forty-foot beach at Mossel Bay and this puts the beginning of the Middle Stone Age during the last (i.e. Riss-Würm) Interglacial. The later "Stillbay" facies plunges beneath the present beach at East London. The facies, then, is dated as that of a Würmian beach not less than 10,000 years old. Thus all later ages are left for the development . . . of Late Old Stone Age (parallel to the Mesolithic in Europe), as well as Neolithic, Copper, etc. In these later ages there was also an evolution of Late Old Stone Age art—in various stages—both engraving and painting. Some of this art seems to me . . . as old as some of the Spanish Levantine paintings and of the diagrammatic art which followed on after the Levantine.

'Thus, the rock-paintings of southern and South Africa would not be the descendants of those of Spain, but "cousins", at first contemporary with some of the Levantine frescoes and then, later on, continuing right up into the nineteenth century. . . .

'Similar human reactions were produced in parallel fashion, in similar circumstances. In such conditions, the Bushmen played their part as did other but unknown peoples who were neither Negro, nor Bantu, nor Hottentot. Some came from the borders of Egypt and perhaps lost (maybe through the action of the tsetse fly) their flocks and herds by the way. Others were possibly only visitors, traders driven down from the Persian Gulf by the monsoon which swept men along from the early days when the Sumerians (about 3000 B.C.) built the first sailing-vessels which could take the high seas. Paintings in South Africa seem to represent such visitors, Semites and others—the forerunners of those Arabs, Indians and Chinese who were to come later on.'

The problems of extinction are as puzzling as those of origins. Why did dinosaurs die out? Why did the Maya civilization of the highlands fade away? Why did the splendid naturalistic art of Late Old Stone Age western Europe crumple up into scribblings on pebbles? Let us say 'climate' as an all-in explanation and no doubt it is plausible enough. Did the quickening of art in the neolithic Near East owe anything to culture-streams through Africa? Yet, why should we seek always for contacts? If art, pictorial art, was 'invented' once, why could it not be 'invented' again? Art was apparently invented independently in pre-Columbian America, why not in and among the new agricultural communities, dating back to perhaps 7000 B.C. in the Near East where new ways of life called forth new ideas of magic and religion? The rites and ceremonies of a hunting community are not those of one sowing and reaping, keeping flocks and herds . . . and, with rites and ceremonies, art changes, mirroring, maybe, new ideas or at least helping to induce them.

Here is Breuil's opinion on one essential feature of African rock-art:

'It seems to me that, in addition to hunting-magic and rain-making (the latter sometimes associated with human sacrifices, even that of a royal personage), we must also recognize that an important place was reserved in African rock-paintings for "historical pictures" (i.e. those of migrations, battles with other peoples, cattle-thieving, feasts and successful hunts) and for more day-to-day events such as courtships, quarrels, reconciliations, initiations, special relationships and contacts, all of which are well represented both in the Tassili n'Ajjer and in South West Africa. It was not for nothing that Frobenius wrote about the "painted rock archives" of ancient African history.'

Without seeking to minimize the results of Breuil's African prospections and explorations, it is fair to say they were not and could not have been comparable with the achievements of his prime. In southern Africa he was confronted with an immense mass of material and he had not the time to do more than scratch the surface, but his work on the geology of the coastlines, on the river-deposits, on the chronology of the rock-paintings, was of high importance though in a measure that of a pioneer. Then his ideas on the antiquity of the African rock-art, on the penetration of art-influences and on the connection between African and European prehistoric art were, perhaps, in some cases, too hurriedly proclaimed.

It is most probable that the origins of southern African prehistoric art do go back to a period of maybe 10,000 years ago or even more, but it is doubtful if many, if any, of the existing paintings are as old as this, though the engravings may be older than the paintings.

Breuil carried on a controversy with Schofield about the age of the paintings and in 1956 Van Riet Lowe got into the dispute and qualified the Abbé's theories about the White Lady herself as 'romancing' and he put the age of the Tsisab frescoes at rather A.D. 1500 than 1500 B.C., though before he died Lowe had retracted his objections and as far as the Tsisab was concerned came round to the Abbé's point of view. It was indeed a point of view that changed a good deal in the last years of Breuil's life. He kept to his datings—in a general way—but as to the origins of the artists, their presumed sources of inspiration and the phases of artistic evolution, he came to recognize that there was much more to be said. Indeed he modified his former rather too dogmatic statements. The fact was, and we must admit it, he tackled the whole African prehistoric problem rather late. Had he been able to do in the years following his first visit in 1929 what he attempted to do nearly twenty years later no doubt his conclusions would have been different, but then he would have been withdrawn from the European scene where he could ill have been spared. As it was, his achievements in Africa were of the highest interest and remarkable for a man of his age working in a harsh climate . . . and we must not underestimate those achievements.

In the last of all his public pronouncements at the Wenner-Gren symposium on 'Comparative Prehistoric Art', held in 1960 at Burg Wartenstein in Austria, he showed that he was, in the words of one of his most devoted disciples and friends, Dr. Léon Pales, 'Freeing himself from the only intolerance he ever allowed himself—that in prehistory'.

14

Art and Record

'Painting cleanses the mind and curbs anxiety, augments
future good, causes the greatest delight, kills the evil of
bad dreams and pleases the household divinity. It is the
best of all arts and is conducive to right conduct.'

From an ancient Indian treatise

FROM time to time there are recovered from the Danish
peat-bogs remarkably well-preserved human bodies, mostly
of men, but occasionally also of women. These bodies are
generally naked with the exception of a cap on the head. The
Borremose Man, found in 1946, and the Tollund Man, discovered
in 1950, were both strangled and then thrown into a marsh or
swamp. The leather thongs employed for the killing were
plaited round the men's necks like torques. The victims seem
to have been sacrificed, probably to the Earth Goddess, and
certainly to some divinity who did not like bloody offerings. These
Danish relics date only from the Iron Age of northern Europe;
that is to say, from about the beginning of our era.

Now let us jump back, say, 15,000 years, and see something
which makes prehistoric ethnology vivid and real. Inside the
Addaura Cave on the slopes of Monte Pellegrino just outside
Palermo in Sicily there is one of the most remarkable of all prehistoric pictures. Monte Pellegrino is historic ground. Here-
abouts Hannibal's father had his encampment. Down below is
the plain, the fertile sweep of the Conca d'Oro, the Golden Shell,

in which are the mosaics of the Capella Palatina and a little farther away at Monreale all the Christian story exemplified in glittering Byzantine wall-pictures.

Until a few years ago the prehistoric engraving was hidden by a cave-filling, the upper layers of which were neolithic. Breuil visited this site, studied it and wrote two long articles about it, one a description and the other an approving comment on A. C. Blanc's interpretation of the enigmatic scene depicted.

There are seven men and a woman dancing, or, anyway, let us say performing some sort of, apparently ritual, set of movements. Two of the men have raised arms. Others appear ready to leap. The woman's head is hidden by an object either a bulky mask or some cumbrous head-dress. One of the dancers brandishes a lance or maybe a bow. In the middle of the circle are two other men, unmasked, naked and it would seem bearded. Their necks are caught in thongs pulled tight to joined ankles so that the bodies are bent backwards in an arc. The legs are flexed and the arms outstretched. The male organs are erect, but there is no ejaculation as there would be had strangulation been effected.

What is the reading of the pictures? Acrobats, it has been suggested. An homosexual act, others have said. An initiation? An execution? A human sacrifice? Almost certainly the latter. The twin themes of cannibalism and human sacrifice run right through our story. Anyway, at Addaura we are in a world of complicated and developed rites.

The Abbé's comment was:

'Baron A. C. Blanc's theory seems to me to be very plausible. Two of the men are obviously being subjected to torture by strangulation effected with the cords that join the necks to the feet ... in a number of cases [Breuil is referring to the dancers] the face has a pointed chin, and this may be interpreted as a bird-mask, however, in other cases, there is the tip of a beard as well as indications of a nose ... the single figure identifiable as a woman is carrying a heavy burden on her shoulders, while a man,

some way away from her, appears to be armed with a long lance.
... The human figures at Addaura are of very great importance
both because of their exceptionally high quality as drawings and
because ... there is some depiction of joint ceremonial action
accompanied by ritual dances.'

Ritual strangulation in Sicily 15,000 years ago, ritual strangulation in Denmark 13,000 years later. It seems impossible there
should be any connection between the two, but rites have a
long life, and maybe it was sought to propitiate something, both
there and here. No, prehistory is not all datings and chipped
stones, it is also no doubt men of like passions with ourselves.

Scenes such as this filled the dark recesses of some prehistoric
caves. It looks as though, from very early times, Man indulged in
some sort of ritual; that is a set of acts performed with no direct
physical object, acts that are reassuring, of psychosomatic value,
for we need to have our apprehensions calmed. To the other
definitions of Man—the mammal that walks upright, the tool-
maker, the cannibal, the talker, the myth-maker—we may add the
apprehensive animal.

The decorated caves of the Late Old Stone Age do not date
back to more than about 30,000 years ago, and most of the prehistoric picture galleries are more modern than that. It looks as
though pictorial art was an invention of *Homo sapiens* (and, as far
as we can see, in western Europe), still it is well to keep an open
mind. The Neanderthaloids certainly practised complicated rites,
and, on occasion, buried their dead with grave-gear; they may
well have done a little painting and engraving. Why not? At the
Mousterian (i.e. neanderthaloid) sites of La Ferrassie, Pech de
l'Aze, Combe-Capelle and Le Moustier itself (all in south-
western France) there have been discovered several pieces of
colouring matter (notably red ochre and blue-black manganese
ore) showing traces of having been scraped with a flint tool or of
having been worn down on a hand-scraper. Of course such
pigments may have been used for adorning the body, though

P

body-painting and wall-painting may well be kindred arts. At La Ferrassie were two rough stone slabs showing traces of paint—dotted and ribbon-like patterns in brown and black—as well as a slab with small marks and scrawls together with indented bones. At Mousterian sites in south Germany (horse's jaw with indentations and a mammoth's tusk also indented) and Czechoslovakia (a piece of deer-horn incised with geometric designs) there are indications that the Neanderthaloids did some engraving. There has been reported from central Asia (Uzbekistan, the same province in which about twenty years ago were found in the Teshik Tash Cave the remains of a neanderthaloid boy buried amid a number of wild-goat horns) a cavern 'with engravings 100,000 years old'; that is to say going back to the Riss-Würm Interglacial. The report can be taken as indicating no more than a possibility that the site may be neanderthaloid, but even if it is it may not be '100,000 years old', for it looks as though Neanderthaloids may have lingered on in parts of Asia after they had disappeared as a distinct type in western Europe.

In any case, it may be with pictures as with tools, if only to this extent that not all men of any given type produced the same sort of art. What were the other *Homo sapiens* doing when in France and Spain their fellows were executing fine paintings?

When we think of prehistoric art our minds turn at once to the cave-paintings and engravings, to the often exquisite chattel-art, to the statuettes. But some of the chipped-stone implements are works of art. The superb laurel-leaf blades of the Solutrean culture are remarkable by any standard. The men who fashioned them were obviously highly skilled artists. In fact, when the first Australopithecine chipped the first crude pebble-tool he was creating, however humbly, a work of art, and tool-making implies the existence of some sort of language, since the knappers must be able to explain to others how and why the implements are chipped—in fact, to impart know-how. It is in the making of things we prove our 'humanity'. Man, the tool-maker.

It takes rather an effort on our part to realize that a number of basic skills were acquired countless ages ago, and it is not always realized that when we come to the art of the Late Stone Old Age, we are among men who, in some areas anyway, and at some periods, had a quite highly developed cultural life. We may take it that the men who fashioned—200,000 years ago and more—the excellent Acheulian tools (and all stone-knapping is an arduous and difficult art) must have not only possessed articulate language, but have been cunning hunters (with all that implies) and have had ideas about themselves and the world they lived in. The elementary problems of living were solved long, long ago; the few remaining Bushmen—now relegated to the Kalahari Desert—live more or less as their ancestors did 50,000 years ago, and they could give most of us points in tracking, hunting, finding water, adapting themselves to circumstances, looking after their families, organizing their communal life and in general coming to terms with their surroundings.

Owing, probably, to the rather sudden revelation of the great prehistoric painted caves, the idea became current that naturalistic drawing and painting came before any other. However, the oldest manifestations of pictorial art which we can attribute to *Homo sapiens* are not naturalistic but abstract, symbolical 'non-organic', pre-figurative and most probably of symbolical significance. A preoccupation with symbols is a constant with Man and long before he became (in a very few regions of the world) an accomplished artist, he must for long ages have been concerned with ideological imaginings.

We have only to reflect an instant to realize that the easiest way, the way most readily adopted by an unskilled craftsman, to figure a 'horse' is to scratch a few lines—and not to produce a 'naturalistic' picture. In his exciting little book *Del' Astratto al Naturalistico*—'From the Abstract to the Naturalistic'—the late A. C. Blanc developed his contention that 'stylized' art comes first and 'naturalistic' afterwards. Breuil wrote an introduction to Blanc's book and expressed agreement with the author's views.

At Minateda (in Levantine Spain) Breuil discovered a phase of schematic art he considered to be (chronologically speaking) 'pre-naturalistic'. At the Romanelli grotto in southern Italy there is a wealth of complicated graffiti and sexual figurations. Blanc thought that at Romanelli we had evidence of a 'real and primitive sacred writing'. In fact 'symbolic homoglyphs' pave the way to real writing.[1]

It looks extremely probable that if a man had the skill to manu-facture such a fine object as a fully developed Acheulian hand-axe, he had also the skill to use this for scratching lines and designs on a rock-face. Again, men must from very early times have recognized, in natural shapes of rocks and stones, resemblances to living things. The so-called *pierres figures* (that is bits of stone suggesting forms of animals and touched up by hand) are now rather discredited but certainly in Late Old Stone Age times men did use natural cavities, bosses and ridges as foundations for paintings that were in part 'sculpture'. In the dark recesses of Niaux Cave in the Pyrenees—on the old smugglers' route to Andorra—as you make your way to the mysterious black lake which lies at that cavern's end, you pass a hollow in the walls which was touched up in prehistoric times to present a striking image of a deer's face with antlers. On the clay floor of the same cave is a bison engraved. On its body are three holes made by drips of water, three wounds; certainly the holes were there first and the picture drawn for them.

Among the oldest man-made markings in the prehistoric caves are traces of fingers dragged through a clayey surface—maybe imitations of marks left by cave-bears' claws so it has been held. But the finger tracings also include meandering, interlacing

---

[1] *Quelques notes sur l'origine de l'art* ('Some Notes on the origins of Art') is the title of Breuil's introduction to Blanc's book (Rome, 1958). In *L'Art Vivant* of May 1929 Breuil contributed a paper on *L'origine de la peinture et de la gravure* ('The Origin of Paintings and Engraving'). At the international congress of Prehistorical and Protohistorical Sciences (London, 1932) Breuil read a paper on 'The Evolution of Painting in the Upper Palaeolithic' and embodied this study in the second edition (written in collaboration with Obermaier) of his *Altamira*.

patterns including the so-called 'macaroni' lines. Often super-imposed on these are real engravings, simple outline drawings of beasts—generally with the eye omitted. These sketches look almost as though a stone scraper had been passed around the shadow of the animal and they are vigorous enough.

It is, in fact, probable that men amused themselves by making shadows permanent outside in the open and on suitable rock-faces. There is an oft-quoted example of a young gorilla in the London Zoo who was observed, on three occasions, to run his finger around his own shadow on his cage-wall. Men's shadows loom large in art and in religious belief. . . .

Associated with these simple outlines are vague geometric patterns—magic symbols? Also from very early times date the hand-stencils that stare at us from so many cave-walls. In some caverns these hands are very numerous. There are, for instance, fifty-five at El Castillo and no less than 124 at Gargas, the great majority of left hands and many of them mutilated. The 'stencils' were produced either by rubbing the hand in pigment and then placing it against a wall or by putting the outstretched hand against the rock-face and then spraying or blowing colouring matter over it. . . . Various explanations of the custom have been proposed such as that the hands are 'symbols of possession', but such interpretations are valueless, though it is certain that hand-imprints have been made throughout the ages, in many parts of the world and right up to the present . . . pilgrims leave impressions of their hands in some Italian sanctuaries.

It is generally said that it is impossible to produce the effect of a mutilated hand by just doubling back a finger, the digits must really have been chopped off, yet W. J. Sollas seems to have re-produced 'palaeolithic hands' by doubling back a finger. However, chopping off a joint, or a whole finger, is a wide-spread practice among 'primitive' peoples even today, either to indicate mourning (a propitiatory sacrifice?) or to secure, maybe, 'good luck'. At the Le Placard site were found isolated phalanges—did these come from the quick or the dead?

The area of the painted caverns seems to be greater than was thought only a short time ago, for in 1960 came the announcement of prehistoric pictures in Bashkiria south of the Urals and not far from the industrial centre of Magnitogorsk. However, practically all the European painted caverns are in France and Spain and the areas in which these caves are found are so relatively small that they look as though they were the creation of certain definite tribes, maybe with a common 'religion'.

In the latter part of the Old Stone Age, the period of cave-art, only the entrances and fore-parts of grottoes were used as dwellings, the openings were, no doubt, protected by shelters of twigs and branches and in Magdalenian times, anyway, men occupied 'tents' in the open at some seasons of the year. Tent 'circles' have been known in Germany for some time and since 1960 have been recognized in the Dordogne.

The paintings and engravings, however, are mostly in the far recesses. There are some apparent exceptions to this rule. At Altamira the Bison Ceiling is quite near the entrance but it is not the one used by Old Stone Age Man. Lascaux main hall is also quite near the entrance though this, again, is probably not the original one.

At Niaux the first paintings are 700 yards from the entrance. At Nerja there is a steep slope at the end of a series of halls and the painted galleries begin some distance after a hole at the top of that slope. In some caves you must crawl through long, narrow passages, in others swim a river. No one could ever have lived, or no community of men could ever have lived, for long in such remote and ill-ventilated retreats: the air filled with torch-smoke would soon have become unbreatheable.

Breuil defined two main art-styles in late palaeolithic Europe:

(1) Aurignacian and Gravettian (Perigordian).

(2) Solutrean and Magdalenian.[1]

(1) preceding (2) by several thousands of years.

[1] No painting or engraving can with certainty be ascribed to the Solutrean culture-phase but there is a considerable amount of Solutrean sculpture.

The oldest true paintings of animals are merely coloured outlines or are in flat-wash, then came modelling, in monochrome or polychrome. Both mineral (e.g. iron oxide) and earth (e.g. ochre) pigments were used—blacks, reds, oranges from delicate yellow to darkest brown, even violet, but no true blues or greens.

However, exciting as are the great naturalistic animals of the Aurignacian and Magdalenian artists, these paintings are extraordinarily isolated. There are very few 'scenes' (the Lascaux scene of the man and the bison—see p. 192—is an exception) in the paintings—though this is not true of the engravings—there is nothing but the (generally static) animals and their accompanying symbols.

It is these symbols which are more and more attracting the attention of prehistorians. Breuil recognized clearly enough that some of these symbols were of a sexual nature, but some he held were 'graphic puns', others 'huts' or 'blazons'. The signs have received names that are merely descriptive, e.g. pectiniform because 'comb-shaped' or claviform because resembling 'clubs'. These latter Breuil guessed might be 'boomerangs', while Obermaier thought some of the 'huts' were 'spirit-traps' (this latter interpretation a daring guess suggested by modern usages in some 'primitive' societies).

These abstract signs accompany the pictures at nearly all sites from the Dordogne to the Pyrenees, from Cantabria to La Pileta. Are these symbols a sort of 'writing' in the widest sense of the term? Are they writing such as we use today to give a picture a title? Are they 'sign-posts' or an integral part of the pictures they accompany? One French prehistorian[1] has advanced the theory that the pictures in prehistoric caves were not distributed at random but that the caverns were organized as units with certain signs at the beginning and at the end of a 'sanctuary'.

In any case there is not much doubt that many of the signs are conventionalized representations of the male and female genitalia, while the female signs seem very often to be associated

[1] Professor André Leroi-Gourhan of the University of Paris.

with a bison and the male signs with a horse. Furthermore, it is highly probable that the signs, the symbols and the paintings themselves bear witness to beliefs in Man's relationship to the animals about him, some sort of vision of the world in terms of our connection with the beasts, maybe a physical as well as a 'spiritual' one. We may remember the Trois-Frères and some simulated or real conjunction.

Possibly these signs could be 'read'. Every picture is, in a measure, writing: writing which can be read by all whatever is the tongue we speak, the language we think. If the signs could be read, then they could also be chanted, perhaps in some sort of ritual. Of course, the chants may not have been in phrases susceptible of semantic analysis; chants and enchantments developed language.

Obviously pictorial art is the forerunner of writing even though writing as we know it may have developed (as in Sumeria) as a device for identifying temple offerings and priestly property, or (as in ancient China) as a means of oracular consultation with the spirits; writing is the essential of civilization and it looks as though Late Old Stone Age Man had some sort of writing. Here is the Abbé's conclusion on prehistoric painting:

'If art was to exist among "primitive" populations in the world of long ago, it must embody the essential preoccupations of hunters and herdsmen—hunting-magic, multiplication of game and rain-making—and then the hope of a future life and the Cult of the Dead in Egypt and in the ancient and medieval Christian world. But these considerations do not explain either the birth of figurative art "out of the void" nor the cult of the beautiful for its own sake. "Art for Art's sake" alone would have provided no livelihood for the artists but, although they placed their skill at the service of Magic and Religion, the artists were not, because of that, prevented from enjoying their own creations, nor were their contemporaries prevented from enjoying the artists' work. Thus, the artists produced beautiful things which, because of their beauty, stir and move us still. There had to exist a spring of intense visual emotion before the powerful and plastic paintings (evoked by the dangers of big-game hunting) could be so enriched.'

So painting may have developed as a device to secure, through magic, highly desirable material things, but painting must also have fostered both the growth of magic and of 'religious' feeling. Pictures, once created, live on a life of their own—we may remember the part they have played in the formation of dogma and historical myths. Pictures do not change our environment, they do more, they change us. The pictures talk back with as imperious a voice and in as masterful a manner to their authors as to anyone else . . . and then, as Baudelaire wrote, '*En art la part laissée à la volonté de l'homme est bien moins grande qu'on ne le pense*'—'In art the part left to the will of Man is much less considerable than is thought.'

15

The Father of Prehistory

H E W A S much moved as he stopped in front of a magnificent bison-head. His memory, for once, failed him and
he imagined he had forgotten to copy it. There was a
broken-down chair nearby and those with him propped it up so
that he could sit. He whipped out a pencil from his pocket and
fumbled for a piece of newspaper. And then, with all his old
art, swiftly, admirably, surely, he drew the engraving and with
astonishing veracity.

It was 13th August 1954, and Breuil was paying his last visit
to the Trois-Frères Cavern where he had spent so many days and
which he considered among the most significant of the prehistoric
caves—significant for what it tells us of the manners and customs,
the rites and maybe the beliefs of our remote ancestors.

Despite his seventy-seven years he made his way through all
the galleries including the upper ones which are still difficult to
reach. He moved from one rock panel to another, stopping
before each picture, saying a word to each maybe: the lions, the
ibex and the mammoths; the reindeer and the presiding sorcerer,
shaman or god, draped in a beast's skin and antlered ('the
mysterious stags whose horns disappear and then appear again'),
robed and crowned.

Then he moved slowly away, leaning heavily upon his stick,
his bowed figure weighed down with the thought that this was
the point of no return.

Two years later, it is true, he was at Rouffignac,[1] but that cave is easier to negotiate and it had not for Breuil the nostalgic charm, or indeed the scientific significance, of the Trois-Frères.

In 1957 the Abbé's eightieth birthday was celebrated at the Museum of Man. There was a great gathering to do him honour. Dr. Pei, his old friend of Peking days, arrived, bringing with him the lower jaw of *Gigantopithecus*, a large meat-eating ape with rather a 'human' sort of mandible which lived in south-western China about the same time as Peking Man. Before this jaw was discovered the ape was known only from teeth which looked so like those of a man that the creature was, for some time, known as *Giganthropus*. Not 'giant ape' but 'giant man'. But it certainly was an ape and a meat-eater like ourselves and unlike any other sort of ape we know sufficiently well to judge of its diet.

Breuil, indeed, in his later years, was a frequent visitor to the Museum of Man. Once or twice a week you might come across him, accompanied by Harper Kelley, up in the prehistoric section ('behind the scenes' of course, and not in the public galleries), making his way to Dr. Léon Pales's laboratory. The Abbé's eyes had fully recovered from his accident down at Brive in 1940 and, in fact, retained their brightness and sharpness until almost the end. He did in later years wear a curious pair of reversible spectacles when reading or writing—for most of his life his eyes were capable of standing almost any sort of strain—but he could still, with the unaided eye, decipher the intricacies of lines and drawings. But his own writing often baffled him. Still, he turned over to Pales the four tons of engraved stones from the La Marche grotto which are astonishing in their variety and depiction of men and beasts. This material will, when published, throw a great deal of light on the manners and customs of Stone Age Man. And as Pales did not fail to point out, some of the La

[1] Rouffignac, about ten miles to the west of Montignac, has a number of outline paintings of animals (including a doubtful 'rhinoceros frieze'). Breuil, then in his eightieth year, thought the pictures authentic but added they presented many puzzling features. Some of the pictures are almost certainly fakes.

Marche human profiles are every bit as 'Semitic' as those on southern African rock-paintings: what could be deduced from that about 'foreigners'? It is true that Late Old Stone Age western European paintings of human figures are rare, but engravings of such are plentiful enough, and they afford a pretty complicated picture of palaeolithic profiles. The fine Magdalenian male portrait painted on a stone slab that Dr. Dorothy Garrod and Mlle. de Saint-Mathurin discovered at Angles-sur-l'Anglin has rather a snub nose, so we can be sure enough that there were no 'pure races' or 'pure types' 10,000 or 15,000 years ago, and doubtless for long before that.

The four tons of La Marche engravings represent just a part of the new material the 'prehistoric ethnologists' have to work on—and naturally more will be forthcoming. Laboratory work was, generally speaking, what the Abbé disliked, though we could say that the prehistoric painted caves were his laboratories for years of his life.

Of course it was the human figures on the La Marche stones that attracted most of Breuil's attention. Sometimes, after examining realistic representations of embraces, couplings and of intertwined figures, he would remark, with a smile for the Magdalenians, 'I think these must be marriage certificates.'

As long as he could travel he kept on moving about. On 25th September 1956 he read at Düsseldorf a paper—'Sixty Years of Discoveries of Early Man and their Influence on Ideas'—at the meeting held to celebrate the hundredth anniversary of the discovery of Neanderthal Man. In 1955 he had wanted to go to Livingstone and take part in the third Pan African Congress on Prehistory, but he could not. Still in January and February 1957 he was again at Lisbon. In 1958 he went off to the La Chapelle-aux-Saints and with the two Bouyssonie brothers celebrated their great discovery of 1908 (see p. 70).

Breuil suffered, as the years swept on, little of the in-folding, the withdrawal into self, that so often make an ageing man but a shadow of what he was. And his mind was remarkably clear to the last. A man, after all, is his memory. It seems our brain-cells do not develop after we are about the age of twenty, but that if they are kept active they will go on functioning (barring accidents) until extreme old age; though if the pyramidal cells of the brain are allowed to lie fallow they disconnect and never can link up again. Breuil never allowed his to snap apart. And his memory was, unlike many old men's, almost as good for recent events as for those long past, though he could think far back.

Only a few months before the Abbé's death Harper Kelley said he had not realized a certain type of prehistoric implement known as an 'Asturian pick' occurred outside Spain: 'Oh yes, it does, I saw several of them at Isturitz in the Basses Pyrénées when, with Cartailhac, I was on my way to Altamira in 1902.' And he went on to describe just where he had found them.

In his old age, as in youth and middle years, he 'let himself think' and still spent long hours at his desk—as all must do who really write and study—and prepared books on his explorations, one of which appeared after his death.

In his last years his deafness increased and as he would wear no hearing-aid he would sometimes answer at random just because he had not heard the question—and thus led some to think he was getting senile, but he was not. When he was sitting on committees, especially, he would interject apparently irrelevant remarks either because he found a subject silly (he was always inclined to joke if conversation flagged, or got too pompous or boring) or because he had not caught what had been said. He was also obstinate about gadgets. He was allergic to cybernetics, computers and the like. Voting in the board-room of the National Research Council is not by means of bulletins in an urn, but by mysterious dials which have to be manipulated like those of a telephone. Magical figures then flash on an opalescent screen. Sometimes the contraption would get out of order. This delighted the Abbé. So electronic gadgets could break down after all. Anyway, he would have no truck with them. He would ask a neighbour to manipulate the thing for him and as he had rather a tendency, as have many deaf people, to shout, his decisions—and the reasons for them often expressed in forthright terms—were clearly audible all over the room.

Against his doctor's orders, in August 1960, only a year before his end, he insisted on going to Austria and there taking part in the Wenner-Gren Foundation's symposium on 'Comparative Prehistoric Art'. While he was at Burg Wartenstein he celebrated Mass served by two Spanish ethnologists, one of whom took an impressive photograph of the aged Abbé pronouncing the last words of the liturgy, ITE MISSA EST—a message of dismissal and farewell.

On 11th May 1961, feeling his time was approaching, he wrote, in rather less illegible hand than usual, a codicil to his will in which he declared: 'If I die away from Paris I ask my relations to provide for me a very simple grave. If I am buried at Belleu I desire that my funeral should be very plain—no flowers, no wreaths, no speeches.'

His last public appearance was characteristic of the man. On 30th of this same month of May he fought a last fight, and won it, defending the cause of the research attachés at the National Research Centre—whose numbers it had been proposed to reduce radically. One of those present at the meeting has written:

'Researchers who, perhaps tomorrow, may criticize his work in the light of new knowledge and progress achieved, you should know that it was to safeguard your future and secure your moral rights, that he, deathly pale, enfeebled, indignant, standing though nearly dropping from exhaustion, fought his last fight—for you.'

A little later in that summer of 1961 he had an attack of pleurisy at his country home but refused to be moved to hospital until a Tunisian Moslem doctor, one of his disciples and a close friend, called and carried him off. When the Abbé got home again he was better but suffered a relapse some weeks later.

He died quietly. His physician had given him an injection to stimulate the heart. His secretary turned away to lower a blind and screen him from the glare of a summer morning's sunlight. When she looked back he was dead. It was 14th August 1961. He was eighty-four years and six months old.

If we ask, 'Just what, after all, did Breuil *do*?' the answer is simple. He gave us prehistory as we understand that word today. He established a firm foundation for history. When he began his career he had before him a mass of confused evidence. When he ended his career that evidence had been welded into a coherent whole. No inconsiderable achievement for one man's lifetime.

His first triumph was the placing of the Aurignacian culture-phase (which had been more or less lost sight of since Lartet's death in 1869) in its right place before the Solutrean. Breuil was then twenty-nine.

The paper he read at the Geneva Congress in 1912 on the 'Sub-divisions of the Upper Palaeolithic' established a framework which was elastic enough to accommodate new discoveries but which has remained valid in all its essentials today, more than fifty years later, fifty years full of remarkable accessions of new knowledge. In this paper he laid down the principles for systematic research in the geology, the ethnography and the geography of the Upper Palaeolithic. And twenty years later he succeeded in grouping all the Magdalenian material into six classes unevenly distributed in different sites with evidence of this remarkable culture.

But he recognized that with new knowledge must come re-adjustment:

'Our classifications are far from being intangibly dogmatic, every scientific worker in the field has his own contribution to make especially if he will set about his work in the right way, and the first of all requirements is an open mind about all those facts which may escape him at first but which, in the field, he comes slowly to recognize.'

In the revised edition of the *Subdivisions* (published in 1937) he wrote: 'I dedicate this second edition—*slightly* revised and touched up, though insufficiently—to my pupils and my colleagues in the hope that they, in their turn, will go farther than I have.'

But all this was only a beginning. He directed his attention to the Lower Palaeolithic, forsook the caverns, and betook himself to areas where there is evidence of glacial conditions—the regions of the Pyrenean foothills, northern France and south and south-eastern England—the main areas of western Europe where such evidence combined with proof of Man's settlement is abundant. Now geology was to furnish him the master-key. The timetable of man-made implements can be accurately fixed only by study of the successions of the different types of implements and by interpreting the story presented by the regions near the ice-front.

From the very beginning of his career he was fascinated by the problems presented by the forms and shapes, by the morphology, of palaeolithic implements in stone. But he held that attention directed exclusively to form and shape might also be a source of error. The *type* of technique is the main thing, exact *shape* depends upon the raw material utilized. Some communities may jump some stages, while other communities, ultra-conservative, may linger long in what he called 'industrial mediocrity'. In this highly technical and complicated field of man-made-tool classification, Breuil was the undoubted master, his experience vast, his judgement sure.

It was a joy to see him settle down to a table spread with *cailloux*, or 'pebbles' as he called them, and with extraordinary rapidity sort them out, discarding some (by just tossing them

Q

over his shoulder very often!) and arranging the others according to type; to a casual onlooker, however, one *caillou* might seem much like another.

In the field he was extraordinarily intuitive and he was often able to identify and classify discoveries made by others who could not interpret what they had found.

However, this was very far from being all. Breuil revealed Old Stone Age art to the world and his marvellous copies still serve to illustrate all the phases of that art from the caverns to the rock-shelters and the later paintings of Spain which mark 'the transition from the figurative to the schematic—awaiting the invention of writing'.

And Breuil, despite his eminence as a geologist, as an authority on stone implements, as a physical anthropologist, was essentially, as his title at the I.P.H. indicated, a 'prehistoric ethnologist'. He presented the evidence for religious and moral conceptions of men of the 'Reindeer Age'. He changed our picture of early Man, and of the remote past of our race, and this changed picture has had a profound influence upon our thought.

During his long career most of the problems—and most of the discoveries—in prehistory were submitted to him and he never failed to illuminate the evidence before him. His range of experience, of knowledge and of learning was so vast that he could make bits of stone exciting even to those with little or no acquaintance with prehistory at all. And we must not forget the work he did in inspiring others. No one who had been his disciple failed to bear the master's imprint.

Breuil was not the first of the prehistorians but he was the first man to devote his whole life to prehistory from youth to extreme old age. His industry was prodigious. Not only did he publish over a thousand scientific papers, but he wrote a number of books many of them as exciting and as attractive to the man in the street as to the specialist.

But he was the last representative of the heroic age of prehistory. No scientist of the future will be able to embrace every aspect of Man's prehistory. Now the time has come for intensive laboratory work such as Breuil found restricting and, indeed, rather tiresome, but there had to be a Breuil. Without him, without his unflagging energy, his extreme accuracy, his intuition and his powerful, and thoroughly French, ability to synthesize, it is no exaggeration to say that prehistory as we know it today would not exist.

He was, as he said, 'the perfect example of the generation to which he belonged'. One could hardly express oneself more proudly—and more humbly—than that.

And if we ask 'What is the use of prehistory?' we must answer ourselves with another question: 'What is the use of history?' Well, one of the uses of the imposing and rather terrifying story of Man is to remind us of our essentially human condition. We may be manœuvring ourselves into a state that puts too great a strain on our brains and bodies, and our bodies, at least, are no stronger than those of forefathers we may choose to look on as little better than animals. In any case history and prehistory are one, though this fact is still not always realized, but prehistory at least is not vitiated, as is so much of history, with the written word, almost always tendentious, on occasion misleading and sometimes absolutely untrue.

The Dates

1877. Henri Edouard Prosper Breuil born at Mortain in Normandy, 28th February.

1883. Breuil at school at Clermont de l'Oise.

1887. At the Collège Saint-Vincent, Senlis.

1895. At the Issy-les-Moulineaux Seminary.

1897. The first 'Tour of France'. At the Saint-Sulpice Seminary.

1898. The second 'Tour of France'.

1900. Ordained priest. Digs at Sordes and the Abri Dufour.

1901. Discovery of Les Combarelles and the Font de Gaume.

1902. At Altamira with Cartailhac. Périgueux Congress.

1903. *Licencié ès sciences naturelles* of the University of Paris. With Commont at the Bultel-Tellier gravel-pit, Amiens.

1905. *Privat-docent* at Fribourg.

1907. At Bédeilhac with Cartailhac where Harlé had reported paintings.

1908. Discovery of the La Chapelle-aux-Saints neanderthaloid skeleton. With Peyrony at Le Ruth.

1909. Prince of Monaco at Covalanas and Altamira.

1910. Foundation of the Institut de Paléontologie Humaine with Breuil as professor of prehistoric ethnography.

1911. Breuil in England.

1912. Discovery of the Tuc d'Audoubert. Breuil presents his paper 'The Subdivisions of the Upper Palaeolithic and their Significance' to the Geneva Congress. Breuil at La Pileta. With Sollas in South Wales and the Channel coast.

1914–18. Breuil in Intelligence in Spain.

1916. Discovery of Les Trois-Frères.

1918. Receives the Order of Santhiago of Portugal and the Gold Medal of the Lisbon Geographical Society. Officer of the Order of Saint-Charles of Monaco.

1920. Litt.D. *honoris causa* of the University of Cambridge.

1921. Receives the *Jeton d'Or* of the *Société d'Archéologie du Midi*.

1924. At the Igritz Grotto in Transylvania. Commander of the Order of the Crown of Rumania.

1926. Lectures at Oxford.

1927. Discovery of *Sinanthropus* tooth at Choukoutien. Breuil LL.D. of Edinburgh University and member of committee to investigate the Glozel frauds.

1927–8. *Chargé de Cours* at the Institute of Ethnography of the Sorbonne.

1929. Breuil in South Africa. Professor at the Collège de France.

1931. Breuil in China.

1932. In Moravia. At Swanscombe gravel-pit in Thames 100-foot terrace.

1933. In Abyssinia with Teilhard and Monfreid.

1935. Second visit to China. Receives Flinders Petrie Memorial Medal, London.

1936. At Saccopastore with A. C. Blanc.

1937. Gold Medal of the Society of Antiquaries, London. Georg Schweinfurth Medal, Frankfort.

1938. *Chevalier* of the Order of Leopold of Belgium. Elected member of the *Académie des Inscriptions et des Belles-Lettres* (Institut de France), Paris.

1940. Discovery of Lascaux.

1941. Breuil in Portugal. With Neuville and Ruhlmann at Casablanca, Morocco. Visiting professor at Lisbon University.

1942. Breuil in South Africa. Receives the great Gold Medal of the National Academy of Sciences, Washington.

1945. Breuil returns to France.

1946. Retires from the Collège de France. Huxley Medal of the Royal Anthropological Institute, London. Visits Arcy-sur-Cure.

1947. At Nairobi for Pan African Congress.

1948. In South Africa. Receives the Joseph Prestwich Medal of the London Geological Society.

1949. Medal of the Royal Belgian Geographical Society.

1950–1. Breuil in Africa.

1952. Breuil in Algeria. Receives the Geoffroy-Saint-Hilaire Medal of the Société d'Acclimatation, Paris.

1954. Grand Cross of the Spanish Order of Alfonso el Sabio.

1956. At Düsseldorf. At Piette's tomb.

1957. At Rouffignac. His eightieth birthday celebrated at the Musée de l'Homme, Paris.

1958. Commander of the French Order of the *Palmes académiques*. Albert Penck Medal of the Quatärvereinigung. Commander of the Legion of Honour. At La Chapelle-aux-Saints.

1959. The *Salle Breuil* opened at the Saint-Germain Museum.

1960. At Burg Wartenstein for the Wenner-Gren symposium on 'Comparative Prehistoric Art'.

1961. 14th August. Breuil dies at his house in L'Isle Adam and was later buried at Belleu (Somme).

Breuil was a member of nineteen foreign learned societies and academies.

Bibliographical Note

In addition to his numerous books Breuil wrote hundreds of papers and articles and he went on writing to extreme old age. Just as an example of this remarkable activity here are a few titles for the years 1949–54, and the list is by no means exhaustive, for we may remember that at this time he was preparing his big books on cave-art in general and on his various African prospections and explorations. Moreover, he kept up his writing until almost the last months of his life.

'Des Cavernes peintes d'Aquitaine aux Fresques rocheuses de l'Afrique australe' in the *Reports of the Académie des Inscriptions et des Belles-Lettres*, Paris, 1949.

'La Paléolithique du Harrar' in *L'Anthropologie*, 1951.

Les Hommes de Pierre ancienne, paléolithiques et mésolithiques (with R. Lantier), Paris, 1951.

Boucher de Perthes, ses Précurseurs et ses Continuateurs, Abbeville, 1951.

'Souvenirs sur le Prince Albert de Monaco et son Œuvre préhistorique', *Bulletin de la Société préhistorique française*, 1951.

A la Recherche de la Mentalité préhistorique, Paris, 1951.

'Cavernes ornées' in the *Bulletin of the Société archéologique et historique de Chelles*, 1953.

'Peintures rupestres de l'Afrique et d'Espagne orientale' in *L'Anthropologie*, vol. 57, 1953.

'Prolegomène à une Classification préhistorique' in the *Bulletin de la Société préhistorique française*, 1954.

'Le Magdalénien' in the *Bulletin de la Société préhistorique française*, 1954.

La Evolución del Arte parietal de los Cuevas y Abrigos ornamentados de Francia, Saragossa, 1954.

'Le Paléolithique ancien' (with Harper Kelley) in special publication of the *Société préhistorique française*, 1954.

Index